COMMUNICATION
for modern management

J. BARRON WILEY

THE BUSINESS PRESS
Elmhurst, Illinois, U.S.A.
1966

THE AUTHOR

From a varied background of experience in business and military service, combined with comprehensive schooling in business education and specialized study in the use of audio-visual materials in business and education, Dr. J. Barron Wiley acquired a broad fund of information on communication as a significant, basic factor in business management.

After graduating from the University of Denver in 1940 with a degree of Bachelor of Science in Commerce, Dr. Wiley spent brief periods with Firestone Tire & Rubber Company, Standard Oil Company of Indiana, and Matador Land & Cattle Company, a large cattle ranch in Texas. From April 1942 until November 1945 he was with U. S. Army Air Force. During the next three years, while employed briefly by a floor covering firm and the Continental Air Lines in Denver, he studied for his masters degree at the University of Denver. The degree was awarded in August 1948, in airline-airport managment.

Following three years as head of the business education department of the Colorado Woman's College in Denver, Dr. Wiley was recalled to active duty by the U. S. Air Force during the Korean War, from May 1951 to July 1954. Part of this service was as Air Force ROTC instructor at Indiana University. While at the university he completed his work for a Doctor of Education degree, which was awarded by Indiana University in June 1956. The degree included a major in audio-visual instruction and a minor in business education administration. In September 1956 the author joined the staff of the California State Polytechnic College as assistant professor of education and audio-visual specialist. He was promoted to associate professor in 1962.

Taking a sabbatical leave during the first six months of 1964, Dr. Wiley engaged in a post-doctoral study at the University of California at Los Angeles. He prepared a research study of the practices of industrial organizations in the Los Angeles area in their use of the audio and visual media in various communication situations.

An honor indicating recognition of his specialized knowledge in the field of communication came to Dr. Wiley in March 1965, when he was appointed to the National Advisory Board of the Brooks Foundation, Santa Barbara, Calif. The purpose of the Brooks Foundation is to increase the quality and effectiveness of communication in business, industry, government, and education.

FOREWORD

Today is a period of rapid expansion in the use of the graphic media of communication. Visual and audio media have become so commonplace that we have ceased to be astounded by them. However, if we take a moment to consider the mass media of communication, it will readily become apparent how important they have become in the modern world. Almost every magazine advertisement has one or more illustrations, generally photographic and often in full color. Some of the most popular magazines are those which provide a large part of their content in the form of photographic reporting. Newspapers are constantly increasing the proportion of space allotted to illustrations. Graphic billboards confront us at every turn. Motion pictures inform and mold opinions as well as entertain people. Television and radio bring the message of the advertiser into nearly every home. Many millions of dollars are spent annually by business organizations for the purpose of conveying their messages to others. There is a need for people who are aware of the potentialities of these newer media of communication and who know how best to utilize them.

In the past, the educated person was the one who was fluent with words, primarily in the written form. Today's educated person must know how to communicate in many different media and how to choose the most effective one for the particular situation.

Where is industry to get these people who are fluent in the various media? At the present time very few are being prepared specifically for this sort of work by colleges and universities. The majority move into these positions from related areas—graphic art, photography, training, advertising, etc. It is to be hoped that more collegiate institutions will introduce courses and perhaps majors in industrial communications with emphasis upon the part that the audio-visual media can play. The author teaches such a course to technical arts, business, and engineering majors and the skills learned in this course have helped a number of former students move into responsible positions rather more rapidly than they might otherwise have done.

What about those who are already in the industrial field and are called upon to participate in or even to direct communication of an audio-visual nature? A company may want to make use of the knowledge possessed by its own employees with regard to its products and company policies. These people may have only limited familiarity with the use of audio-visual materials in communication. They need information as to the medium that will best solve their communication problem and how to make the best use of that medium.

It is hoped that the present volume will be of value both to college students and those people who may be embarking upon the production and/or utilization of these materials. Up to the present time, nothing has appeared in print which covers the whole range of industrial communication using the audio-visual media. There are many books which are concerned with these media as they relate to elementary and secondary school teaching. There are also magazines, such as *Industrial Photography* and *Reproduction Methods,* which are concerned with certain limited aspects of the media, but nothing which covers all of the types of communication of an industrial nature that fall under the general heading of audio-visual.

This book is not intended for the expert in the audio-visual media. He will have already met and solved the problems that are discussed. At the same time it is not a how-to-do-it type of book. References in the chapter bibliographies indicate sources of information of this nature. Rather, it is intended to serve as a guideline to the college student or the person just entering the audio-visual field. It will indicate to him the areas of communication which could take advantage of the increased efficiency which is made possible through the wise use of these media, and the various tools and techniques of communication, including the advantages, disadvantages, and problems involved in their planning, production, and utilization.

Perhaps some advance in the art of industrial communication will come about as a result of some reader's use of the material in this book. If so, the time spent in writing it has not been in vain.

J. BARRON WILEY

San Luis Obispo, California
January, 1966

CONTENTS

CHAPTER 1

INTRODUCTION

The Nature of Communication

Civilization requires an increasing amount of communication—between persons, between organizations, and between governments. The fields of business and industry are no exceptions to this trend. Increasing complexities of manufacturing processes, corporate structures, and the system of laws and taxation demand that efficient methods of conveying information from one person or organization to another be developed.

Many misunderstandings and errors occur in business because the people concerned have not communicated: that is, there has not been a real meeting of the minds.

Fig. 1 is a simplified diagram of what occurs when one person attempts to communicate with another. The communicator's message

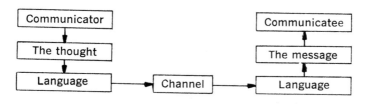

FIG. 1. The Communication Process.

is a thought which he wishes to convey to the communicatee. Before he can communicate this thought, however, he must express it in some form of language. This language may be the ordinary oral or written language of everyday conversation or it may be the special-

1

ized language of such disciplines as mathematics, music, or engineering. At any rate, the abstract thought must be expressed in tangible language.

Having chosen the appropriate language, which must be understood by both of the parties, the communicator must choose the proper channel through which to convey his thought to the communicatee. The choice of the channel is an important decision, because the quality of communication depends directly on it. The message and the nature of the person whom the communicator is trying to reach will determine the choice of the channel. If the message is general and intended for large numbers of people, then a diffuse medium such as a newspaper, general circulation magazine, radio, or television will be utilized. If the message is for a more selected group, other channels will be used. Always, however, the attempt is made to reach the desired persons and communicate with them as efficiently as possible.

Words spoken or written, mathematical symbols, musical notes, or engineering specifications do not have meanings of their own—only those meanings that the principals involved in the communication process bring to these symbols. Therefore, both must apply the same meanings to the symbols—otherwise they have not truly communicated. Both, then, must understand the language used in the communication. If they do not, the message which the communicatee receives may be quite different from that intended by the communicator.

Also involved is the factor of "noise." Noise is anything which interferes with the transmission of the message. It might be actual physical noise interfering with an oral message, static disrupting a radio signal, the quality of reproduction of a photograph, or the quality of the handwriting in a written message. The communicator should choose the channel for sending the message least likely to have so much noise that it prevents the successful receipt of the message.

Persons in the business world do a great deal of communicating with others. These others may be employees, fellow employees, customers, management, stockholders, or governmental agencies. Anything that can increase the quality of these communications will save a great deal of money. Many of the tools of communication which can facilitate the exchange of ideas are those known as audio-visual materials.

What Are Audio-Visual Materials?

The term "audio-visual materials" generally includes all media of communication other than the simple printed page and face-to-face spoken words. It includes models and mockups, demonstrations, exhibits, motion pictures and television, still pictures, and radio and recordings. The availability of these varied media makes it possible to choose the one most appropriate for the type of material to be transmitted and the people sending and receiving the message.

What Has Been the Experience in the Use of Audio-Visual Materials in Education?

Audio-visuals of many sorts have been used in business for a number of years, but little has been made public about the success of using these communication tools. However, educators have made many investigations of the value of these materials in the schools, and findings of these studies are applicable to business communications. In a general summary, these are the results of a large number of research studies.

1. When the appropriate audio-visual materials are used, students learn more of the subject matter and retain it longer than do those who do not have the advantage of these methods.
2. Attitudes can be modified by the use of audio-visual materials.
3. Students who learn by audio-visual methods have greater insight into relations of ideas and facts.
4. The "change of pace" which occurs when an audio or visual device is introduced into the teaching routine increases interest and lengthens the attention span.
5. Concepts which are quite difficult to understand can be made a great deal clearer by the use of the proper visual devices.
6. People who are slower to learn seem to gain more proportionally from the concrete presentation of data through proper use of audio-visual instructional materials.

Applications of Audio-Visual Materials to Business Communications

Business organizations in the United States spend many millions of dollars every year to convey information to others. The people in charge of the communication activity must use available media to the best possible advantage. They must select the types and avenues of communication which will carry the greatest possible amount of information to those people who are their "targets," at the least cost per hit on the target.

Advertising via the printed page has, of course, been used by business for a great many years. Until fairly recently, this was practically the only way to contact large numbers of people with a sales or other message. Newspapers, magazines, circulars, flyers, catalogues, and direct mail advertising were the media used by most businesses to carry their messages to the people. These were combined with personal demonstration and persuasion to sell the merchandise or the idea.

The last few years have brought into general use media of communication that supplement, and in some cases replace, the written word as the chief means of disseminating information. Radio and television, the graphic arts, and photography in all of its forms (including motion pictures), combine to make the visual method of communicating a powerful competitor to vie with the written word for the attention and the imagination of the person to whom the message must be transmitted. A communicator who ignores the potentialities of these newer media is failing to communicate as efficiently as he should.

Listed below are some of the situations in which a business needs the best communication that it can get. With each one is an indication of a few of the audio-visual devices that will assist in the communication process. Each of these categories will be discussed in a separate chapter.

Employee Recruitment and Training. (Chapter 2) Every company wants to hire the best employees it can. In order to interest these potential employees in the company, it is necessary to tell them what the company has to offer them.

Brochures and booklets give much of the statistical background of the company and describe what it expects of employees and what it in turn offers them.

Motion pictures can convey to the prospective employee something of the philosophy and atmosphere of the company while it is showing him the physical appearance and operation of some of the plants.

Photographs of the plant and of the products can form a basis of discussion and assist in the development of rapport between the interviewer and the prospective employee.

When the new employee begins work for the company, he is not yet ready to produce. There must first be a period of training and indoctrination into the company's methods of operation. Another period of training may be involved after the employee has proved his potential and is ready to be upgraded into a more responsible position.

On-the-job training is often used when the duties are rather easily learned or when the new employee is well versed in the work when he is employed. Photographs, diagrams, drawings and charts may assist in developing the new employee's understanding.

Vestibule training is commonly used when the new employee must develop a large body of skills and it is not desirable to slow down production by letting him gain those skills in the regular production line. Demonstrations, motion pictures of equipment operation, photographs of the steps in the production process, and samples of the product in various stages of completion will help the new employee grasp the procedures more quickly.

Employee Relations. (Chapter 3) After a company has spent time and money to train an employee and bring him up to full productive output, it is concerned about keeping him and maintaining high morale, thereby reducing turnover and training costs. In addition to such things as equitable pay and promotion policies and good working conditions, there are contributions which good communications techniques can make. A house organ or company magazine can make the employee feel that he is part of the group and that the company is interested in him. Bulletin boards can do much besides remind employees of working hours and union meetings. Motion pictures can help employees gain a more accurate concept of the entire company and its operation.

Public Relations. (Chapter 4) Every company is quite conscious of the "corporate image" it presents to the general public. This image is built up through many channels, not the least of which are those of an audio-visual nature. Brochures are printed to tell the public something about the company and what it is attempting to accomplish. Motion pictures can tell the company's story in an entertaining and informative manner. Commercial radio and television provide an entry to the person's home and the opportunity to tell him about the company.

Sales and Promotion. (Chapter 5) Telling prospective customers about the company's product is essential to the success of any organization. In the majority of cases, communications of an audio-visual nature provide excellent ways of telling others about what one is trying to sell. The choice of the media to be used will, of course, depend upon the product and the prospective customers. Television presentation of the sales message reaches a wide but unselected audience and is suited to a product that is of widespread use. Motion pictures go to a smaller but more selected audience and in an extreme case may be shown to a single person by means of a compact projector unit on a desk. At conventions and conferences of people interested in the company's product, many forms of presentation can be used, including slide projection, overhead projection, charts and flipsheets, exhibits, and audio recording. These varied media make it possible to provide infinitely diverse types of presentation to suit the product being sold.

Reporting to Management. (Chapter 6) The magnitude and complexity of many of today's business organizations make it extremely difficult for individual members of management to be conversant with all phases of the operation. Also, the executive has many demands on his time, and the less time he has to spend digesting the information he receives the more time he will have for reaching decisions. Motion pictures, slides, graphic presentations, and models (of such things as proposed plant remodeling, etc.) can summarize, condense, and concentrate the information the executive needs in order to reach sound decisions.

Reporting to Stockholders. (Chapter 7) Much of the stock of today's corporations is held by people who have little or no knowledge of the technical aspects of the production phases of their companies, and only a slight appreciation of the business principles involved. Yet these people have the right to information about the company's operations in order to understand something of the soundness of its policies and the security of their investments. The concern in this chapter will not be with the choice of information to present to stockholders, but with the proper presentation techniques to the corporate owners who can attend stockholders' meetings and those whose information must reach them through the mail. In addition to the operating statements, which are a vital part of the annual report, charts, graphs, and photographs of the company's operations will make these materials much more informative to the stockholders—especially those who are not skilled in the reading of financial statements.

The Tools of Audio-Visual Presentation

Efficiency in business communication depends upon the choice of the proper channel to carry information from the communicator to the communicatee as shown in Figure 1. The choice will vary from one situation to another, but the best choice is always that form of dissemination that will transmit the message with the greatest possible amount of clarity and the least chance for misunderstanding or misinterpretation.

Visualization of Information. (Chapter 8) Most people other than artists, photographers, and audio-visual practitioners have had little training or experience in conveying information by visual means. Yet more and more the ways that we think and the things that we buy are influenced by those who are adept in this medium. Many of the barriers to good communication can be overcome by the proper use of visual or audio devices. They can get and hold the viewer's attention, provide him with background experience, and provide precise and vivid presentation of materials so that they are remembered longer. The following chapters describe suitable media for this communication.

Photography. (Chapter 9) Photographic presentation can convey the visual impression of an object to a viewer. It may, in some cases, be superior to actually viewing the object itself. The original may be too large or too small to see and understand directly. It may exist for only a short time, or may change so rapidly that the only way to keep a record of it is photographically. The "reading" of a photograph provides a common experience to a group of people who might have much more diversified experiences if they observed the actual object.

Motion Pictures. (Chapter 10) This special category of photography adds a dimension that still pictures do not have—that of time. While the still picture freezes an instant of time and shows things as they exist at that moment, the motion picture enables one to recreate visually a flow of events so that they may be observed in their sequence. Industrial applications of motion pictures include such things as time and motion study, recording the results of experiments, and the preparation of advertising material.

Slides and Filmstrips. (Chapter 11) This specialized application of still photography utilizes a transparency and a projector which produces an enlarged image of the picture on a screen. This type of presentation is particularly suitable when simultaneous viewing by a group of people is desired.

Overhead Projection. (Chapter 12) Several advantages are gained by the use of the overhead projector in business or industrial situations. The construction of the projector permits the projection of a large, bright image from a short distance. This means that the person using the machine can do so in a fully lighted room and while standing at the front of the room where he can maintain eye contact with the members of the group.

Opaque Projection. (Chapter 13) The opaque projector has the unique advantage of being able to project an image of material that is not in the form of a transparency. Material in a book or typed or written on paper can be reproduced so that a group can see it. Specimens, samples, and small mechanical assemblies can also be projected. Enlargements of materials may be made so that they can be reproduced graphically.

Flipsheets. (Chapter 14) Charts and graphs form excellent means of reducing masses of information to forms that are more easily understood. They summarize and compare, and demonstrate the implications of large quantities of data. One method of presenting such data is on flipsheets. Flipsheets consist of large sheets of heavy paper hinged across the upper edge. They are attached to a stand or easel in such a way that the individual pages may be successively turned over. The material must be large enough for all of the group to see it directly.

Audio Recording. (Chapter 15) The recording of narration, sounds, and music can be accomplished as a method of making another instructional devices more effective, or it may carry the burden of the communication process by itself. The most generally used method for making the original recording is on magnetic tape. The final release form may be that of a motion picture sound track, a phonograph record, or a magnetic tape. Each form has its own advantages. The emotional impact and the amount of information gained from most visual media can be substantially increased by the use of sound.

Exhibits. (Chapter 16) A summary of the operations of a department, a company, or an industry can very often be made in the form of an exhibit. The exhibit utilizes many of the different types of audio and visual materials and synthesizes them into an organized presentation of related information. Photographs, models, samples and specimens, drawings, moving parts, written materials, and a sound track or narration can combine to produce a meaningful exhibit.

Television. (Chapter 17) Anyone in business knows the impact which commercial television has had on advertising and public relations work in the United States. Other forms of this electronic communication system are also very important to the industrial communicator. Employee training can utilize closed circuit television to demonstrate the operation of certain machines in the plant. It is also possible to observe warehouses, perimeter fences, and traffic in the various corridors from one central location in the plant by means of closed circuit television.

Teaching Machines. (Chapter 18) The efficiency of automated teaching in the education systems of the United States is being proved repeatedly. Applications of these same principles can increase the quality and speed of the training of new employees and can put them into productive positions much sooner.

Facilities for Audio-Visual Presentation. (Chapter 19) Just as with any tool, audio-visual devices work best when used under optimum conditions. Regardless of whether the room is used for training or for other types of presentation, certain things should be provided for the sake of efficiency. The room itself should be capable of being completely darkened, well ventilated, and equipped with chalkboards, projection screens, tables, and comfortable (but not *too* comfortable!) chairs. Sufficient electric outlets should be available and controls for dimming the lights and operation of projection equipment should be easily accessible from the rostrum. In addition, all types of projection, sound, and display equipment should be easily and quickly available, preferably in an adjoining room. A photographic studio and darkroom and a room for production of graphic materials should also be easily accessible from the projection room.

BIBLIOGRAPHY

Brown, James W., Richard B. Lewis, and Fred F. Harcleroad, *AV Instruction Materials and Methods,* Second Edition, New York, McGraw-Hill Book Company, Inc., 1964, 592 pp.
  Chap. 1 Learning and Communication

Dale, Edgar, *Audio-Visual Methods in Teaching,* Revised Edition, New York, The Dryden Press, 1954, 534 pp.
  Chap. 5 What Can Audio-Visual Materials Do?

Kinder, James S., *Audio-Visual Materials and Techniques,* 2nd Edition, New York, American Book Company, 1959, 592 pp.
  Chap. 1 The Way of Audio-Visual Education

Sands, Lester B., *Audio-Visual Procedures in Teaching,* New York, The Ronald Press Company, 1956, 670 pp.
  Chap. 1 Audio-Visual Teaching

Strauss, L. Harry, and J. R. Kidd, *Look, Listen, and Learn,* New York, Association Press 1948, 235 pp.
    Chap. 1 Why Use Audio-Visual Materials?
Wittich, Walter Arno, and Charles Francis Schuller, *Audio-Visual Materials: Their Nature and Use,* Third Edition, New York, Harper & Brothers, 1962, 500 pp.
    Chap. 1 The Teacher and Communications
    Chap. 2 How People Learn

CHAPTER **2**

EMPLOYEE RECRUITMENT AND TRAINING

Every business organization is in competition with others for the best potential employees as they come onto the labor market from the high schools and colleges of the country and from other sources, such as married women returning to work after having been out of the labor market for some years. The company's representative has the duty of selecting those people who appear to have the most to offer as employees. In addition to this, he must present the company's story in such a way as to make the prospective employee choose this company as the one with which he wants to make his career rather than one of the others competing for his services. To obtain the services of these desirable people, the company representative needs tools and materials.

Methods Used in Recruiting

The methods used to locate prospective employees vary according to the nature of the company, its location, and the type of employee desired.

Many companies use the classified advertisement section of newspapers to tell the public about positions available in the organization. Whatever information deemed necessary to get people to apply is given in the advertisement. Other information is generally presented to the individual when he applies for the position. Brochures explaining company benefits—vacation policies, retirement plans, recreational facilities, fringe benefits—are given to him to study at his leisure.

A second group of people is composed of those who have had some previous knowledge of the company, but are making their first personal contact when they walk into the employment office to com-

11

plete a job application. Having been partially sold on the company
and what they believe to be its personnel policies they are good
prospects.

The third group of prospective employees are those interested
in employment with the particular company because friends or rel-
atives already work there and have recommended it as a good place
to work. These people are already favorably disposed toward the
company, and the work of the employment representative will be
to select applicants in accordance with the positions available.

The fourth group is composed of college students majoring in
fields of interest to the company, who will soon be completing their
college careers. This group is the one from which the company hopes
to select the great majority of its future executives and officials. It is
for this group that the greatest competition is evoked and for whom
the company will put out its most potent appeal. This is the group
upon which the greatest amount of time and money will be spent
to prepare them for their future responsibilities. They must be most
carefully selected. One phase of this selection is the interview at the
college or university by the company representative.

The interviewing representative will want to talk to each prospective employee individually, in order to assess his potential value
to the company. This also gives the applicant the opportunity to
ask questions about the company in a confidential atmosphere. In
addition to these interviews, the representative may arrange a general meeting for all interested in employment with the company.
Motion pictures and slides illustrating the company and its operation
may be shown, and brochures and other informational materials
distributed. In many instances this group meeting is informal, somewhat like a social affair—but it helps both the company representative and the applicant to decide whether or not to proceed further.

Motion Pictures. Motion pictures produced to aid in recruitment
are designed to interest prospective employees in working for the
company. The film will show the company in the best possible light
with respect to working conditions, possibilities for advancement,
and other things a person should know when considering the choice
of a company for which to work.

Some of the things a recruiting film might include are:

1. A short history of the company, including something about the
   founder, his dreams, and his accomplishments.
2. The company's product and why it is superior to those of its
   competitors.

3. Plant and district office locations.

4. Company policies for advancement and promotion.

5. Satisfactions to be gained from doing the particular kind of work.

6. Insurance and medical plans provided for employees.

7. Retirement plans.

8. Future plans for the company's operations.

A film of this sort will probably be rather general in scope. If it does delineate one kind of job, it will do so merely as an example of the general situation.

Some examples of company sponsored motion pictures which serve useful purposes as recruiting and general informational films are:

1. *The Du Pont Story.* This is a 40-minute, color, sound motion picture produced in 1951 and is available in both 16mm and 35mm versions. It traces the development and expansion of the company from its founding in 1802 to the present time and stresses how the growth of the company was tied to that of the country.

2. *Growing Places.* This 26-minute, color, sound, 16mm film was produced in 1958. It is the biography of the Minnesota Mining & Manufacturing Company, tracing its development and explaining its policies of diversification and research.

3. *The Magic Wheel.* This is a 30-minute, color, sound, 16mm (also available in 35mm) film, produced in 1956. It is the story of National Cash Register and was designed to interest sales and factory recruits in working for NCR. In addition, it serves as an orientation film for visitors to the factory and as a documentary film for luncheon clubs and other groups.

4. *Outside that Envelope.* A 43-minute, color, sound, 16mm motion picture, made in 1957. Sponsored by the Connecticut General Life Insurance Company, this film is not a history of the company; instead it tells of the satisfaction to be derived from helping others in a crisis. An employee's wife, who had felt her husband should change jobs, realizes that he should keep his present position.

5. *The Whole World Over.* $22\frac{1}{2}$ minutes, black and white, sound 16mm, produced in 1957. This film tells the Pan American Airways story through stories about employees. It tells of the company's operations as they see them and gives the viewer an impression of what it is like to work as a pilot, scheduler, training instructor, main-

tenance man, dispatcher, or other flight and ground service personnel.

Filmstrips. A filmstrip can in many instances, be as effective as a motion picture in presenting a company's story. When combined with a sound recording it can take on many of the characteristics of the motion picture, through the use of music and speech, and by pacing the presentation to suit a particular viewer or group of viewers. The company representative may encourage questions and discussion of the material shown as he presents the filmstrip. Each frame may be projected for as long as necessary for a complete understanding of the material, instead of, as with motion pictures, being restricted to the pace determined by the producer.

The materials included in a recruitment filmstrip would be essentially the same as those in a motion picture intended for the same purpose.

Brochures. Motion picture and filmstrip presentation of the company's recruitment story are excellent ways of helping the prospective employee to understand the organization's history, background,

FIG. 2. Recruitment, from Procter & Gamble. *(Photo Courtesy of Proctor & Gamble)*

and prospects, but because such a large amount of information has been presented in so short a time, they may confuse more than they clarify. In order to make an intelligent choice of an employer, the applicant must have tangible materials to which he can refer. The brochure provides this source of information.

Much of the material contained in a recruiting motion picture or filmstrip can be summarized in the brochure. In fact, the brochure may be taken directly from the projected materials and can serve to recall to mind the information presented by them.

An attractive cover design for the brochure will help to interest the prospective employee in the company. The cover should be dignified and should evoke the reader's interest. Figure 2 illustrates one approach to the cover design and contents of the recruitment brochure.

Upon opening the brochure, the reader has the right to expect to find a logical, clearly illustrated statement of the company's viewpoints as they affect an employee's career.

Charts, graphs, and diagrams should be used where appropriate to illustrate the ideas brought out in the brochure. The organizational chart of Montgomery Ward & Company reproduced in Figure

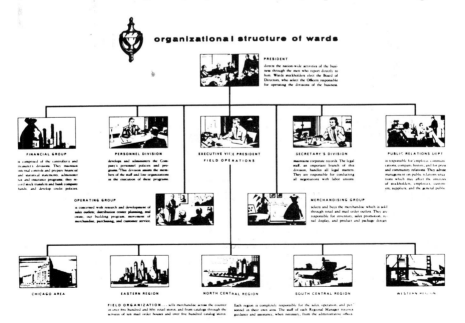

FIG. 3. Organizational Structure of Wards. *(Courtesy of Montgomery Ward & Co.)*

3 is illustrative of an informative and well illustrated chart. Drawings and descriptions of the various activities of the company bring the chart to life.

Illustrations in the brochure are generally more effective when they show people and work activities rather than things. This allows the reader to identify himself with the person he sees in the brochure and imagine himself in that position. Some sample pages from the Parke, Davis & Company brochure (Figure 4) show the type of approach used by this company.

FIG. 4. Pages from *New Horizons at Parke, Davis*. *(Courtesy of Parke, Davis & Company)*

The recruitment brochure should contain the information necessary to enable the person who is looking for a company with which to establish a career to find the answers to these questions;

Keeping in mind my interests and education, does this company's activities offer me a challenge?

Are there opportunities for advancement in my field?

Is it possible to continue to advance my knowledge of my specialty?

Is the company one which will continue to operate through my lifetime?

What benefits does the company offer in addition to the salary?

What are the arrangements for retirement income?

Frank, informative, and truthful answers to these questions will help the prospective employee make up his mind about the company while the company is making up its mind about him. This will help reduce dissatisfaction and employee turnover.

Methods Used in Training New Employees

A new employee is seldom profitable to his employer immediately. In almost every case there must be a period of indoctrination and training to teach the employee about his special responsibilities, how his position fits into the overall organization, and how he is expected to act in various circumstances. The new person goes on the payroll upon commencing work, but he must learn his duties before he repays the company's investment in him. Someone will have the responsibility of getting him started. During the "starting" period the older employee will not be producing at his normal rate. Being inexpert, the new employee will damage or consume materials which will not result in an acceptable product. All of these things add to the expense of getting a new employee started. Training methods should be selected with the objective of putting the new person into full production as quickly and inexpensively as is consistent with safety and quality standards.

On-the-Job Method. This training method involves placing the new employee under the charge and guidance of a worker who is experienced and skillful in the performance of his duties. Under this person's direction, the new employee gradually learns the operation of the job. As the new person learns various procedures, the more experienced person gives him diminishing attention until finally the new employee is working entirely on his own. This method works best where the operation is a fairly simple one or the new person comes to the job with a good background knowledge, and where his initial slowness will not interfere with the production of others in the department.

The efficiency of this method is generally quite low. During the early part of on-the-job training, the new employee takes nearly the full attention of the person teaching him, resulting in a 1:1 instructor-student ratio. In addition, if the older employee is disgruntled at having to do this instruction work, or if his instructional ability is not equal to his productive ability, an optimum learning situation cannot result.

In some instances the new employee is assigned as an apprentice to help, to do the simple parts at first, and to take over gradually the more involved portions of the work.

Vestibule Training. In many types of operation, an inexperienced person cannot be utilized on the production line without seriously affecting the efficiency of the entire organization. In this case it is imperative that he build up his skill to the production standard before he starts to work on the actual product. In a situation of this sort, the company will generally operate a training department where the appropriate skills can be learned without affecting the normal production. Instructors who are skilled and who like to teach are assigned from the production line to the training department. Machines and equipment are identical to those which the employees will be operating when they have finished their training. The materials consumed in this training are, for the most part, a loss. However, as the employee nears the end of his training period, his output should be of a quality that can pass inspection and it will help to pay a part of his training costs.

The physical separation of the training function from production makes possible the use of audio-visual materials as they are used in other school situations.

Much of the instruction will be carried on by means of demonstrations. The instructor shows the students how to adjust and operate the various parts of the machine and how to obtain maximum quality in the product. The students, following instructions and example, perform the same operations. Manuals and other printed information help to organize the information in a logical manner.

Motion pictures can be utilized with excellent results in such a training operation. Close-up motion pictures can enlarge small parts of the machine so that the entire class can observe the adjustments made. Slow motion photography can reduce the speed of actions that occur too rapidly to be seen, and make it possible to analyze them. The manufacturer of the equipment being used probably can supply "how-to-do-it" motion pictures on getting the most out of his product. As the learner gains skill, motion pictures of his operations can make self-analysis possible thus enabling him to eliminate unnecessary motions and further increase his skill.

Enlarged still pictures placed on the walls of the vestibule training room allow students to check their machine settings against the ideal.

Samples of properly prepared materials give standards against which the learner and his instructor can gauge the learner's skill. He can readily see how his skill compares with that which he must develop before he can move into actual production.

Small-scale models of the plant can be utilized to show the flow patterns of materials and products. Cutaway models of machines can illustrate the operation of internal parts.

Flipsheets are useful to teach the various phases of the construction, operation, and adjustments of the machines. Cutaway drawings, adjustment instructions, and specifications for the machines are some of the materials that can be used successfully on the flipsheets.

General Indoctination into Company Policy. A new employee has many questions that must be answered before he is fully a part of the operation, such as:

FIG. 5. *About Purina,* published by the Ralston Purina Company.
(Courtesy Procter & Gamble)

What is appropriate clothing for my work?

What should I do if I am ill and cannot report for work?

Is there a company cafeteria?

What are the working hours?

How and where do I report for work?

Is there a designated parking area for my car?

How are pay scales determined and modified?

Many of these questions are answered by the personnel represent-ative, the new employee's supervisor, or his fellow workers. Much confusion and many errors can be avoided, however, if such ques-tions are answered in a booklet which the employee can keep and study at his leisure. This may be a small pamphlet covering things of general interest to all employees, or there may be a number of specialized booklets applying only to certain categories of employees. An example of the latter is the group of booklets issued by the Ral-ston Purina Company and titled *About Purina*. The scope of these informational publications is indicated in Figure 5.

FIG. 6. Pages from *P & G and I*, Published by Procter & Gamble.
(Courtesy Procter & Gamble)

These publications should be easy reading, giving the reader the necessary information with a minimum of study. A figure with which the new employee can identify will help to tie the various parts of the booklet together. This technique was used by Procter & Gamble in its publications, *P&G and I*. The figure for the "I" was carried through the pamphlet and represented the individual. Pages from this publication appear in Figure 6.

Following the New Employee's Progress. Unless conscious effort is made to follow the progress of the new employee as he finds his

DUN & BRADSTREET, INC.
INTRODUCTION CHECK LIST

See General Personnel Instruction
4C-18. Numbers following same
items refer to reference material in
"Welcome to Our Company"

NAME OF EMPLOYEE _____

WHEN TO BE DONE	INITIAL WHEN DONE	WHAT IS TO BE DONE	SUGGESTED PERSON TO HANDLE
Day before Employee arrives		Prepare Supervisor for arrival; have Supervisor review application blank.	Dept. Head
		Prepare future immediate associates.	Supervisor
		Have desk cleaned out and supplies ready.	Supervisor
		Have instructional materials ready.	Supervisor
		Have initial work ready.	Supervisor
		Arrange for first-day luncheon companion.	Supervisor
1st Day On Arrival (Estimated time - numbers 1 - 9; 30 minutes)		1. Have employee fill out duplicate application form and withholding certificate if not done previously.	Dept. Head
		2. Give the new employee a copy of the booklet, "Welcome to Our Company". If not done previously, review the function of Dun & Bradstreet along the lines of pages 3-5 in the booklet.	Dept. Head
		3. Briefly review the job - give its title.	Dept. Head
		a. Sketch the duties.	
		b. Stress its importance - how it fits in with other jobs.	
		c. Where the work originates.	
		d. What employee and others in department do with it.	
		e. Where it goes.	
		f. Relation of job with others in the department - with others in the office.	
		4. Give assurance that employee will learn quickly - that we recognize there is much to learn - that employee will have adequate and friendly supervision.	Dept. Head
		5. Explain who immediate Supervisor will be - something about her or him. Stress importance of Supervisor in all employee - employer relationships "your instructor, your supervisor, your representative in Management".	Dept. Head
		6. Review compensation.	Dept. Head
		a. Amount per week or month.	
		b. When is pay day.	
		c. Mention briefly deductions required by law; these will be explained on pay day. ("Welcome" booklet 10-12)	
		1. Federal Withholding (Income) Tax.	
		2. State or City Income Tax (if any)	
		3. Federal Old Age Benefits (Social Security)	
		4. State Disability Insurance (if any)	
		5. State Unemployment Insurance (if any)	
		d. Explain policy on payment for short-term absences.	
		e. Salaries are confidential.	

BE BRIEF, CLEAR, NON-TECHNICAL!   LISTEN PATIENTLY!   ENCOURAGE QUESTIONS
4C-22 (29677)

FIG. 7. Dun & Bradstreet, Inc., *Introduction Check List*. (Page 1 of 4 pages)
(Courtesy of Dun & Bradstreet, Inc.)

place in the organization and settles down into the routine of his job, he may feel lost and discouraged. To counteract this tendency, a definite and planned procedure for introducing the person to his fellow workers and to his job routine should be followed. In the Dun & Bradstreet, Inc., organization, a definite routine is established by means of a checksheet which indicates what is to be done, when it is done, and by whom. The person responsible for this step in the routine initials the proper place after it has been accomplished. The first of four pages of the *Introduction Check List* is reproduced in Figure 7.

The abilities of the new employee, his personality traits, any personality conflicts he may have with his fellow workers or his supervisors, and his methods of working, all will affect the way in which he fits into his new environment. The sooner such things can be determined, the sooner they can be corrected or reinforced. A periodic rating sheet for the new employee, completed by his supervisor, helps focus attention upon any problems which may be developing, so that they may be corrected before they become too deeply involved. The Dun & Bradstreet, Inc., *New Employee Progress Report,* reproduced in Figure 8 is an example of such a rating sheet.

After the new employee has had an opportunity to learn his job and begin to produce, he is scheduled for a performance interview with his supervisor. His work is reviewed and he is told how he is progressing. To help him prepare for this interview, he is given a form to guide his thinking about himself in relation to his job. This form, reproduced in Figure 9, not only asks the employee questions about his performance in his job, but also calls for suggestions he may have for improving working conditions or any other matters.

Training for Upgrading of Employees

Employees who do outstanding work at the entry level positions are the ones who should be given prime consideration when an opening occurs in a more responsible, better paying position. Morale of employees and their desire to perform well increase when they realize that their accomplishments will be recognized in such a tangible manner. In some cases, however, superior performance on one level of operation does not prepare the employee for the next level. Further training must be provided to enable the person to move up to the better position. Some companies work in cooperation with

NEW EMPLOYEE PROGRESS REPORT

DUN & BRADSTREET, INC.

NAME_____ OFFICE NAME_____ DATE_____

JOB TITLE_____ DEPARTMENT_____

DATE EMPLOYED_____ DATE LAST PROGRESS REPORT_____

INSTRUCTIONS

1. In making your judgments, consider this employee in relation to his or her length of experience on the job. Try not to be overly influenced by single incidents -- rather think of the employee's general performance and standing on each of the qualities listed.

2. Concentrate on only one quality at a time. Do not allow your judgment on any one quality to be influenced by your decision on another quality.

3. Read over the descriptive phrases several times so you will fit in your mind the range of the scale for that particular quality.

4. Each line is a continuous flow from low to high. Note that the two lowest sections are not subdivided, whereas the three higher sections are divided into two or three degrees. Place a check mark in the space above the horizontal line (not on a dividing line) which most nearly expresses your judgment on each quality.

5. If any words or phrases under the section you select are not inappropriate, line them out.

6. In the spaces provided, give whatever statistics or comments you feel are necessary to support your checked decisions.

QUALITY OF WORK -- (Do not consider amount of work.) Is work done correctly and accurately? Does work meet the required standards of quality? Are errors more frequent than normal in this stage of training?

| Work is carelessly done or not done correctly. Makes errors frequently. | Work not up to standards. Has to be checked frequently to get required results. Work not always accurate. | Does acceptable work. Results meet normal quality standards. | Performs work of high quality. Makes few errors. Can be depended upon. | Work is of higher quality. Very accurate. Does job exactly as it should be done. |

Specific training and supervision needed:_____

QUANTITY OF WORK -- (Do not consider quality of work.) Does employee apply himself or herself to the job? How does employee compare in production with others doing same job with same level of experience?

| Slow worker. Stalls around. Low Production. | Takes it easy. Requires some pushing. Below normal production. | Works fairly steadily. Does job in reasonable manner. Does normal amount of work. | Works hard. Steady at job. Does more than others doing same job. | Outstanding for amount of work accomplished. |

Supporting production statistics:_____

ABILITY TO UNDERSTAND AND FOLLOW INSTRUCTIONS -- Does employee understand instructions? Can employee remember what to do? Does employee actually do what he or she was told to do?

| Requires and needs constant instruction. | Needs detailed instructions on every point. Must be reminded of original instructions. | Understands instructions reasonably well. Requires only normal follow-up. | Rarely has to have instructions repeated. Understands and follows instructions. | Seems to anticipate instructions. Understands with great ease and follows through. |

Supporting comments:_____

4C-296 (8a)

ATTITUDE TOWARD SUPERVISION -- What is employee's attitude toward supervisor? How does employee react to instructions? Does employee cooperate willingly? Does employee take criticism open-mindedly?

| Negative reaction to supervision and criticism. At times uncooperative. | Not too happy to have contact with supervision. Reluctant to cooperate with supervision. | Normally accepting instructions and criticism. | Normally cooperative in accepting instructions and criticism. | Pleasant and cooperative. | Fully cooperative. Does it willingly. | Fully cooperative. Tries to be helpful. |

Supporting comments:_____

PERSONALITY -- Is employee accepted by fellow workers? Does employee get along with other workers? Does employee have any objectionable characteristics which affect others?

| Not fully accepted by fellow workers. May cause friction or trouble. | Tolerated by group. Not particularly tactful or cooperative with fellow employees. | Accepted as one of the group. Gets along normally with fellow workers. Cooperates with others. | Well-liked by fellow workers. Cooperates readily. Makes favorable impression. | Liked by everyone. People react to work with him or her. |

Supporting comments:_____

HEALTH AND PHYSICAL CONDITION -- How does employee's health and physical condition affect his or her work?

| Poor health. Physically unadapted to job. | Not in the best health. Some physical impairment which affects job. | Has reasonably normal health. Able to do work. | Has good health and energy. Keeps in good physical shape. | Always in. Has pep and energy. No physical handicaps. |

Recent absence and punctuality record:_____

GENERAL COMMENTS -- What is needed to help this employee develop into a satisfied and productive member of our staff?

_____

_____

_____

_____

This Progress Report was discussed with the employee on_____

_____

Supervisor's Signature

FIG. 8. Dun & Bradstreet, Inc. *New Employee Progress Report. (Courtesy of Dun & Bradstreet, Inc.)*

PREPARING FOR YOUR
PERFORMANCE REVIEW   Name _____   Date _____

Shortly you and your Supervisor will sit down together for a periodic review and discussion of your performance. The two main objectives are . . . to help you review and improve your performance and to help you and your Supervisor understand each other better in relation to your work with Dun & Bradstreet.

This form might well be called a "self-appraisal." It is intended to assist you in thinking about your performance and about your job in general. You will not turn this form in, but you should make notes on it and bring it along as a reminder of the points you want to discuss. With this preparation you and your Supervisor will be in best position to share views and to talk over matters of importance to you both, and to the Company.

General Personnel Department

1. How well do you feel you are doing your work?

    a. In relation to Quality . . .

    b. In relation to Quantity . . .

2. What do you especially like about your work? Can you explain why?

3. Is there anything you especially dislike about your work? Can you explain why?

4. Are there any steps you feel you can take to do your work more effectively . . . to increase your production or improve your quality?

OVER

4C-81(2-72)0

5. What can your Supervisor do, not do, or do differently to assist you in working more effectively and getting more satisfaction from your job?

6. Are there any parts of your work on which you feel you need more training, information or guidance? What are they?

7. Can you suggest any changes in procedure that might enable you to work more effectively?

8. What is and how do you feel about your . . .

    a. Attendance Record:

    b. Tardiness Record:

9. What other job or jobs, if any, would you like to have in our office? Why? Are you now qualified for that work?

10. How can we make our office a better place in which to work?

11. What other matters d . . . want to discuss in your performance review?

FIG. 9. Dun & Bradstreet, Inc., *Preparing for Your Performance Review*, Pages 1 and 2. *(Courtesy of Dun & Bradstreet, Inc.)*

APPRAISAL WORK-SHEET

NAME _____ DATE _____

Our Summary Appraisal program has two main objectives — to help you review and improve your performance results and methods, and to help you and your Manager understand each other better.

This work-sheet is intended to assist you in thinking about your performance, about the plans you have for your work and about your aspirations. The notes you will make as you review the various captions and questions will make it possible for you to contribute most importantly to the discussions you will have with your Manager.

General Personal Department

PERFORMANCE RESULTS — *What do you feel you have accomplished since your last appraisal in meeting objectives, achieving standards, improving performance, reducing costs, expanding responsibilities?*

PLANS & GOALS — *What major objectives in your present job have you set for yourself for the months immediately ahead . . . what do you want to accomplish, what improvements do you plan to make, what problems are you going to move in on? Name specific projects. Include starting and completion dates you have set.*

OVER

SELF-IMPROVEMENT — *What personal plans do you have for expanding your knowledge and skills, improving your personal performance, enhancing your career potential?*

ASPIRATIONS — *What are your aspirations in the business, immediate and long-range?*

ASSISTANCE — *What do you think management can do to help you in the above areas?*

MISCELLANEOUS — *Is there anything else you want to discuss in your appraisal interview?*

FIG. 10. Dun & Bradstreet, Inc., Appraisal Worksheet, Pages 1 and 2. *(Courtesy of Dun & Bradstreet, Inc.)*

local school systems, colleges, and universities to develop courses in areas that will assist their employees to qualify for promotion. Others develop such courses within their own organizations, where they have complete control over the courses and who takes them. The types of study offered will be as varied as the kinds of duties performed or anticipated. Regardless of the subject matter presented, a well planned course of this sort will make optimum use of the appropriate audio-visual materials.

Motion pictures may be used as bases upon which to build discussions of problem situations. They may present new concepts and procedures. They may show special aspects of the company's operations which not all personnel have the opportunity to see. They may be used to help employees recognize and identify the best ways of accomplishing certain ends.

Filmstrips and slide sets can present much of the same material as motion pictures (except where a knowledge of the motion is important), and have the advantage that a single frame can be held on the screen for any length of time during discussion. Even with a sound filmstrip, the sound track can be stopped or turned off during the discussion. Slides have an advantage over filmstrips because their order can be rearranged to make them fit the needs of the group.

Overhead projectors are excellent devices for this sort of program. Their flexibility, use in a fully lighted room, and the ease of maintaining eye contact with the audience while using them, make them valuable tools for conducting a meeting where discussion is encouraged.

Flipsheets can show many of these same things. Their advantage is that they do not require additional equipment (projector and screen), and they can be used where projection is not feasible.

Tape recordings of actual counselling or work performance interviews (with adequate precautions to preserve the anonymity of the individuals involved) can form the basis for discussions of ways to handle certain situations. Such interviews may also be staged for recording purposes in order to bring out more clearly the problem that is to be discussed. The audience should be told in advance whether or not the recording is of an actual interview.

Continuing Education

Progress in most lines of endeavor is so rapid that continuing study of the field is necessary merely to keep abreast of innovations. As Lewis Carroll said in *Alice in Wonderland,* we have to run as fast as we can just to stay in one place. Particularly where the work is technical, there should be a method of informing personnel of new developments in the field. One such method is used by Merck & Co., Inc., by showing during the noon hours, in the company cafeteria, appropriate motion prictures describing developments in medicine and pharmaceuticals. Announcements on company bulletin boards inform all employees of film showings. Attendance is not required, but good programming and the desire to improve knowledge of the job make employees want to attend. Announcements of two of the programs are shown in Figure 11.

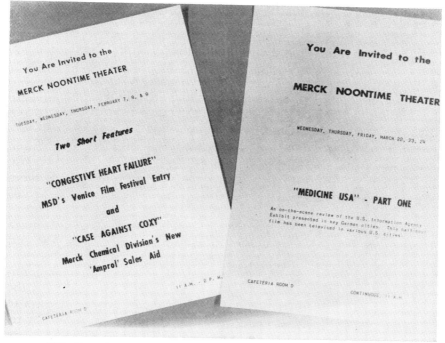

FIG. 11. Invitations to the Merck Noontime Theater, Merck & Co., Inc.
(Courtesy of Merck & Co)

Developments of general interest to company employees may be published in leaflet or pamphlet form. A loose-leaf binder with dividers for different categories of materials can be provided. Filing under the proper category makes the material easily accessible when

it is needed. An employee working in one phase of a company's operations can maintain a knowledge of developments in other areas and
can thus foresee and prepare for their effect on his department.

Summary

Recruitment of the best potential employees is necessary if a company is to grow and improve. Recruitment involves two more or less
simultaneous phases. One is the selection of prospects who will fit
into the company organization and contribute to its efficiency and
productivity. Interviews, aptitude tests, and examination of the person's past achievements are the tools for this phase. The second
phase is the process of selling the person on the company as a place
to establish his career. The recruitment interview is an important
part of this and it is supplemented by motion pictures, brochures,
other informational materials, and tours of the plant.

Employee training is a continuous process from the time a person is selected for employment until he leaves the company through
retirement or for any other reason. Interest in what the company is
trying to accomplish and enthusiasm for its products are aroused
by keeping the employees informed. Information is carried to the individual employee through departmental meetings, individual conferences with supervisors, and materials sent directly to the employee. Some of the tools of this communication process are motion
pictures, brochures and pamphlets, filmstrips, recordings, bulletin
board materials, and the spoken word.

CHAPTER 3

EMPLOYEE RELATIONS

Purposes of Employee Relations Activities

Maintenance of a good relationship between a company and its employees is an important aspect of the work of the personnel division. The responsibility, however, goes beyond this department, for all of management must consider this as part of its area of accountability.

A company that enjoys good relations with its employees has less turnover, less absenteeism, greater loyalty, and greater employee pride in being a part of the organization. It would seem to be axiomatic that every company would do its utmost to promote so many advantages to itself and to the people associated with it.

A new employee generally has a good attitude toward the company and its policies. It should not require a great deal of effort on the part of the management to build and improve upon this favorable start as time goes by. Some organizations, however, seem to make no effort to maintain favorable employee attitudes.

Like morale in a military organization, favorable employee relations are built up by many little things—none particularly important alone, but contributing to the general overall feeling. Some of these things can be deliberately fostered by the company; others seem to be spontaneous. In any event, the management should be alert to the evidence of good or bad personnel relations and take steps to improve them.

Poor personnel relationships, like poor relationships in many other areas, are often due to lack of proper communication between the different parts of the organization. Naturally, a company cannot divulge all of its affairs to all employees. This would make it possible for competitiors to learn too much of the company's business, since there are bound to be leaks somewhere. Also, in many instances the work of one department is not of the slightest interest to members of other departments. However, truthful, candid information should be supplied to the personnel on issues concerning them directly, especially when their jobs, working conditions, pay, or other direct interests are involved.

Audio-Visual Methods Useful in Employee Relations

In personnel relations, as in every other type of business communication, the amount of information management can give employees can be greatly increased by the use of proper audio-visual methods.

Motion Pictures. In many large corporations the average production worker has never even seen the president of the company. To this worker the president is merely someone who sits in a paneled office and pushes buttons to hire or fire factory people. Perhaps he is thought of as a sort of ogre who delights in keeping those below him in fear of their jobs. One motion picture approach to better employee relations might be for the president to make a series of short talks to the employees on motion picture film. This might help employees realize that he is a human being, too.

A company that has operations in various parts of the country or the world cannot be understood in its entirety by people located at a single plant or office. A newsletter in the form of a weekly or monthly motion picture film showing the far-flung operations can act to develop employees' pride in being a part of the organization. New products new processes, laboratory and field research, newly operating units, company personnel who have distinguished themselves in some way—all these can form the raw material for a film report to employees. One such film series was prepared by Kaiser Steel Corporation. In these 28-minute, sound, color films the viewer is taken through the various plants of the Kaiser Steel Corporation to see the overall operations of the company. The films include talks by the president, taking all employees into his confidence on problems that can be solved by cooperation. The title of each film is *Report to Kaiser Employees,* 1957 . . . 1958, etc.

Some other films which have proven to be successful in the development of good employee attitudes are listed in following paragraphs. In most cases, these films are for use within the company only and are not available for outside distribution. The brief descriptions are simply to indicate their character.

Examining the Will to Work is a 14-minute, sound, black and white film that was produced in 1956 by the Esso Standard Oil Company. It was designed to provide first-line supervisory personnel with the latest industrial research findings on factors that motivate employees to high levels of productivity. The supervisors are urged to examine their own leadership practices in terms of those brought out in the film.

Here Today, Here Tomorrow deals with the psychological factors affecting absenteeism. It offers first-line supervisory personnel suggestions for preventing conditions that lead to absenteeism. This 15-minute, sound, color film was produced in 1956 for the Ethyl Corporation.

The Inner Man Steps Out is designed to help management personnel do their own thinking and solve problems in working with people. It is designed to be followed by a period of discussion. It was made by the General Electric Company in 1951, is sound, black and white, and runs for 34 minutes.

The Communication Casebook. This is a kit consisting of film sequences from *The Inner Man Steps Out.* A Leader's Guide is included. Each of the four filmed sequences deals with a different problem.

CASE I — *The Case of the Tuned-Out Mind* points up the two-way nature of all communication and illustrates that a profitable exchange can only occur when both parties are interested, receptive, and respectful of each other.

CASE II — *The Case of the Wrong Wave-Length* shows the necessity for considering individual differences between people.

CASE III — *The Case of the Chain Reaction* demonstrates the importance of sensitivity to other people's emotional reactions. It emphasizes the immediate and · long-range consequences of the way an order, or any other communication, is transmitted down the line.

CASE IV — *The Case of the Silent Yell* examines the effects of unspoken attitudes.

These film sequences are available on either 16mm or 8mm film from Harry Strauss Distributing Corp., 31 West 53rd Street, New York 19, New York.

More Than Telling is intended to develop in supervisory personnel a realization of the importance of two-way communication between them and the people they supervise. This is a 22 minute, sound, black and white film, made in 1955 by the New York Telephone Company.

A sequel to the above film, *No One Answer,* points out the importance of day-to-day, informal communications in developing employee attitudes. It stresses the necessity of recognizing individual differences and dealing with people according to the ways in which they react. It is also concerned with the opportunities for developing constructive relationships through informal communicating on the job. This was also made by the American Telephone & Telegraph Company in 1957, runs 23½ minutes, is in sound and black and white.

The Time Is Now was a 29-minute, sound, black and white film made by the Mutual Benefit Life Insurance Company as a public service to industry. Although it has now been withdrawn, it was part of a complete management program directed chiefly at members of lower and middle supervision. The aim was to stimulate a realization that a man's most important assets are internal and intangible—those qualities of integrity, self-reliance, initiative, and leadership which he has built out of his past experiences.

Proper utilization of these motion pictures by the appropriate personnel can assist in improving employee relations. It would be unrealistic to expect any one thing, including the use of films, to cause this improvement, but this medium can work in combination with others to provide the desired effect.

An employee relations film carefully planned for maximum effectiveness in presentation is *Missing Person,* prepared by the Westinghouse Electric Corporation. It is designed to help supervisors at all levels improve their relations with subordinates. To be most effective, the viewing group should consist of 25 or fewer supervisors. The program begins with a four-minute introduction by J. K. Hodnette, formerly vice-president and general manager of Westinghouse. His remarks are as follows:

At a recent stockholders' meeting a shareholder who was also a veteran Westinghouse employee took the floor to say that something was missing from the Company's relations with its employees something had happened to the old spirit of friendliness and cooperation which used to prevail among our people. He said everyone feels he is on his own—the boss isn't interested in him anymore.

The speaker was expressing something that has been and is a major concern of all of us. And we're going to do something about

FIG. 12. *Missing Person* Manual Cover. *(Courtesy of Westinghouse Electric Corporation)*

it—and by we, I mean you, me, and every member of management.

We are going to restore that spirit of friendliness and cooperation and group loyalty—not only because we want good, stable,
healthy employee relations, but because it is good business.

As supervisors, the attitudes of the people you manage are your
direct and first responsibility. As a part of your job as a supervisor
you are personally responsible for the creation of an atmosphere of
cooperative understanding among your people—an atmosphere in
which the will to work is motivated from within, not superimposed
from without.

In too many cases we have forgotten that to produce we must
lead. The result is that employees are left to their own devices—the
rumor committee works overtime—the dissenters and detractors take
over. Insecurity, futility and poor performance can be the only result.

You are going to see a film presentation that has just one purpose
—to start you thinking about your leadership responsibilities. After-
ward you are to discuss methods of correcting whatever man-management problems exist in your departments. I shall have a few more
words to say at the conclusion of this meeting—meanwhile I'm count-
ing on your participation to make this effort a real success.

After this introduction, the main body of the film is shown. The film is animated and runs for 19 minutes. It commences with scenes of confusion and argument and points out that this is happening because a man is missing—the supervisor. He is not missing physically, but is doing work he considers more important than managing his people. Man-management is the supervisor's most important responsibility because it is through people that he can achieve quality of product, delivery on time, and a high level of productivity. The supervisor must recognize and accept his responsibility to lead and to create a climate of confidence. This means that he will observe his people in order to be aware of their reactions, encourage employee participation in developing plans, keep employees informed, and maintain fair standards of performance. He must practice man-to-man management; he must start every new employee off on the right foot, encourage long-term employee development, listen to and help with employees' personal problems, be consistent in administering discipline or praise, and encourage individual initiative by avoiding too close supervision. He must also build good group relations and develop a good team spirit within his organization. Extra personal efforts on the part of the supervisor will not increase the productivity of the department very much, but time spent in encouraging, motivating, and managing the department people *will* increase productivity.

Following the showing of the film, a 45- to 65-minute discussion period is planned to reinforce and intensify the viewers' impressions. To structure the discussion, a series of 12 flipcharts indicates a series of questions to be considered.

1. In the film we have just seen, much reference was made to the term "man-management."
    What does this term mean to you?
2. The film stated that a supervisor must—
3. *Accept* his leadership responsibility!
4. Create a Climate of Confidence!
                    by
    Encouraging employee participation
    Keeping employees informed
    Maintaining fair standards of performance
5. Practice Man-To-Man Management
                    by
    Being employee centered—treating each employee as an individual

Putting the right man on the right job
Starting new employees off on the right foot
Training and re-training
Counseling, coaching, and encouraging
Listening to employees' personal problems and being helpful
Administering discipline when necessary
Praising when deserved
Avoiding too close supervision

6. Develop Good Group Relations!

by

Recognizing that each employee is a part of many groups
Seeking out employee leaders and getting them on your side
Building team spirit

7. From your experience, which of these points which were brought out in the film, and we have just discussed, are the most important?
Why?

8. Good man-management, this is, employee-centered management, means considering fully the impact our decisions and actions will have on employees.

9. What are some practical steps that we, as individual supervisors, can take to improve our man-management performance?

10. What benefits accrue to (1) the supervisor and (2) Westinghouse as a result of employee-centered management?

11. You may feel that to improve your own man-management performance, some decisions must be made, some policy must be clarified, or some action must be taken by higher management.

12. What three questions pertaining to the how, the what, the why, or the who of any phase of man-management would you like to have answered by top management?

At the conclusion of the discussion period, the group decides on three questions directed to the company's management. One way to do this is to divide into smaller groups and ask each subgroup to come up with one question. The entire group then chooses three of the questions for referral to top local management.

After the question shave been selected, the last portion of the film—Mr. Hodnette's concluding remarks—is shown.

This meeting is just the beginning of a program that we feel will have far reaching benefits for all of us.

Make no mistake about it, we are determined to build the best employee relations in American industry. We depend upon you as our "man-managers" to do it. From time to time we'll offer advice and instruction. We'll back you with authority and with our confidence. We'll give you every support we can think of—but *you* have to do the job.

Our employees are working under long-term contracts. The situation is right; the time is right.

You will be seeing more of us and we expect to be seeing more of you—not buried behind your desks in routine chores, but out on the production floors, or out in the offices, in the company of your people.

Remember this—to your employees you are management. You are their hope for security and advancement and prosperity. A little understanding from you goes a long way in job satisfaction and peace of mind.

Yours is a serious responsibility and a great opportunity. We're depending upon you to make the most of it for yourself, for your people and for a name we all want to be proud of Westinghouse.

At the conclusion of the meeting a copy of the manual, *Missing Person,* is given to each of the supervisors. The manual contains the introduction and concluding remarks by Mr. Hodnette, a scene-by-scene review of the film, and a list of the important discussion questions used following the film.

About one month following the film and discussion program all of the supervisors meet with the local top management to hear them discuss and answer the questions that were raised by the small groups of supervisors.

This meeting has utilized several of the available techniques of audio-visual presentation. The central feature was, of course, the motion picture. This provided a common experience from which the group could draw examples and base their discussion. The introduction and concluding remarks, although they were on film, were not structurally a part of the film presentation .They served to motivate and hold the attention of the audience because of the authority of the speaker and the respect in which he is held. Flipcharts help to structure a discussion and insure that the talk does not go off on a tangent. Passing out the manuals at the conclusion of the program provides the participants with something tangible to remind them of the different points brought up and the ideas developed for improving their techniques of supervision. By holding them until the discussion is completed, the leader insures more complete concentration on the questions as they are discussed. If the materials were passed out any sooner, the people would be reading them during the discussion. The follow-up meeting with local management serves to underscore the importance of the program.

Filmstrips. Filmstrips often can serve just as well as motion pictures in helping to maintain good employee relations. One of their chief advantages is the way in which they can be used to struc ture discussion. Since they do not have to be projected at any pre-determined rate, the presentation can be tailored to fit the audience. They lend themselves to many variations in structure and composition. They can be used to:

Introduce a new product to the employees
Initiate a change in company procedures
Explain the reasons for a change in company policy
Demonstrate safety campaigns

Sound filmstrips introduce the added dimension of music, narration, and indigenous sound to augment the emotional impact of the visual. Proper integration of the various aspects of a filmstrip can achieve much of the effect of a motion picture.

Overhead Projection. The overhead projector is an excellent tool for presenting employee relations material. By use of successive overlays, ideas can be developed while the image is on the screen. Additional information, geared to a particular group, can be added to the transparency with a grease pencil and later removed with a soft cloth.

Opaque Projection. By means of the opaque projector, it is possible to project on the screen documents or other objects which do not lend themselves readily to reproduction as transparencies. Thus, labor agreements or other timely materials can be shown to a large group as soon as they are typed or otherwise prepared. Changes can be pencilled or inked in as they are acted upon by the group.

Materials from books or in other forms too small to use with a large group can be enlarged with the opaque projector on a piece of cardboard and a drawing made by tracing over the projected image. This is an excellent means of making eye-stopping illustrations and announcements for employee bulletin boards.

Brochures. Booklets may serve as devices to improve employee relations. They may be distributed to all of the employees or to certain groups, such as supervisors. Typical of this class of publications is the Allis-Chalmers pamphlet illustrated in Figure 13.

Audio Recording. Sound recording is primarily a tool to make other communication media more effective through synchronized

FIG. 13. Employee Relations Brochure Issued by Allis-Chalmers.
(Courtesy of Allis-Chalmers)

sound, narration, and music. It can also be used by itself to bring talks to the employees from the company officials. Although not strictly in the audio-visual communications line, recorded music played in work areas helps people relax and increase their production.

Bulletin Boards. Strategically placed bulletin boards (usually located near time clocks or drinking fountains) can keep employees informed on developments within the company. Prompt publication of information of interest to employees can build employee morale by preventing the spread of rumors. To be effective, the material must be kept up to date. Material should be evaluated at least weekly and removed if it is out of date or has lost is interest.

The Borden Company keeps its employees informed by use of the *Borden Reporter* and other publications posted on their bulletin boards.

FIG. 14. Borden Reporter. *(Courtesy of The Borden Company)*

Summary

Many companies carry on employee relations activities in order to sustain morale and reduce training costs by lessening turnover.

Audio-visual media can facilitate communication between management and all levels of personnel. When the employee believes that management has an interest in him and his welfare, he is likely to repay that interest with loyalty to the organization.

Use of audio and visual devices will not in themselves insure good employee relations. They can only be means to that end. However, they can make communication more effective and generally more pleasant for the employees.

CHAPTER 4

PUBLIC RELATIONS

Purposes of Public Relations Activities

Every company, like every individual, wants to be held in high esteem. Large corporations spend millions of dollars in their effort to develop a desirable "corporate image" in the public mind.

For the purposes of this discussion, we shall separate the field of public relations from that of sales promotion. Although the two are very closely tied, we shall consider public relations to be concerned with increasing the public acceptance of the company on an institutional basis and not necessarily with the translation of this goodwill into sales.

Aluminum Company of America sets out the following functions as belonging to their public relations department. As specialists in the field of communications this department is responsible for:

1. appraising public attitudes toward the company;
2. recommending positive and practical programs by which the public may be informed regarding Alcoa's corporate activities; and
3. developing or assisting in the development of specific communications methods through which such information may be transmitted to the public concerned.[1]

Public relations communications take many forms because there are many different types of information to communicate and many different types of people with whom to communicate.

Audio-Visual Devices Useful in Promoting Public Relations

Motion Pictures. Just as in other areas of business communica-

1. *Alcoa's Public Relations.* Unpublished memorandum, Aluminum Company of America, July 1, 1960.

tion, the motion picture is a powerful medium for telling the public relations story of the firm or an industry. The impact of the large picture on the screen, the elimination of distractions, and the acceptance of this medium through past conditioning—all contribute to the effectiveness of the motion picture in the dissemination of public relations material. Many excellent public relations films have been produced by companies in all lines of business and industry. A few typical of this nature are listed and described in following paragraphs.

1. *Company Manners.* This is a 27½-minute, sound, color film, produced in 1958 by the Union Pacific Railroad. It explains the importance of good public relations and emphasizes that public relations is everybody's job. It points out the operations of the press, radio, and television departments in disseminating material. It also stresses the importance of individual contacts between employees and the public in maintaining good public relations.

2. *Birth of a Giant.* A 30-minute, sound, black and white, film, produced in 1958 by the Canadian Government. The film tells the story of the building of the largest aircraft carrier ever produced in Canada, the CL-28 (Argus), and its impact on the Canadian Community.

3. *Crisis in Lindenville.* Produced in 1958 by the National Association of Manufacturers. It runs 28 minutes, is in sound, black and white, and is available in 35 mm as well as 16 mm. The president of a small company fights to save the plant for his community, acts promptly to kill wild rumors through frank talks with employees, community leaders and fellow executives. Shows dynamic leadership at work within the board of directors.

4. *Flight 803.* A 26-minute, sound color film produce by United Air Lines. Brings together three great names in aviation—United, Douglas, and Pratt & Whitney—in the development of the DC-8, and traces through a coast-to-coast flight services on the plane, the work of the weather center, flight training, engineering maintenance, etc.

5. *Holiday in Hawaii.* A 29-minute, sound, color film produced by United Air Lines. It tells the story of a holiday on the islands of Oahu, Maui, Kauai, and Hawaii—covering major attractions from deep sea fishing to luau banquets. It also shows the seldom seen Polynesian fire dance, and singing by the Haili Choir of Hilo.

6. *Industry on Parade Series.* A series of 13½-minute, sound motion pictures produced by the National Association of Manufacturers.

It includes more than 400 television reports about people, products, processes, and plants, and the changes brought about by science and industry.

7. *Experiment: Solar Energy.* A 23-minute, sound film produced by the National Association of Manufacturers. Science is directing the power of the sun, which already provides all our food and fuel, into new and exciting services to mankind. Between scenes of concentrated sunlight melting steel and creating oxygen from algae for possible submarine and space travel, the camera tours university and industrial research laboratories to report on such things is sun-powered radios, solar heating and cooling of homes, distillation of sea water and purification of organic wastes.

8. *A Product of the Imagination.* A 26-minute, sound, color film produced by the Aluminum Company of America. Aluminum, from the beginning of time to the penetration of outer space, has evolved as truly *A Product of the Imagination.* Narrating the film, the imaginary "Adam and Eve" explain how aluminum lay locked for eons in rocks, ores and clays and how man's curiosity finally sought it out and revealed a boundless new adventure in ideas. Viewers take a highly entertaining journey through the aluminum industry's past, present and future. Colorful scenes include mining operations and manufacturing plants where aluminum is forged, rolled, drawn, extruded and impacted. From today's practicalities the film turns to tomorrow's possibilities for the light, versatile metal. The Alcoa FORECAST collection opens entirely new concepts in aluminum design for home and family.

9. *Outboard Outings.* A 19-minute, sound, color film produced by Aetna Life Affiliated Companies. Over forty million Americans are boating enthusiasts today and more millions join them every year. Boating safety rules are often blithely ignored or forgotten at the dock. This film highlights the safety precautions that should be observed, boaters' rules-of-the-road, fair and foul weather boating techniques, and similar pointers designed to make boating a safe nd pleasant experience. This film should appeal to the neophyte and experienced boater.

The purpose of each of the films described in preceding paragraphs is to enhance the public acceptance of the company producing it. Direct selling of the company's product is not a function of this type of film. In many cases the only mention of the organization which produced the material is the company's trademark appearing at the beginning and end of the film. This is not to say that in a film having to do with a subject area in which the company manufactures equipment, this company's equipment will not appear. However, this fact will not be continually brought to the attention of the viewer.

Choosing the Audience. To determine the general approach and appeal of the material, an organization planning to produce a public relations film must first consider what groups of people are to be reached. Examples of typical groups follow:

School classes (from kindergarten through college)
Youth groups (Boy Scouts, Campfire Girls, YMCA)
Adult hobby groups (hunting clubs, photographic groups)
Service clubs (Lions, Rotary, Kiwanis)
Occupational groups (union, Grange, trade organizations)
Church groups
Professional groups (doctors, teachers, engineers)
Community organizations (PTA, taxpayers' groups)

The entire approach of the film will vary according to the group which the company considers its prime audience. For instance, a film which might go very well at a hunting club could be a complete failure at a PTA meeting. On the other hand, a production that attempts to appeal to all groups may not reach any of them successfully.

Running Time. The question of running time of a public relation motion picture is an important one. The film must be long enough to be informative, yet short enough to be interesting. Like the old-fashioned vaudeville act, the film should quit while the audience still wants more.

If the film is intended for use in school classrooms, it should be remembered that the usual duration of a school class is from 45 to 55 minutes. In order to allow for the normal class routine of getting the period under way, introduction of the film, and discussion afterwards, 30 minutes should be the maximum running time for this sort of a film. If the film is intended for use in the primary grades (kindergarten through third grade), it should be limited to about ten minutes, to fit the short attention span of these youngsters.

Some public relations films are produced to be broadcast from commercial television stations. Television programming is in segments of 15 minutes and its multiples, and the desired lengths of running time for materials are 13 to $14\frac{1}{2}$ minutes or 27 to 29 minutes. This allows a short time at the beginning and end of a film presentation to bring in announcements or remarks concerning the film.

Standard sizes of 16mm reels and their running time at sound speed determine the lengths of many productions. The standard reel of 16mm motion picture film is 400 feet, which runs for approximately 11 minutes on the screen.

Reel capacity	Number of "reels"	Running time
400 feet	1	11 minutes
600 feet	1½	16 minutes
800 feet	2	22 minutes
1,200 feet	3	33 minutes
1,600 feet	4	44 minutes
2,000 feet	5	55 minutes

FIG. 15. Running Time for 16mm Sound Motion Picture Film.

Color versus Black and white. Most public relations films being made today are photographed on color film. A motion picture film in color holds the interest of the viewers better than the same film in black and white. Audiences have become accustomed to color in films and a black and white film may not satisfy them. Esthetic values of color may also outweigh the slight extra cost. Some films, planned for distribution in black and white, are orginally photographed in color because of the better tonal qualities gained by utilizing this method. Also the distribution can be changed to color whenever desired.

As color television becomes more prevalent, films intended for showing solely through TV channels will shift from black and white to color.

Sound versus Silent. This is practically an academic question, since virtually all public relations motion pictures utilize sound tracks. However, the choice does exist and occasionally a silent 16 mm film is made commercially.

Filmstrips. Filmstrips, at a much lower cost, can often do as effective a public relations job as motion pictures. Either silent or sound filmstrips can be used in the production of public relations materials.

Silent filmstrips rely upon printed information included with the pictures on the frames or upon a commentary from the person showing them.

Sound filmstrips are accompanied by a recording of the commentary, music, and other appropriate sounds. The recording is on a disc record or a magnetic tape. Signals to change frames may be audible (this tends to disturb the audience) ; they may be subsonic vibrations to which the changer mechanism is sensitive, which provides automatic, silent changing of the frames; or they may be printed in a manual so that the projector can follow the narration and advance the film at the appropriate time.

Where movement is not a part of the significant material in the subject being presented, the filmstrip can do quite as good a job as a motion picture. However, the motion picture has the advantage of holding the attention of the viewer.

Filmstrips lend themselves very well to either photographs or graphic techniques or a combination of both.

Most filmstrips are produced today on color film. The difference between the cost of black and white and color film is proportionately a small part of the total production cost, and the increased interest in color will more than offset the price differential.

Brochures. Projected means of communication are excellent for presentation of information to large numbers of people simultaneously, especially when the desired message is one of general impressions rather than specific, detailed information. However, when people cannot be assembled in large groups or when the information is detailed in nature, a better approach is through printed materials. They can be retained by those concerned and referred to at any time that the information is desired. The same sorts of information that would be shown by means of the projector can be distributed on the written page with the exception, of course, of the motion involved in the motion picture. The advantages of both methods may be obtained by passing out printed materials immediately following the motion picture or filmstrip showing. The same message may be repeated in the brochure, to be read as reinforcement of the projected material. Detailed information remains for reference at any time.

Public relations brochures are generally issued to cover areas, closely related to the company interests. For instance, the Deere & Company bi-monthly magazine, "the Furrow," pictured in Figure 16, covers various activities vital to farmers and concerning which the company can offer advice and help to them. This magazine also serves a sales function in informing farmers of new products and new applications of the older ones.

Exhibits. Public relations exhibits are made for a wide variety

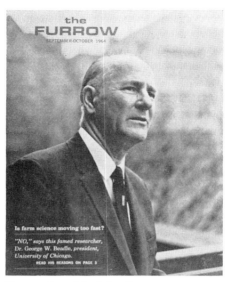

FIG. 16. The Furrow, Issued by John Deere. *(Courtesy of Deere & Company)*

of uses and levels of interest. The purpose is generally to acquaint the viewer with such things as:

Manufacturing processes
Operation of a machine
Explanation of a theoretical concept
Uses of a product
A method of accomplishing some activity (such as how to lay out lines for contour plowing)
The interior construction of some object
"Before and after" some action

The public relations exhibit often involves a combination of audio-visual techniques. Some which lend themselves to the preparation of an effective exhibit are the following:

Motion pictures—often with a rear-projection screen to save space and to make possible use where room darkening is not sufficient for regular projection.

Filmstrips and slides—on a continuous automatic projector which changes slides without attention.

Models and mockups—for use where the original cannot be shown or where it needs simplification.

Specimens or samples—to show the actual product or the materials that go into it.

Charts and graphs—to call attention to and explain concepts that would otherwise be difficult to understand, such as statistical compilations.

Audio recordings—to add the dimension of sound to that of sight. Can be broadcast by means of loudspeakers or provided individually with earphones or telephone handsets.

Whatever combination of approaches is used to make up the exhibit, it must be kept in mind that everything should be directed toward the same single end. The exhibit which makes one major point and utilizes every appropriate device to emphasize that point will be more successful than one which has a divided message.

Some of the places where public relations exhibits may be found are the following:

School classrooms
Fairs and expositions
In the lobby of the company's office or manufacturing plant for the orientation of visitors
Museums of science and industry
Conventions and conferences
Showrooms of dealers handling the product
School audio-visual libraries
Chambers of commerce

Photographs. Photographic presentation of the product, manufacturing process, or other phases of the company's operation may make an excellent public relations device. In addition to the motion picture, filmstrip, and exhibit use of photographs, there are other ways in which pictures can be presented effectively.

Study prints are used by school classes in learning about many subjects. These are individually mounted photographic or half-tone engraving prints that are at least 11x14 inches in size. This is the minimum size that will permit all students to see at the same time. These prints are utilized in several different ways, as follows:

The teacher may hold them up or place them on an easel so the entire class can see and discuss them at the same time.

Pictures may be passed around the room individually so that each student can study them in detail.

Photographs and other materials may be put on the bulletin board in such a way as to point up the relationships between the items involved. The bulletin board presentation may be left up a week or so to give each student the opportunity to study it at his leisure.

Exhibits may be centered around several pictures that tell the story and relate the parts of the exhibit to one another.

Photographs may be filed according to subject and made available to students for preparation of their reports.

Photographs may be projected with an opaque projector to provide an image large enough for all students to see details at once.

Examples of materials of this sort that are made available to schools are *History of Mail* and *Historic Planes* study print sets prepared by United Air Lines. As might be imagined, these show the development of mail transportation and that of aviation through the years.

Of a similar nature are the study folders distributed by the Douglas Aircraft Company, Inc., illustrated in Figure 17.

FIG. 17. Study Print Sets Distributed by the Douglas Aircraft Company, Inc.,
Famous Douglas Missiles, Famous Douglas Military Aircraft,
Famous Douglas Space Vehicles, and *Famous Douglas Commercial Aircraft.*
(*Courtesy of Douglas Aircraft Company, Inc.*)

Publicity releases are generally accompanied by suitable photographs of the persons or objects that are the subject of the publicity. The usual purpose of these is to illustrate the newspaper or magazine article in order to increase the readership and the interest in the material. This type of photograph should be technically correct, clear in what it is trying to convey, honest, and correctly captioned. Although most publicity photographs are staged in order to get a good picture, they should be about an actual, true situation or happening in the organization.

Pictures prepared for use as parts of exhibits must be planned in such a way that they fit into and increase the effectiveness of the story that the exhibit is designed tells. For this reason, they should be planned for and taken as a definite part of the preparation of the exhibit and not as an afterthought.

Summary

Activities intended to improve the public's regard and approval of an organization can be made more effective through the use of appropriate devices of an audio-visual nature. Motion pictures and filmstrips can tell the story to large groups in an interesting and attention holding manner. Sound can increase the effectiveness of a filmstrip just as it does for the motion picture. Brochures are valuable when the target audience cannot be assembled or when detailed information is to be transmitted. Combinations of the two are even more effective than either one singly. Exhibits can make use of a variety of audio-visual devices to tell the company's story in the classroom, fairs, conventions, and other gatherings of people of somewhat similar interests. Photographs are used as components of other devices or separately to tell a story. Study prints and publicity releases are two of the ways in which photographs can be used in public relations.

BIBLIOGRAPHY

Strauss, L. Harry, and J. R. Kidd, *Look, Listen, and Learn,* New York, Association Press, 1948, 235 pp.
Chap. XI Audio-Visual Aids in Public Relations.

CHAPTER 5

SALES AND PROMOTION

Purposes of Sales and Promotion Activities

All of a company's activities have one ultimate end—that of making a favorable showing on its financial statements. In the planning of all activities this end must be kept in mind. Preparing the sales campaign activities is one of the important steps in which management must engage in order to insure a successful year's operations.

An important part of the planning of a sales and promotion campaign is the selecting of the communication channels through which the company will go to tell its story to prospective customers or those who may be able to influence purchases.

Why use audio-visual devices to help in this selling activity? Why not just tell the people about the product and demonstrate it to them? In the first place, just telling them about the product might not be enough. More persuasion may be necessary than merely talking about it. Demonstration of the actual object might be impractical or impossible. It might be too small, too large, too dangerous, too far away, too complicated, too fragile, too offensive in odor, or too unmanageable for one to carry it to a person and say, "Here it is. Would you like to buy it?" Or it may be that what you are selling is intangible and cannot be shown or demonstrated. In any of these situations, intelligent use of the proper audio-visual methods of communication will help to get the sales message across.

Sales and promotion activities are of two general types—internal and external. Internal sales and promotion activities are directed toward the members of the selling organization. They are the dealers, salesmen, representatives, and others who call upon the prospective customers. Audio-visual presentations to these people usually take the form of instructions in the proper approaches, things to stress, and ways of convincing the prospects to buy. External sales and promotion activities are aimed directly at the prospect and are for the purpose of convincing him to buy.

Internal Sales and Promotion

A primary purpose of internal sales and promotion activities is to inform the selling personnel about the advantages of the company's product and its superiority over those of the competitiors. In order to function productively, each sales person must have the latest information about the material and its features at his finger-tips. Thus a more or less lengthy period of indoctrination and training must take place before he is ready to represent the organization and its product. Naturally, the more complicated the article and/or its use, the longer will be the period before the person is ready to commence selling.

Many companies call in their representatives to headquarters periodically to brush them up on sales techniques and knowledge of the latest developments in current products and those which are to be marketed in the near future. This is a rather expensive procedure for a company to undertake, considering the cost of transportation and the fact that the representatives are not producing sales during the time of the meeting. Consequently the information to be presented must be important to the company, must be presented in the most efficient way possible, and be directly applicable to the problem of selling the product to the customer. Audiovisual methods of presentation cannot do much about the first of these three conditions, but they can help to improve the other two.

A common feature of a sales conference is a preview presentation of materials that will be shown to prospective customers. In addition they can be provided with information that will supplement that given to the customer and go into more detail on the various technical aspects. Thus, if a customer desires further explanation on some point, the salesman will be able to supply him with the data desired. Short-comings of competitors' products may also be demonstrated to convince the personnel further of their own product's superiority. All of these things can increase the salesman's confidence and build up his sales effectiveness.

Another advantage of the internal sales meeting is that it increases the drive of salesmen and "fires them up" to go after more orders. Association with other sales people and executives in the sales division of their company can act as a stimulant to their own sales activities.

How can the various audio-visual methods assist in making the internal sales promotion activity more effective? Some of the general advantages are as follows:

1. Preview of materials to be used with customers enables the salesman to anticipate reactions and adjust his sales approach accordingly.
2. A knowledge of the appearance, utility, etc., of products yet to be introduced will help in planning future individual sales activities.
3. The emotional impact of properly used audio-visual devices can enhance the motivational aspect of the sales meeting.

Motion Pictures. The attention getting and holding properties of motion pictures make them valuable devices for presenting sales information to company representatives. Steps in the manufacturing processes, historical information, and testing activities which prove the quality or efficiency of the product all may be illustrated. Suggested or proper ways of using a product may be shown to help sales representatives to give the right advice to customers concerning use of the product. Motion pictures have the capability of presenting information in a way that will assure vivid recollections for a long time. The use of this medium, then, will add to the effectiveness of the sales meeting.

As an example of an excellent use of the audio-visual approach for several years Republic Steel Corporation has been holding "Order Makers Institutes." The need for a program of this sort was felt in 1954 when Norman Foy, Republic vice-president (sales) and Larry Hamaker, general sales manager, found that Republic's production of steel pipe was greater than the demand. Salesmen for distributors of the pipe products for the most part have little or no formal training in sales. If the distributors' salesmen could be helped to do a better job, obviously Republic would benefit. OMI was born, with Republic furnishing all the materials needed, even a leader to conduct the discussions. A careful investigation of the complaints of steel customers helped to shape the presentation. The end purposes of the OMI are to help steel salesmen to sell better and to create a growing demand for what they have to sell. During the institute, which covers six training sessions, the problems of selling the product are diagnosed to determine their causes, so that a treatment can be recommended to bring about a cure.

The materials consist of a series of specially produced 16mm motion pictures, flip charts on which the faults of salesmen are recorded, and printed materials that become parts of the salesmen's files.

A typical film in the series is titled *The Care and Handling of Buyers*. Buyers and sellers who were the top people in their various fields were asked how buyers should be handled. The results of the investigation indicated that these bits of advice should be incorporated into this film:

1. Make friends . . .
   by entertaining
   by building confidence
   by listening
2. Be helpful . . .
   by having something interesting to tell
   by selling your company in terms that benefit your customers
   by taking inventory
   by consulting with other departments
   by following through
3. Be tactful . . .
   by building back
   by calling personally
   by finding the best time to call
   by thinking of big "little" things
   by knowing when to be personal
   by finding the proper procedure
4. Be purposeful . . .
   by saving customers' money
   by saving customers' time
   by providing special service
5. Be flexible . . .
   by accenting the positive
   by holding down the pressure, but
   by not holding it down too low
   by knowing when to leave

Following the showing the the film, a discussion is held to emphasize the points brought out. Brochures passed out at the conclusion of the meeting provide material for review and comment. Booklets and other data are illustrated in Figure 18.

Filmstrip. The filmstrip can be used in internal sales promotion in the same manner as a motion picture—plus the added advantage

FIG. 18. Materials Used in Republic Steel Corporation's "Order Makers Institute."
(Courtesy of Republic Steel Corp.)

found in the fact that questions can be answered and discussions can be held during the projection. The motion picture projector can, of course, be stopped during the showing for discussion, but this is generally not done because of the tightly-knit sequence of scenes that make up this form of presentation. The filmstrip, on the other hand, particularly the form in which the person leading the presentation reads the narration aloud, lends itself very well to answering questions and discussing relevant side issues that arise during the showing. The leader must decide for himself how far to let the discussion stray from the "bare bones" treatment that is usually found in the printed narration that accompanies a filmstrip. Sometimes the most fruitful parts of the showing are found in the exploration of the ideas brought out by someone's questions or comments during the filmstrip's showing. In the case of the sound filmstrip where the narration is on a recording or a magnetic tape, there is more of the tendency to let it run on through, just as in the case of the motion picture. One method of handling a situation of this sort is to play the filmstrip and soundtrack through once without interruption, then repeat the filmstrip without the sound track and encourage discussion of the frames as they appear. Motion picture producers sometimes utilize a technique similar to this when they make a filmstrip to follow the film. On the filmstrip they reproduce key scenes from the film and superimpose questions for discussion.

The Caterpillar Tractor Company has prepared a number of sound filmstrips which they use to keep their dealers and salesmen informed about their products and the ways in which they are manufactured. One such filmstrip is *Heat Treatment*. It is intended to inform the salesman about the quality of parts and products manufactured by Caterpillar so that he can sell with more confidence. It describes the processes of heating, quenching in water and in oil, annealing, hardening, and tempering, and tells the effect of each on different types of steel. The filmstrip also tells of the care with which Caterpillar handles its steel parts to insure the proper hardness and toughness characteristics in each piece of steel that goes into one of their tractors—depending upon the type of strain and wear that part will have to resist. At the end of each section, the script instructs the leader to turn off the sound track and lead the group in a discussion of the material they have learned. A series of frames of the filmstrip is projected to guide the discussion.

An advantage that the filmstrip has over the motion picture for this sort of discussion is that the operator can easily flip back to a particular frame for further discussion during the question and answer peiod of the program. When using a motion picture, it is difficult to locate a certain scene once it has been passed.

Some typical sales and promotion filmstrip announcements and manuals are illustrated in Figure 19.

Brochure. Used either by itself or in conjunction with a film or filmstrip, a brochure or booklet is an excellent means of disseminating material that is complicated or which otherwise is difficult to remember in detail. The brochure can be studied at home or when there is a lull in work activities. If a question should come up during a sales talk with a customer, a quick reference to the booklet can disrlose the correct answer.

An example of this sort of publication is the booklet (Figure 20) published by the training department of Montgomery Ward to acquaint sales people with their Airline brand of stereos, phonographs, tape recorders, radios, televisions, and other sound devices. In order that the sales person understand the product he is selling, the booklet starts with basic information about sound reproduction. It answers

FIG. 19. Some Filmstrip Announcements and Manuals Issued by the
Caterpillar Tractor Co. *(Courtesy of Caterpillar Tractor Co.)*

such questions as, "What about UHF? Tube or transistor . . . is there is difference?" It also discusses such things as the function of the cabinet, the speaker system, the amplifier, and the record changer. The major portion of the booklet contains photographs and technical descriptions of the various units of Airline merchandise interspersed with selling hints to help convince the customer. The format and information make it useful to all salesmen in this department regardless of the experience they may have.

Flipcharts. Efficient use of a motion picture or filmstrip can be attained even though the operator may not be an expert in the subject matter being shown. The sound track or printed narration, along with the visuals, carry the burden of imparting the information to the viewer. The flipchart, on the other hand, requires that a person using it be quite familiar with the material that is being presented. The flipchart provides a means of summarizing, emphasizing, and illustrating the information that is being given orally by a speaker.

It is a very useful auxiliary device but it will not accomplish a great deal of instructional work by itself.

Material to be covered during the talk is printed on successive sheets of heavy paper and the sheets are hinged together at the top. An easel or tabletop stand holds the sheets at the correct height for reading by the audience. As each point is brought home (or at other strategic steps of the talk) the appropriate sheet is uncovered by turning the previous one over to the back. The printing, drawing, or other material should, of course, be large enough for the most distant person to see. In the event that the instructor wishes to add information as he talks, appropriate pages may be left blank and the date drawn or printed with a felt pen, china-marking pencil, crayon, or paper chalk. Such additions during the talk can add much to the spontaneity and interest of the presentation.

The application to the internal sales and promotion activity would be in meetings designed to instruct and inspire salesmen to increase their sales.

Combination Approach. Utilizing the "change of pace" made possible by approaching the subject through several different media, a meeting of sales people can be made much more interesting and informative. Dissemination of different types of information can

FIG. 20. Montgomery Ward 1965 Feature Guide. *(Courtesy of Montgomery Ward & Company)*

be accomplished by using the medium that is best suited to each. Also different people respond to different approaches. By varying the approach, the best all-round results can be obtained.

The problem of informing personnel about a new development was handled excellently by the American Telephone & Telegraph Company in its promotion of the interphone. This is a modification of multiple telephone instruments in a home to permit communication from room to room or answering the door, as well as the normal use for outside communication.

Instructions for familiarizing the company personnel with the new service are included in the "Home Interphone Marketing Kit." The kit consists of:

A set of slides and taped narration
Marketing program presentation
Descriptive material: home interphone promotion pieces
Cost and ordering information
Actual samples of promotion pieces

FIG. 21. "Home Interphone Marketing Kit" Prepared by the American Telephone & Telegraph Co. *(Courtesy of the American Telephone & Telegraph Co.)*

Prints of counter card, envelope design, truck poster designs
Designs for demonstration displays
Publicity releases
Ordering instructions for glossies (photographs)
Suggested newspaper ad layouts and copy
Leader's guide—marketing presentation

With such packets of material sales staff members are made thoroughly conversant with all phases of the new promotion before any of the materials are released to the general public. Those people who will work with customers in selling the new idea and others who will be less directly concerned with this activity will have full particulars well in advance of the time when they will have to answer questions and make explanations. Figure 21 illustrates the materials included in the "Home Interphone Marketing Kit."

The United States Plywood Corporation has an unusual training program for its dealers. The program is built around a series of programed booklets. These booklets (Figure 22) carry the dealer or

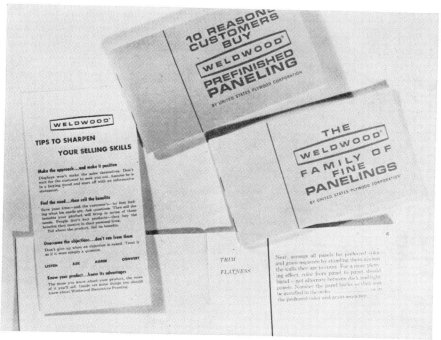

FIG. 22. Weldwood Dealer Programmed Booklets Prepared by the United States Plywood Corp. *(Courtesy of the United States Plywood Corporation)*

his salesman through the various types of information that he needs in order to advise his customers on the values and applications of the Weldwood brand of paneling. When he finishes the course he knows that he can do a better job of selling and satisfying his customers in their use of these plywood products.

Overhead Projector. By preparing transparencies of materials for use in the internal sales and promotion acitivity, it is possible to present the materials in a dramatic and challenging way. Projection in a fully-lighted room encourages the audience to participate more actively than when the room is in semi-darkness or darkness. Through the use of overlays, information can be added and the presentation developed as the group watches. Information also can be added during projection by writing on the transparency with a china-marking pencil and the marks can be removed by wiping them with a soft cloth. The speaker standing at the front of the room maintains eye contact with those to whom he is speaking, thus maintaining rapport. It is not even necessary for him to turn away to point out certain things on the screen. A pencil or other sharply pointed instrument can be used to indicate the point being discussed on the transparency and the shadow will point it out on the screen. Working parts of the merchandise can be reproduced in clear, colored plastic and the projected image will show the operation. Objects that are not transparent can be shown in silhouette. Occasional cartoons illustrating points in the sales story can be brought in to bring some humor into the presentation and at the same time underscore the major ideas that is to be put across.

Opaque Projector. The opaque projector is useful in sales meetings because material to be projected does not have to be modified in any way or reproduced as a transparency in order to be projected. Pages out of a catalog, price lists, instructions, photographs of merchandise, samples or small objects, sample forms, and letters are but a few of the types of materials that might be projected during a salesmen's meeting. The necessity for nearly complete darkness for efficient projection is a limiting factor. In many cases no room is available with sufficient light control to allow use during the daylight hours. Also, it is difficult to take notes when the room is completely darkened except for the projected image.

Audio Recording. Audio recordings may be used to supplement other methods of presentation, such as a filmstrip, or they may be used to do the job themselves. An application of this latter use may be when one of the company officials records a message to be played to sales personnel for purposes of indoctrination or as an inspirational talk at the beginning of a selling campaign. An individual salesman may use a tape recorder for self improvement by recording an interview with another person acting as a potential customer and then playing it back and criticizing his performance or having it rated by his fellow employees.

Exhibits. Company salesmen can be helped in their selling activities by a more thorough knowledge of the organization and its products. Well constructed exhibits can help in instructing the salesmen by showing them facets of the company's operation with which they are not familiar. Some of the types of exhibits valuable in this application are the following:

The different raw materials that go into the product
Steps in manufacturing
The varieties of products the company manufactures
Applications of the company's product
Testing processes for quality control
Steps involved in product design (such as an automobile, for instance)
Comparisons of the product with competitive products
Comparisons of good and poor quality in the manufacturing process and the consequences.

These exhibits can provide the salesmen or distributors with a knowledge of certain parts of the company's operation that it would otherwise take a long time to learn.

Television. Closed circuit television, in which the signal is not broadcast but sent to the receiving sets through a cable, is adapted to internal sales promotion by saving time for the ones who are receiving the information. For instance, the cost of bringing a group of salesmen in from the field is great. The greater the speed with which the message can be gotten across to them, the less the cost will be to the company. A tour of the plant to see a new process or new product would be informative but costly, considering the transportation cost, time away from the job, etc. By use of a series of television cameras, strategically located, the manufacturing process can be shown as it occurs, without the necessity of the group moving from their instruction room. Furthermore, by the use of closeup shots, members of the group may be able to see even more of the process than they could have seen at the actual site. Manufacturing areas are often very noisy, making communication with a group impossible. By bringing the picture into the meeting room, explanations can be made and questions answered without noise interference. Perhaps the manufacturing process is carried on in an area where space is limited. A group of people would interfere with the process, but one cameraman with a small television camera might not be in the way. The operation will appear more natural than if the crowd were filling up all of the space.

Bulletin Boards. Any place where employees gather is a good location for a bulletin board that can stress selling. Employees' rest rooms, smoking areas, time clocks, freight elevators, drinking fountains, cloak rooms, locker rooms, snack areas, and cafeterias are all places where personnel tend to linger for a few minutes from time to time. Hints, suggestions, and reminders placed in these locations will be seen time after time and by sheer repetition will stay in employees' minds. Gimbels in New York utilizes this method to keep their selling employees aware of the things that management wants them to keep in mind while they are waiting on customers. Small bulletin board notices (Figure 23) keep calling these things to mind.

FIG. 23. Bulletin Board Reminders from Gimbles-New York.
(Courtesy of Gimbels-New York)

External Sales and Promotion

Carrying the sales message to the people who do the purchasing of one's product is an important factor in merchandising. The size of the advertising industry in the United States today is a testimony to the importance of this function in the business world. Audio-visual communication methods make it possible to carry the message to the prospective customer with clarity, directness, and in a convincing manner.

In some instances the article that is being sold is its own best advertising, but more often the buyer is not in a position to test and analyze the material for quality or suitability. The choice in this case is made after weighing the available information and taking into account such things as pride of ownership, style, and other factors that influence one's choice.

In some cases what is offered for sale is intangible—a service for instance—which must be sold on the basis of an action rather than a piece of merchandise.

In situations such as this, the seller must search out the effective methods of communicating with prospects. Audio and visual communications often provide the answer. Practically all of the audio-visual devices are used by one organization or another in carrying its sales story to the prospects.

Motion Pictures. Advertising motion pictures, made for the purpose of setting out the desirability of merchandise and convincing propects to become purchasers, comprise a large segment of the films made by business organizations.

The reason for producing this sort of motion picture is recognition of the appeal that motion pictures have for all ages. No other communication device captures the imagination and attention as well as motion pictures. What, then, are some of the things that are unique to the motion picture as a communication device in sales promotion?

Through the use of color, motion, and sound, the motion picture can reconstruct reality to the point where the observer feels himself to be a part of the activity portrayed. This identification with the subject of the film can be a powerful factor in the development of a desire to have the goods or service being demonstrated.

Choice of background setting for the motion picture makes it possible to show the product being used under the conditions with which the seller would like to have it become associated. For instance, a film about the quality of an automobile would show it in front of a modern home, at a country club, and other places that would give it a connotation of quality. If the narration stresses the quality of the product, this emphasizes it, or if no mention is made of the quality, the film points it out by implication.

Similarly, the people who are shown using the product are carefully chosen for the effect they will have on the viewer. As an example, when filters for cigarettes were introduced, there was a fear on the part of some tobacco companies that it would be considered effeminate to smoke a filter cigarette. To avoid alienation of the men smokers, some of the companies instituted an advertising campaign that featured tattooed, outdoor, "he-man" types smoking their brands of filtered cigarettes. By implication the persons shown are the types for whom the product is intended.

Selling motion pictures can show the process of manufacturing a product. They can stress the quality of raw materials, the care with which the product is made, the distribution process, or whatever is considered of importance to the prospect.

The dramatic capability of the motion picture permits emphasizing certain features of a product in order to increase desirability. This can be done by stressing beauty, glamor, utility, value in an emergency, or whatever is appropriate to the particular material.

Allis-Chalmers has made a series of motion pictures intended to show the quality and desirability of the equipment they manufacture. Four of the films that have been made for this purpose are presented below:

1. *It's Got To Be Good.* This is a ten minute black-and-white film showing the tests that Allis-Chalmers equipment is put through on the proving grounds and in the laboratory before it is put on the market.

2. *Looking Ahead.* A 20 minute color film showing the research laboratory of the Tractor Group.

3. *A New High.* A ten minute color sales film on the WD-45 tractor, featuring animation on the principle of the Power-Crater engine and demonstrating the Snap-Coupler hitch, Power-Shift wheels, Traction Booster system and Two-Clutch Power Control.

4. *Engineering in Action.* An 11 minute color sales film on the WD-45 Tractor, LP gas, diesel, gasoline, big-capacity implements, disc plow, disc harrow, 4-bottom plow, Power-Shift wheels, Traction Booster system, and hydraulic ram control.

Motion picture films of this type provide the following advantage over other methods of presenting sales information to a prospect:

1. The viewer's interest is held easily by the motion picture technique.
2. Color, motion, and sound combine to make the viewer feel that he is actually involved in the action.
3. Narration can provide simultaneous viewing and hearing the explanation of material covered.
4. Seeing the equipment in actual operation through the eye of the camera is more convincing than merely reading about its utility.
5. The product is portrayed under the best possible conditions.
6. Rhythm, speed, and sequence of operations can be conveyed to the viewer.
7. Working of internal parts can be shown by means of cutaway sections or animation.
8. Applications of the equipment that are spread over a year or more can be shown in a few minutes.
9. The camera can show angles and areas of view that would never be seen otherwise.
10. Embarrassing situations, such as the failure of the product to act as expected, are avoided.
11. Proper choice of camera angle and action can emphasize or even exaggerate certain features or actions.
12. The film can show exactly what it is wanted to show, no more, no less.
13. The narration is exactly as planned, using the words, inflections, etc., which are deemed to be most effective.
14. The sales message is repeated as many times as it is desired without variation visually or audio-wise.
15. The company can control the circulation of the film and recall it when the information becomes obsolete.

Filmstrips. When motion is not a part of the sales message or when the interpretation of the motion can be made by means other than depicting it exactly, a filmstrip can do the sales promotion job almost as well as a motion picture.

The qualification in the assessment of the filmstrip's ability is not because of any shortcomings it has but merely because the motion picture has a particularly potent attention-riveting quality.

This filmstrip has many of the advantages of the motion picture as a device in sales promotion. In addition, the filmstrip can be produced for a small fraction of the cost of a motion picture. Even with an accompanying sound track in the form of a phonograph record or a magnetic tape, many filmstrips can be produced for the cost of one motion picture.

In addition to lower cost, the filmstrip has the advantage of requiring less costly equipment for projection. The equipment is also lighter and more easily portable.

The filmstrip is smaller than a reel of motion picture film and can be more easily transported from one showing site to another.

Because of the smaller unit cost of the filmstrip, the seller often gives them to users rather than asking for their return. An advantage in this situation is that the dealer or other user is much more apt to make use of the filmstrip if he has it immediately available than if he has to send for the material in advance of the intended showing. If the filmstrip is handy and can be projected with a minimum of previous planning, it can be used whenever the opportunity presents itself.

A filmstrip (or more likely a slide set) can easily be produced by a local dealer to show applications in his own area. If a customer has installed a piece of equipment and is satisfied with its operation, probably he would not mind having it photographed for showing to prospects. Such a photgraph would have a stronger sales appeal than one taken in another community. The most effective method of presentation is to show the generalized version made by the parent company and then follow with the showing of local applications.

A silent filmstrip sometimes can be made more useful by rearranging the order of showing of frames. The individual frames can be cut apart and mounted in 2x2 inch slide frames. They can then be assembled and projected, even interspersed with slides shot locally, to tie the whole presentation to the needs of the prospects in that particular area.

By using a magnetic tape recorder, a new narration can be made to provide a more professional presentation of the revised filmstrip, including the additional frames and any references that should be made to the local situation and its effect on the product being promoted.

Brochures. A great deal of selling is done through the use of brochures, pamphlets, circulars, and other similar printed materials. They have several unique advantages in this specialized form of business communication.

  1. A brochure is inexpensive to produce, compared with other selling communications.

2. The prospective customer can examine it in the quiet of his own home or office.

3. No projection or other equipment is necessary.

4. It can be sent through the mail inexpensively.

5. Material can be left in appropriate places to be picked up and perused by those interested.

6. Information, such as technical data, can be kept for easy referral.

7. Data from competitive manufacturers can be compared.

8. Photographs, drawing, and descriptive material can be combined to provide a good description of the product.

Figure 24 illustrates some sales brochures produced by the Zenith Radio Corporation for certain of their products. They picture the various items in the particular line, describe the features, use drawings where needed for more complete information, and in some cases indicate prices.

FIG. 24. Zenith Radio Corporation Brochures. *(Courtesy of Zenith Radio Corporation)*

The 3M Company brochure (Figure 25) describes the uses of "Scotch" brand products for offices. Using the same girl to illustrate products throughout the book and commentary in the language that she might use provide continuity.

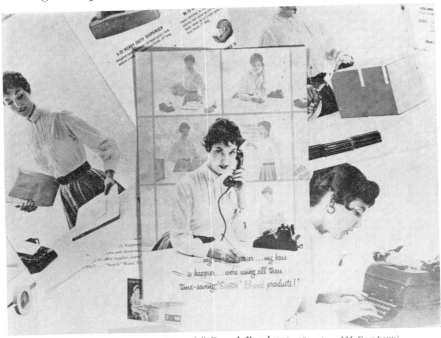

FIG. 25. 3M Company "Scotch" Brand Brochure. *(Courtesy 3M Company)*

Two more types of brochure are those produced by Kaiser Jeep Corporation. Figure 26 shows a brochure intended to remind people that the word "Jeep"* is a trademark of this company and should not be used to designate any product of any other company.

The sales brochure, *Man Moves Forward on Wheels,* (Figure 27) tells the story of the contribution of the wheel as one of the factors that assisted in the development of our civilization. The booklet ends with a history of the "Jeep" and its military and civilian applications.

The person responsible for the preparation of brochures and other selling publications should always keep in mind that the more visual he can make it, with photographs, drawings, charts, and graphs, the better it will communicate its message.

---
* Trademark of Kaiser Jeep Corporation.

FIG. 26. *Let's Not Be Improper* Brochure Printed by Kaiser Jeep Corporation.
(Courtesy of Kaiser Jeep Corporation)

Deere & Co., manufacturers of agricultural machinery of all sorts, prepares brochures (Figure 28) which have the double purpose of giving the readers information about current farming practices and promoting sales of their equipment. These brochures are distributed to farmers and others interested in these matters. The magazine, *the Furrow,* primarily builds goodwill, which will be reflected in increased sales.

Photographs. Photographic reproductions are used in many of the materials previously described. There is no denying that they add to the interest of the materials and tell more about the product than could be conveyed by the printed word alone. However, what is the value of a straight photograph?

Salesmen carry photographs of their various lines of merchandise to show to prospective buyers. It makes it unnecessary to carry the actual product for initial showing to a customer. Often the merchandise may be too large to be moved readily and too distant for the customer to go to it. Photographs make it possible for the client at least to eliminate those that are obviously not suitable. Attention can

FIG. 27. *Man Moves Forward on Wheels,* Published by Kaiser Jeep Corporation.
(Courtesy of Kaiser Jeep Corporation)

then be concentrated on those that have some possibility of being satisfactory. This technique is used a great deal by real estate agents. They photograph each house they have for sale and attach the photo to the file on that house. The prospect can eliminate a number of houses right in the office, without ever having actually seen them.

In the Allis-Chalmers library are more than 70,000 still photographs on all phases of farming. Upon request, 8x10 inch glossy prints will be sent on practically any farming subject. The service is intended especially for teachers, lecturers, authors, editors, and for use on classroom bulletin boards. The photos may be used in illustrating talks, reports, textbooks, magazines, and newspaper articles.

Other companies maintain less extensive files, but generally will supply photographic prints of their product upon request.

Overhead Projection. Communicating sales and promotional information with an overhead projector can be done if room conditions are right and the prospects where the projection is to take place are already interested. Very little information appears to be

FIG. 28. Deere & Co. Sales Brochures. *(Courtesy of Deere & Co.)*

available from business organizations regarding use of this technique in sales promotion.

Opaque Projection. The opaque projector is seldom used in sales and promotion work because of the necessity of quite complete darkening of a room.

Exhibits. On of the very effective methods of putting across a sales message is through the use of an exhibit. Exhibits may be used almost anywhere that people congregate when they are not in a hurry to get somewhere. Stores, fairs, conventions, railroad stations, and amusement parks are examples of locations of this sort. In order for an exhibit to be effective, the viewer must be able to take the time to look at it. The exhibit must have some feature that calls attention to itself and causes the observer to stop for a closer look. Some of the techniques for stopping the viewer are these:

1. Ask a direct question—one that can be answered only by examining the exhibit.
2. Utilize appropriate motion. Have rear-lighted photos flash on successively. Have a working model operating.

3. Have an enlarged or reduced model to catch the eye.
4. Have something that is apparently contradictory or impossible. As an example, a stream of water gushing from a faucet suspended by wires.
5. Have appropriate sound effects coming from the exhibit.
6. Have some part of the exhibit set up in such a way that the viewer can manipulate or operate it.
7. Offer a prize drawing for those who register. This not only induces people to stop and look, but also provides a prospect list for follow-up.
8. Highlight the exhibit with dramatic lighting to call attention to its salient features.
9. Samples, where appropriate, create interest.
10. A properly chosen color scheme can add greatly to the drawing power of an exhibit.
11. Strategically placed and timed advance publicity can make people aware of the exhibit and cause them to look for it.

It must be kept in mind that in most instances other exhibits will vie for the attention of the viewer. The display that has the greatest stopping power and that can then provide material of interest to the viewer will have the greatest success.

There are some things that must be kept in mind in designing an exhibit in order to maintain the interest that has been engendered by one or more of the techniques mentioned. Once the viewer has stopped, he can be kept looking at a display until the story has been told if the following things are kept in mind:

1. Do not attempt to do too many things in one exhibit. One main idea properly communicated is all that one exhibit can be expected to accomplish.
2. Avoid too much detail, even though it may be related to the main point of the exhibit. A person who starts to see an exhibit and finds himself getting bogged down in details is likely to give up and move on.
3. The device used to stop the prospective viewer must be in keeping with the theme of the exhibit. The interest of the viewer must naturally move from the "stopper" to the rest of the exhibit.
4. Proper use of color coding can unify and clarify material in an exhibit. Related processes may be connected with ribbons of a certain color. Colored cards, dots of color, or colored bands may be used to distinguish different processes, materials, routings, or areas.

5. Keep the exhibit manned by someone who knows the subject of the display and who can answer questions viewers might ask.
6. Maintain the exhibit in proper operating condition. Replace burned out lights, keep litter picked up, keep up the supply of handout material, etc.

Exhibits can incorporate many audio-visual devices to increase their communicating possibilities. Some devices that are appropriate are:

1. Motion pictures, preferably using rear-screen projection to cut down the interference from outside light. A continuous loop film will provide for repetitive showing without attention from the personnel.
2. Slides or filmstrips, also using rear-screen projection. A continuous filmstrip loop or a slide projector with a rotating carrier will accomplish the same purpose of freeing the exhibit personnel of the need of constant supervision of the projector.
3. Charts and flipsheets can provide explanations of parts of the exhibit. Flipsheets may be prepared in such a way that they can be changed mechanically and automatically.
4. Audio recordings can be used as an attention getting device and also to explain the material in the exhibit.

Summary

Many audio-visual methods are used to bring sales and promotional messages to prospective customers. One type of sales communication is that which is intended to instruct and inspire salesmen, dealers, and others who in turn will be selling to consumers. Information in sales messages of this sort is intended to acquaint these people with the features of the product, preview future products, familiarize them with materials to be sent to customers, and inspire them to put out more selling effort. Motion pictures, filmstrips, brochures, overhead projection, opaque projection, audio recording, bulletin boards, and television are all channels for the communications of this sort. Often a combination approach will be most effective.

External sales promotion activities are directed to customers. Motion pictures are an important method of carrying the sales message. Also useful are filmstrips, brochures, photographs, and exhibits. Overhead projectors, opaque projectors, and television (excluding commercial entertainment television) are of limited value in this application.

CHAPTER 6

REPORTING TO MANAGEMENT

The manager of a small business is aware of all of the happenings of his business. He knows what his sales for the month are and how they compare with previous periods, how much money he has in the bank, what his current liabilities are, whether or not he is overstocked with merchandise, and a thousand and one other facts about the operation of his business. However, as the business becomes larger in its scope, the manager finds that he cannot handle all of the details himself, and so finds that he must call in others to help. These people carry out the routine decisions, but the manager still is in charge of the operations.

As the business continues to expand, the manager is less and less in direct contact with the happenings and must commence depending upon information sent to him by his subordinates to keep himself abreast of the happenings. Eventually he reaches a point where all of the actual operating parts of the organization are under the direct control of departmental managers, and the original manager, now the general manager or president of the company, is almost completely isolated from the day-to-day routine. This is a logical development, of course, because details and decisions have become so numerous that no one person could possibly attend to them all. It means that the results of operating the business must be summarized in reports that are sent by the departments to the top management. The validity of the decisions reached by the management is dependent to a very large degree upon the accuracy and clarity of the information provided.

The accounting profession has developed procedures and forms for reporting the pertinent facts about a business operation and will continue to devise new ones as needs present themselves. This is a form of communication that utilizes a specialized and formal language. It is not the purpose of the present discussion to consider accounting procedures and reporting except insofar as they are a part of the internal communication process of an organization.

Reasons for Audio-Visual Presentation

A well-devised accounting or statistical report can convey a wealth of information about a business and its operation. However, to understand the report, the person reading it must have the following abilities or backgrounds:

1. A knowledge of accounting procedures, terminology, and reporting.
2. A background knowledge of the particular business organization and its history.
3. Ability to infer generalizations and trends from columns of figures.

It is a rare executive who has all of these abilities in addition to the knowledge of his particular phase of the business operation. Even if the personnel concerned had all of these abilities, another problem would still be unsolved. The busy executive is fully occupied in making those decisions which he must make in order to run his section of the business efficiently. Gleaning information from accounting and statistical reports can take a fairly large amount of time. In most instances, this time could be spent more profitably in pondering decisions of importance to his department than in working out the meanings of figures.

This, of course, is the place where audio-visual devices are of value in reporting to management. If the proper presentation techniques can make it possible for executives to grasp the meanings of reports in less time than it would take them otherwise, they will have more time to reach the decisions based on those reports. Time spent in deliberation would result in more and better quality decisions, hence increase the executive's value to the company.

Methods of Presentation

Most of the normal audio-visual methods can be utilized in reporting to management. There are several considerations which must be kept in mind when reporting at this level.

1. Executives are unusually capable and can grasp information quickly and accurately.
2. Groups are small in number—seldom more than 12 to 15.

3. Press of other work makes them intolerant of delay or of unnecessary detail.
4. They generally disapprove of an unnecessarily costly presentation.
5. They do not want decisions formulated for them as part of the audio-visual presentation. They want all of the relevant facts summarized and stated, but the decisions are to be theirs.
6. They want their decisions to be based on provable facts. Therefore, supporting detail should be available in the event that proof should be called for during a presentation.

Keeping these things in mind, let us consider some of the audio-visual methods which will be of value in presenting information to the management of the organization.

Motion Pictures. The chief value of motion pictures in reporting to management is in showing them facets of the business that they have not had the opportunity to learn for themselves.

As an example, the demonstration of a new manufacturing process might very well be shown to the executives in a motion picture. Some of the advantages of this might be:

1. Lengthy processes can be greatly reduced in time.
2. Processes which take place far away can be seen in the home office.
3. Dirt, danger, and discomfort are eliminated in the observation of the process.
4. Cinephotomicrography (or making motion pictures through a microscope) can show processes not visible to the unaided eye.
5. High-speed or time lapse photography can slow down or speed up processes for better analysis.

A film showing such processes would most likely be a silent one. Sound, with the exception of magnetic striped sound, would increase the production costs, delay the showing, and, if this were a newly-developed and secret process, provide a possible security leak. Some companies maintain their own film processing laboratories to provide additional security measures for the information on motion picture films.

Motion pictures of test runs of products may be shown to the executives to acquaint them with the successes or the difficulties involved in this phase of the research or production process. Failures of tests might be projected and analyzed for executive decision as to the next steps to take. Of course, many other sources of information would have to be consulted in addition to the viewing of the films.

Motion pictures can serve as a liaison device between divisions of a company or between its subsidiaries. Products, new developments, and plant additions are a few of the subjects that might be covered in an intra-company motion picture. It would function to keep management personnel aware of what is happening beyond the areas of their own immediate responsibilities.

Slides and Filmstrips. These forms of projected information can serve many of the functions of motion pictures except, of course, where movement or change must be shown. One advantage lies in the fact that production problems are much simpler, making it possible to present an effective showing of the information much more quickly and at less expense than is possible with motion pictures.

Discussion of the material may be held during the time that individual frames are on the screen. This is more satisfactory than having to wait until the presentation is over, as is the case with motion pictures.

Overhead and Opaque Projection. While these projection methods are generally intended for displaying materials to larger groups, they are also adopted to showing materials in executive meetings.

Charts and Graphs. Detailed information of a financial nature can be summarized most effectively by means of charts and graphs.

The complex financial and organizational structures of today's corporations makes it extremely difficult to keep all of the inter-relationships correctly visualized and straight in the minds of the directors and officers. For this reason, each of the company officials should have organizational charts available for consultation at any time. At the minimum, these charts should include a general one showing the over-all organization pattern of the entire company or organization, plus detailed charts of those parts of the company under the individual's direction. These charts may be in duplicated form and placed in a loose-leaf notebook. In addition to showing the relationships of the various offices of the company, the charts indicate who is filling each position at the moment. Those people who are working with personnel from other divisions and departments of the company may want to have the organizational chart prepared in such a way that it can be hung on the office wall and thus be available for instant consultation. The wall chart should be made of a material that will blend with the office decor, it should be framed, and should have tab holders into which the names of people holding the various offices may be slipped. As people move into different jobs, the tabs can be moved about to reflect the current situation. Figure 29 is a reproduction of the organizational chart of E. I. Du Pont de Nemours and Company, without the names of the individuals holding those positions. This is the over-all type of chart, showing the organization only down as far as the general managers of the departments. The detailed charts in the offices of each of the general managers will indicate the organization from the department manager on down.

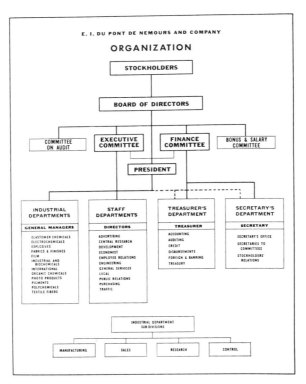

FIG. 29. Organization Chart of E. I. Du Pont de Nemours and Company.
(Courtesy of E. I. Du Pont de Nemours and Company)

Charts showing the business activities of a company are the life-blood of information for the executive who must make the policy decisions that govern operations. These people simply do not have the time to examine detailed reports of sales, turnover, manufacturing costs, etc., make analyses and then decisions. For this reason, they depend upon charts and graphs prepared by personnel in the analysis or statistical sections. Criteria will have been set down by the executive committee to govern the preparation of these materials and reporting methods will remain constant from year to year unless changed by directive of the executive group. This insures that data reported from year to year are comparable and that changes in figures and their relationships are true changes and not merely due to modified reporting procedures.

E. I. Du Pont de Nemours and Company utilizes this method of keeping its Executive Committee (see Fig. 29) informed about company operations. Following are the conclusions regarding the values of this type of presentation:

First, the charts themselves do not utilize narrative explanations. There is no opportunity for one reviewing the figures to bog down under the weight of particular words or phrases that might be chosen to explain a given development. In the course of presenting the charts to the Executive Committee, the chart supervisor answers questions or volunteers answers without question by giving background reasons for significant variations in current data. But the primary purpose of the charts is to point up the trouble spots where further review or attention may be necessary. The charts show what has happened and and what is anticipated in terms of Return on Investment, and "put the finger" on the broad factors that may be responsible for a change in trend of chart curves. Such identification of factors enables the Executive Committee to raise questions with a general manager regarding any possible trouble spots. This frequently leads to further analysis of the underlying facts.

Second, it is comparatively easy to hold the attention of an entire group to one item at the same moment.

Third, rather rigid rules govern the assembly of the data for the chart presentation. To the maximum extent possible, data for all periods shown on the charts are on a uniform basis, so that common measurements of performance are provided for all major product lines. If changing conditions require a revision in current data, then all the data for the five preceding years are revised appropriately. In this way, the charts are kept comparative throughout.

Fourth, a given format is adhered to until it becomes clear that a change would be a substantial improvement. Then a new format is brought into use completely at one time, including a reset for the entire five-year period. Frequent minor changes are avoided.

Fifth, the Executive Committee itself makes the rules governing the division of lines of business into chart series, and the classification of financial data into the several items set forth in this description. To be sure, the Executive Committee requests and receives the recommendations of the Treasurer's Department, as developed in collaboration with the industrial departments. But it is the Committee's decision that is final after full consideration of the pros and cons presented to it. This approach to data presentation, by rules decided on by the top management group by whom the data are to be used, serves to remove a potentially wide area for disagreement on the classification of the basic data to be presented.[1]

Flipsheets. As a method of presenting data to management groups, the flipsheet is very useful. The rate of presentation is entirely under the control of the speaker and material which has been previously covered can be referred to again very easily.

Materials which can be shown efficiently on the flipsheet include the following:

Charts and graphs
Diagrams
Tables of figures
Drawings (including cutaway drawings)

Generally, management groups are small and can easily see the information on even a small flipsheet unit. Such a unit set on a table or an easel can be the focal point of a presentation of material relating to the past or future of a business organization.

Utilization of this form of data presentation has advantages over projection by means of slides, overhead, or opaque projection in that it eliminates the need for darkening the room and setting up the projection equipment. Also, the speaker may feel more rapport with his audience when he does not have the mechanics of the projector to come between him and the group.

Exhibits. In order to convey certain information to the management of a company, an exhibit may be utilized. The exhibit may be used to communicate understandings that are difficult to put across in other ways.

A company may be considering the advisability of making a change in plant layout and the routing of materials through the building from raw materials to finished product and the storage of the product until sold. Written descriptions of the proposed changes would be difficult to understand and visualize. Blueprints and drawings would be clearer, but only if the executive has developed a skill in reading this form of communication. An exhibit in the form

1. *Executive Committee Control Charts,* E. I. Du Pont de Nemours, and Company, Wilmington, Delaware, 1959, p. 33.

of a scale model of the plant after the proposed changes had been made would be much more meaningful to the management personnel and they could see the ways in which the proposed changes would benefit the company in more efficient handling and routing of the material through the plant.

Other exhibits prepared for communication between management and others in the company might include the following:

Steps in the preparation of a new product.

Analysis of the company's product with that of its main competitors.

Products now in the experimental or planning stage.

Shortcomings of the present products with an analysis of why they have failed.

How components made fit into the larger product, e.g., automobile, aircraft, or missile components.

Issue No. 200   A News Bulletin for Key Borden Personnel   August, 1964

SALES AND EARNINGS SOAR TO ALL-TIME HIGHS -- The highest sales and earnings for any quarter or half in the Borden Company's history were reported for the periods ended June 30. Net income for the first half of the year rose to $19,388,192, equal to $1.74 a share on 11,124,976 shares outstanding. This was 17.4 per cent above earnings of $16,507,718, or $1.53 a share on 10,781,017 shares outstanding for the comparable 1963 period. Sales for the six-month period rose 8.2 per cent to $591,974,948 from $547,215,189 a year earlier.
        Second quarter net income rose 16.4 per cent to $11,150,943 or $1.00 a share, from $9,583,101, or 89 cents a share for the same 1963 period. Sales for the quarter increased 8.7 per cent to $302,095,334 from $277,969,394.

BORDEN AND SMITH-DOUGLASS REACH MERGER AGREEMENT -- An agreement has been reached between Borden's and the Smith-Douglass Company looking toward the acquisition by Borden's of the Virginia-based fertilizer/chemical firm. The transaction is subject to the approval of Smith-Douglass stockholders. The plan would provide for continued expansion of the business of Smith-Douglass with improved service to its customers. Smith-Douglass would continue under its present management, retaining its name and organization and would become a division of the Borden Chemical Company.
        Smith-Douglass produces fertilizer and animal feed supplements and a variety of related products including insecticides, pesticides, herbicides and defoliants. It has 15 plants in nine states in the South and Midwest. For the nine months ended April 30, the firm has a net profit of $3,361,381 or $3.10 a share. This is up from $2,918,900 or $2.75 a share in the same nine months the year before.

BOARD OF DIRECTORS DECLARES 218TH DIVIDEND -- Borden's Board of Directors, on July 28, declared the regular dividend of 50 cents a share payable Sept. 1 to stockholders of record Aug. 7. It was the Company's 218th consecutive dividend.

WORLD'S FAIR EXHIBIT ATTRACTING CAPACITY CROWDS -- After a delayed start due to construction problems, the Borden exhibit at the New York World's Fair is now drawing capacity crowds daily. With waiting lines sometimes backed up as long as 45 minutes, the main attraction of the exhibit is Elsie the Cow starring in a musical revue. Elsie,who came into being at the New York World's Fair of 1939-40, has proved that the quarter-century spanning the two great expositions has only served to strengthen her appeal to all age groups. From 30 to 35 times daily she delights packed-house audiences in "All About Elsie" as her "supporting cast" of electronically animated figures surrounds her with songs and gaiety.
        People waiting to see the show find that their time is far from wasted. Demonstrators in the exhibit's kitchen delight homemakers (and family eaters) with practical tips and recipes using Borden products. In a matter of minutes these young ladies create such exotic desserts as Baked Alaska. They show the many tasty

FIG. 30. *For Your Information*, Published by the Borden Co. *(Courtesy of the Borden Co.)*

Printed Materials. Particularly for those members of management who are below the "top" management level, there must be
some way of keeping up-to-date on decisions and developments that
affect the operation of the entire company. One solution to this
problem is to keep these middle management people notified of actions and developments is to send them bulletins or newsletters.
The material is generally condensed and has only the briefest explanations of the news items.

One organization utilizing this form of communication is the
Borden Company. The front page of one of the issues of *For Your
Information* is illustrated in Figure 30.

Combination Approach. In many instances, a combination approach using several of the communication media will get the message across to management personnel better and more efficiently
than any single medium. One advantage is the renewing of interest
that comes about with a change of pace. There is bound to be a certain flagging of interest when information is given in the same manner over a period of several hours. Attention can be aroused again
if some variety is put into the presentation. Lockheed takes advantage of this in its presentation (Fig. 31) called *The Lockheed Road
Show.*

FIG. 31. *The Lockheed Road Show.* *(Courtesy of Lockheed Aircraft Corp.)*

The Executive Meeting Room

In designing the layout and equipment for the executive meeting room, the basic principles and methods of audio-visual communication should be kept in mind. The facilities for more efficient presentation of data will quickly repay their cost through more precise and rapid communication.

Some of the requirements for a meeting room for the board of directors or the executives are as follows: (Numbers refer to features in Fig. 32)

A room that is comfortable, accessible, and suitably decorated.

A table with enough chairs to seat the number of people in the executive group.

Chairs along the side of the room for other people who may be called in to report to the group. (12)

Desk and chair for the secretary who keeps notes of business transacted during the meeting.

Windowless or otherwise capable of complete darkening.

Adjacent room with tape recorder mechanism (7) and with glass ports (6) through which motion pictures, slides, and filmstrips (5) may be projected.

Movable wood panelling on the walls, motor driven, to conceal or expose the following material mounted on the wall behind:

    Projection screen (3)
    Chalkboard
    Bulletin board space (4)
    Organizational charts (1)
    Statistical charts (1)
    Maps (8)
    Refreshment unit (13)

Control console at the chair of the presiding person, operating the following facilities of the room: (9)

    Light level control.
    Movement of the wall panelling to expose the desired segment of information.
    Starting and stopping of the motion picture projector.
    Starting, stopping, and changing of the filmstrip and slide projectors.
    Volume of the motion picture or filmstrip sound track or of a recording.
    Recording and playback of the tape recorder.
    Intercom to the projection room.

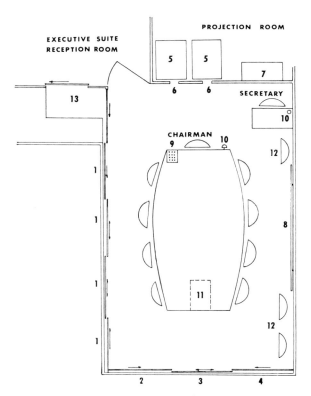

FIG. 32. Executive Meeting Room.

Executive Meeting Room. Further information on features of the executive meeting room illustrated in Figure 32 follow:

1. Statistical charts (1) located behind the movable panels constructed with movable letters and figures so that they can be easily
   kept up-to-date by daily posting as information comes to the
   statistical department. Graphs are constructed in such a way that
   lines can be extended or modified as new data are received or new
   estimates for the future are made.

2. The separate room for the projectors and the tape recording
   equipment eliminates the noise and distraction of the operator
   threading and adjusting machines. Also, it removes the projectionist from the executive meeting room where discussions may be
   under way on subjects that are not yet ready to be made known
   to the rest of the organization.

3. The secretary's telephone (10) does not ring, but signals her with

a flashing light. If she feels that the call is of sufficient importance to interrupt the meeting, she signals the person in charge, also by means of a flashing light.

4. The refreshment unit (13) is accessible from the executive suite reception room as well as from the meeting room. This enables another person to come into the refreshment unit while the meeting is still in session and prepare the refreshments. When preparations are complete, this person can leave as she came. When the meeting is over or a break is called, the panel in the meeting room can be moved aside and the refreshments served. The sliding door arrangement giving access to the outer room also permits executive secretaries to prepare coffee break refreshments for themselves and their executives without having to enter the meeting room.

5. Low level loudspeakers for the sound systems are flush mounted in the ceiling.

6. Microphones for the tape recorder are mounted in the ceiling so as not to be a disconcerting or inhibiting factor.

7. The overhead projector is mounted on a disappearing mount (11) similar to those used to hold typewriters in desks. It is out of sight ordinarily, but can be swung into position instantly.

Use of Rear-Screen Projection Units in the Executive Meeting Room. Translucent projection screens made of a special plastic material can be used to provide for projection from the opposite side of the screen. Motion pictures, slides, and filmstrips can be projected from the rear. An executive meeting room using this type of projection is illustrated in Figure 33.

Features of the executive meeting room with rear-screen projection include the following: (Numbers refer to features illustrated in Figure 30.)

Rear-projection screens. (1)

Random-access slide projectors (2) such as the one illustrated in Figure 62.

Motion picture projector (3) with a front-surface mirror set at a 45° angle to reverse the image for viewing through the rear-projection screen.

Tape recording and playback equipment. (4)

Slide storage cabinet. (5)

Console for operating slide projectors, motion picture projector, and tape recording and playback equipment. (6)

Portable lectern (7) for use in formal presentations to the executive group.

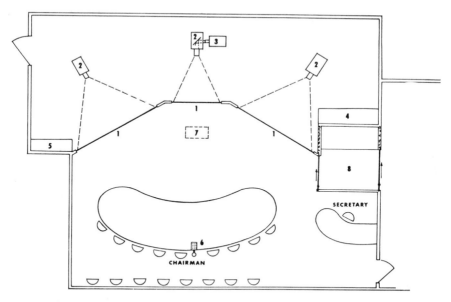

FIG. 33. Executive Meeting Room Utilizing Rear-Screen Projection.

Refreshment unit (8) for preparation of sandwiches, coffee, or other refreshments during protracted meetings.

One company making constant use of a room of this nature is Douglas Aircraft Co., Inc., Santa Monica, Calif. Management was faced with the problem of insufficient space to display the corporate charts vitally important to management personnel in making decisions. The number of charts that could be utilized was limited by the wall space of the room. Also, they were unwieldy to store and transport and gave a cluttered appearance to the room. The decision was made to reduce the charts and other materials to 35m slides that could then be projected with random access slide projectors. Company executives seated in the corporate chart room can call up instantaneously any of 384 slides on four Spindler & Sauppe SLX-750 random access projectors by means of digital selectors. Each of the four projectors has its own rear screen for viewing from within the corporate chart room. When not being used, these screens are covered by framed photographs. The room, with slides appearing on the rear projection screens, is shown in Figure 34.

In addition to the rear screen projection room, a front screen projection room provides for the more conventional type of viewing.

FIG. 34. Douglas Corporate Chart Room. *(Courtesy of Douglas Aircraft Co., Inc.)*

This room is accessible from the corporate chart room and from the outside and contains a motion picture projector, a random access slide projector (controllable from the chart room), sound equipment, and controls for the lighting and for the curtain which normally covers the front projection screen. A speaker in this room makes it possible for the projectionist to monitor the sound of motion picture or tape recorder materials and also enables the executive to give oral orders to the operator.

Some advantages of this type of room over that illustrated in Figure 31 are the following:

1. A higher level of light can be used in the room than with conventional projection onto an ordinary screen.

2. Random-access slide projectors enable the presiding person to call up any information he wants in five seconds or less.

3. A bank of random-access projectors and several screens make it possible to project several slides simultaneously for comparison.

4. Statistical data slides and photographs can be projected simultaneously.

5. There is no interference with the projection beam of light within the room.
6. No attendant is necessary during the meeting to operate the projectors.
7. Materials can be kept up to the minute by replacing certain slides in the projectors while other slides are being projected. Being on the other side of the wall, the person changing the slides is not seen.

The type of facilities selected will depend upon the degree of automation the executives want to have, the types of material they need in order to render their best decisions, and the type of quarters available for the meeting room.

Summary

The executives of a business must be kept aware of the details of company operation. Communication with them must be as efficient as possible because of the limited time they have available and the necessity for as complete information as possible in order to make certain that their decisions are the best ones that could be made. While nearly all of the audio-visual media of communication are appropriate, it must be kept in mind that the executive mentality is a rather special one and that presentations should be prepared to appeal to these people. The materials should present facts as accurately as possible with no unnecessary frills and with no attempt to suggest decisions.

The room in which the executives meet should be designed with the audio-visual media of communication in mind. Those media should be chosen which will provide the best and most efficient communication.

CHAPTER **7**

REPORTING TO STOCKHOLDERS

Purposes of Reporting to Stockholders

Reporting of corporate information to stockholders involves certain problems that are not found in other types of communication. Communicating with these owners of the company, therefore, involves the use of different methods than those used in other communication.

Stock of the average corporation is held by a large number of people. In the case of larger organizations, this runs into many thousands. In addition to the problems imposed by reason of the large number, there is the fact that these people may be located over a wide geographical area. Thus it is practically impossible to get all of the stockholders to one place for a meeting. Even if a large enough building or arena could be found and transportation for the crowd could be arranged, there still would be many communication problems involved.

Conducting business meetings with a group of people numbering into the hundreds or thousands is very slow and inefficient. The amount of time consumed can be very great, particularly when it is necessary to have debate and voting on the issues affecting the company's operation. Theoretically, each stockholder is entitled to ask questions about the policies and actions of management, to make motions, and to cast a vote on each matter that comes up. In general, each stockholder has as many votes on any issue as he has shares of voting stock. Obviously, it would be easy for a meeting to become bogged down in a mass of detail.

Another problem factor is that there are certain kinds of information that cannot be divulged. Theoretically, as an owner, each stockholder should have access to all of the company's records. Practically, however, this cannot be allowed. If it were, anyone with a share or two of stock could demand information about processes, formulas, and other data that had been developed with much trouble and expense. Still, it is the right of a stockholder to receive information about the operation of the company, its earnings, and its prospects. for the future. The difficulty lies in determining just how much information can be disseminated to the stockholders without damage to the company's competitive position.

One method of taking into account stockholder desires in determining the company's policies is to request the stockholders' proxy rights. A proxy is an authorization for some other person to vote a stockholder's shares in a meeting. A stockholder has as many votes as he has shares of voting stock. Someone, usually but not always a major stockholder himself, writes to the individual owners, sending them proxy authorization forms to complete. The person requesting the proxy may make a statement as to how he intends to vote on the major issues, or he may depend upon his reputation and past actions to assure the stockholders of his integrity and good intentions. The stockholder may either give this person the permission to vote his stock or he may withhold it. Also, he may allow the proxy holder to vote as he sees fit or he may specify how his shares are to be voted on certain questions. Often a person who does not own a majority interest in an organization can control it by getting enough proxies to give him sufficient votes. One of the responsibilities of a corporation is to supply its stockholders with enough information for them to choose intelligently to whom they want to give their proxies and to instruct proxy holders how the shares should be voted.

Special Problems Faced in Communication with Stockholders

Two of the problems of communicating with stockholders have already been mentioned—the difficulty in getting them together and the limitations of what can be disclosed to them.

Many of the stockholders in a company know nothing of business activities or the manufacturing processes that are the bases of profits. For this reason any communication must be on a very elementary basis. Conversely, many stockholders will be experts in the field of business and in the operations of the company. The communication must provide information that will be of value to them as well as to the others. Some of the stockholders couldn't care less about the operations as long as the dividends are declared and paid and the market value increases. Others want to follow the company's operations as closely as possible.

Because of distance and other factors communication with stockholders must be largely by mail. Postage costs and the fact that each piece of correspondence is read by only one person make this an expensive way to provide stockholders with the information that they should have.

Stockholders' Meetings. Corporations are required by law to have periodic stockholders' meetings to which every person who owns any stock in the company is invited and is given the opportunity to ask questions and vote in the election of directors and on policy matters.

Audio-visual methods useful in stockholders' meetings are the same as would be appropriate for any meeting of a like number of participants. Some of the media that would be used at a meeting of approximately 1,000 stockholders, for example, would be as follows:

Motion pictures can give the people an overview of the operations of the company and the performance of its products. Sequences might show views of the plant, how the assembly line operates, research and development activities, new products that have been introduced since the last report, employee activities, testing the performance of the product, and such other items that would help interpret the company to the stockholders. This should, of course, be in color and sound and be carefully produced and edited to help convey a favorable impression. The film should not be so elaborate, however, as to raise a question in the minds of stockholders as to its costliness.

Filmstrips and slides do much of the same sort of communication that the motion pictures do. To compensate for the lack of actions, the still pictures make it possible for the president, chairman of the board, or whoever is leading this part of the meeting, to interpolate explanatory remarks as necessary.

The overhead projector is excellent for showing statistical and graphic materials. The image is large enough to be seen from a considerable distance and bright enough to be seen without complete darkening of the auditorium. Development of an idea through several stages can be shown very graphically with this projector.

Flipsheets can be utilized if they are made in a size large enough for spectators in all parts of the auditorium to see. For a large crowd, the overhead projector with its large image will be more satisfactory.

Audio systems are necessary to carry the sound of the motion pictures and filmstrips and to amplify the voice of the presiding person so that he can be heard in all parts of the auditorium. Additional microphones should be strategically located throughout the auditorium for the assistance of those who wish to address the chair to ask questions about the company's operations.

Exhibits of company products and those showing something of the manufacturing process could be set up in the foyer of the auditorium for the stockholders to view before and after the meeting. This would help the owners to learn more about the company's operations than activities that take place in the strictly business discussions of the meetings.

Closed circuit television is useful to carry the meeting to other gathering places when all of the stockholders who wish to attend cannot get into the one auditorium. It is possible (but expensive) to hold simultaneous stockholders' meetings in major cities across the country. By this means everyone can see and hear the meeting as it takes place.

Communicating with Those Who Cannot Attend Stockholders' Meetings

In all but the very closely-held corporations, the number of stockholders who do not or cannot attend stockholders' meetings is much greater than those who attend. Those who do not attend are still entitled to know what occured at the meeting. To inform these people, some corporations publish a condensation of the reports heard and actions taken during the meeting. While such a report is not as satisfactory as attending the meeting, it does help the shareholder to be aware of some of the things that occurred in the sessions. An example of such a report is reproduced in Figure 35.

Annual and Other Periodical Reports

The annual report to stockholders is the chief method used by corporations to keep owners informed regarding activities. Such reports are required by law and serve as a check on the operation of the company by those who have been placed in charge by the

FIG. 35. *Report to the Shareholders of Abbott Laboratories on the 1960 Annual Meeting. (Courtesy of Abbott Laboratories)*

stockholders. Additional reports may be made from time to time to explain unusual happenings that occur in the company's operations, changes in dividend policy, or other information that is of importance to stockholders.

Contents of the Annual Report. Certain information will be found in all annual reports. Other items are added to the report when it is felt that such bits of information will add to the understanding of the company's operations by the stockholders.

Financial statements of the company's operation must be included as a part of the report. The usual statements are the balance sheet and the profit and loss statement. These basic materials are often supported by additional schedules that serve to give more detailed information. Comparison of the current year's activities with those of previous years, as shown in the Lockheed Aircraft Corporation statement in Figure 36 indicates growth and fluctuations over a period of time—in this case, ten years.

Lockheed's consolidated balance sheet shows the comparison of

LOCKHEED CONSOLIDATED HIGHLIGHTS... *A Ten Year Comparison*
Dollars — Other Than Per Share Amounts — Are Stated in Millions

	Sales					Net Earnings			Federal Taxes on Income	Dividends Paid			
	TOTAL	AIRCRAFT AND SERVICES	MISSILES	SPACE PROGRAMS	SHIPS, ELECTRONICS & OTHER FIELDS	AMOUNT	PER AVERAGE SHARE	% OF SALES		TOTAL CASH	CASH PER SHARE	STOCK DIVIDENDS	
1963	$1,990.5	$1,050.3	$478.3	$321.1	877.8	$43.3	$4.06	2.2%	$42.2	$13.9	$1.30	- -	1963
1962	1,553.1	852.8	453.6	370.4	76.3	37.2	3.57	2.1	42.2	9.4	.90	--	1962
1961	1,444.5	650.0	361.1	372.3	61.1	26.1	2.60	1.8	28.0	4.6	.45	--	1961
1960	1,332.3	609.8	397.3	290.9	34.3	(42.9)	(4.37)	(3.2)	(41.1)	2.2	.22	2%	1960
1959	1,304.3	774.0	320.2	192.0	18.1	8.7	.91	.7	8.7	8.9	.29	--	1959
1958	974.7	660.9	177.1	125.1	11.6	18.8	2.15	1.9	19.9	7.2	.89	--	1958
1957	878.9	795.7	58.2	11.6	10.4	16.6	1.92	1.9	17.4	7.1	.89	--	1957
1956	751.4	690.5	50.7	2.0	7.9	15.3	1.81	2.0	15.5	6.8	.86	3	1956
1955	676.3	647.4	23.3	.8	4.8	16.5	1.98	2.4	17.3	8.5	1.07	- -	1955
1954	732.9	722.4	7.1	.1	3.3	20.5	2.49	2.8	21.2	7.2	.89	3	1954

	Stockholders' Equity		Working Capital	Backlog	Research & Development Expense	Property, Plant & Equipment			Floor Area IN MILLIONS OF SQUARE FEET	Employees	Payroll	Avg. Hourly Earnings OF HOURLY PAID EMPLOYEES	
	TOTAL	PER SHARE				NET	ADDITIONS	DEPRECIATION & AMORTIZATION					
1963	$209.8	$19.54	$140.2	$1,422.2	$22.8	$104.4	$27.5	$16.9	20.8	78,296	$603.7	$3.17	1963
1962	177.2	16.79	129.1	1,424.7	18.3	94.3	29.1	16.5	20.0	80,155	652.3	3.04	1962
1961	131.6	12.89	89.6	1,608.8	12.7	82.1	24.6	15.1	-18.1	70,250	536.7	2.95	1961
1960	103.3	10.17	57.6	1,221.3	51.3	73.9	18.0	11.3	16.9	61,050	459.6	2.87	1960
1959	146.9	15.01	75.5	1,155.1	15.1	72.6	21.5	13.1	16.6	57,504	430.0	2.75	1959
1958	138.1	14.84	106.7	1,166.1	18.0	64.5	15.5	12.3	15.7	54,591	358.5	2.82	1958
1957	116.6	13.11	100.1	1,208.7	23.7	61.7	18.9	10.8	14.6	49,165	365.2	2.43	1957
1956	106.8	12.38	109.5	1,609.1	22.2	53.7	22.0	8.2	14.2	61,912	316.5	2.31	1956
1955	96.2	11.39	81.5	1,225.4	9.2	40.6	15.5	5.8	12.8	53,007	283.1	2.20	1955
1954	87.8	10.61	52.7	1,194.0	3.4	31.1	7.5	4.7	12.1	46,894	240.9	2.16	1954

Financial data include Stavid Engineering on a pooling of interests accounting basis for 1959 and prior years and are adjusted for possible renegotiation refunds in the years to which they apply. 1954 and 1955.

Earnings for 1962, exclude a gain of $13.1 million ($1.26 per average share) on disposition of Transamerica stock. All per share data have been adjusted for stock splits (2 for 1 in 1959 and 4 for 3 in 1963) and for stock dividends.

FIG. 36. *Lockheed Highlights,* from Lockheed Aircraft Corporation
Thirty-Second Annual Report, December 29, 1963.
(Courtesy of Lockheed Aircraft Corporation)

LOCKHEED Consolidated Balance Sheet

Assets

CURRENT ASSETS:	December 29, 1963	December 30, 1962
Cash	$ 30,205,000	$ 33,309,000
Accounts receivable — U.S. government (including costs and fees under cost reimbursement type contracts: 1963 — $108,477,000; 1962 — $135,132,000)	189,980,000	207,323,000
Other accounts receivable (including amounts under foreign government programs: 1963 — $8,252,000; 1962 — $23,817,000)	33,395,000	52,560,000
Inventories less advances and progress payments (Note 1)	170,094,000	187,608,000
Prepaid expenses	13,461,000	17,281,000
Total current assets	437,133,000	498,081,000
INVESTMENTS, at lower of cost or estimated realizable value	3,781,000	3,499,000
PROPERTY, PLANT AND EQUIPMENT, at cost (less accumulated depreciation and amortization: 1963 — $127,943,000; 1962 — $118,631,000) (Note 2)	104,359,000	94,271,000
DEFERRED CHARGES	561,000	2,110,000
	$545,834,000	$597,961,000

Liabilities and Stockholders' Equity

CURRENT LIABILITIES:	December 29, 1963	December 30, 1962
Notes payable — banks	$ —	$ 40,000,000
Accounts payable	147,936,000	170,055,000
Salaries and wages	43,712,000	48,175,000
Federal income tax and renegotiation refunds	32,221,000	42,520,000
Other taxes	17,239,000	16,792,000
Customers' advances in excess of related costs	9,207,000	17,411,000
Retirement plan contribution (Note 3)	28,101,000	21,467,000
Other liabilities	18,487,000	20,831,000
Total current liabilities	296,903,000	377,981,000
DEFERRED INCOME (Note 4)	14,070,000	14,406,000
LONG-TERM DEBT — portion due after one year:		
4.50% debentures — due 1976 (Note 5)	22,500,000	24,375,000
3.75% subordinated convertible debentures — due 1980	2,535,000	4,008,000
STOCKHOLDERS' EQUITY: Capital stock, $1 par value: 20,000,000 shares authorized (634,497 shares authorized for employee stock options — Note 6 — and 139,286 shares reserved for conversion of debentures at $18.20) Issued at $1 per share	10,737,000	7,913,000
Additional capital	63,166,000	62,743,000
Earnings retained for use in the business (after deducting stock dividends) (Note 5)	135,923,000	106,535,000
Total stockholders' equity	209,826,000	177,191,000
	$545,834,000	$597,961,000

See accompanying notes.

FIG. 37. Consolidated Balance Sheet, From Lockheed Aircraft Corporation
Thirty-Second Annual Report, December 29, 1963.
(Courtesy of Lockheed Aircraft Corporation)

LOCKHEED Consolidated Earnings

	YEAR ENDED December 29, 1963	December 30, 1962
SALES AND OTHER INCOME:		
Sales (including costs and fees under cost reimbursement type contracts)	$1,930,488,000	$1,753,074,000
Other income	2,619,000	2,143,000
	1,933,107,000	1,755,217,000
COSTS AND EXPENSES:		
Cost of sales	1,713,186,000	1,552,626,000
Administrative and general expenses	108,779,000	100,278,000
Research and development	22,782,000	18,326,000
Interest	2,946,000	4,618,000
	1,847,693,000	1,675,848,000
EARNINGS BEFORE FEDERAL INCOME TAX	85,414,000	79,369,000
PROVISION FOR FEDERAL INCOME TAX (Note 7)	42,160,000	42,170,000
EARNINGS FOR THE YEAR	$43,254,000	37,199,000
SPECIAL ITEM:		
Gain on disposition of Transamerica preferred stock, less related federal tax		13,135,000
EARNINGS FOR THE YEAR AND SPECIAL ITEM		$ 50,334,000

Depreciation and amortization of plant and equipment was $16,916,000 for 1963 and $16,521,000 for 1962.

See accompanying notes.

LOCKHEED Consolidated Earnings Retained for Use in the Business

(After deducting stock dividends)

	YEAR ENDED December 29, 1963	December 30, 1962
BALANCE AT BEGINNING OF YEAR	$106,535,000	$ 65,[illegible]
EARNINGS FOR 1963	43,254,000	
EARNINGS AND SPECIAL ITEM FOR 1962		50,334,000
	149,789,000	115,912,000
LESS CASH DIVIDENDS: Per share, as adjusted for stock split: 1963 — $1.30; 1962 — 90¢	13,866,000	9,397,000
BALANCE AT END OF YEAR (Note 5)	$135,923,000	$106,515,000

Consolidated Additional Capital

BALANCE AT DECEMBER 30, 1962	$62,713,000
Excess of amounts realized over par value of 93,569 shares of capital stock issued upon exercise of employees' stock options (Note 6)	1,701,000
Excess of conversion price over par value of 67,952 shares of capital stock issued upon conversion of debentures (after deducting unamortized debenture expense)	1,415,000
	65,829,000
Amount transferred to capital stock account to maintain the $1 par value on the additional 2,662,850 shares of capital stock issued in connection with the capital stock split on the basis of four shares for three on June 28, 1963	2,663,000
BALANCE AT DECEMBER 29, 1963	[illegible]

See accompanying notes.

FIG. 38. Consolidated Earnings and Consolidated Earnings Retained for Use in the Business, from Lockheed Aircraft Corporation Thirty-Second Annual Report, December 29, 1963. *(Courtesy of Lockheed Aircraft Corporation)*

LOCKHEED Source and Disposition of Consolidated Working Capital

	YEAR ENDED December 29, 1963	December 30, 1962
SOURCE OF WORKING CAPITAL:		
Operations:		
Earnings for the year	$43,254,000	$37,199,000
Add charges against earnings not involving working capital:		
Depreciation and amortization of plant and equipment	16,916,000	16,521,000
Other charges	1,978,000	3,716,000
Increase (decrease) in deferred income (Note 4)	(336,000)	5,587,000
	61,812,000	63,023,000
Proceeds from disposition of Transamerica preferred stock, less related federal tax	—	17,104,000
Sale of capital stock under employee stock options	1,795,000	1,994,000
Other	—	22,000
	63,607,000	82,143,000
DISPOSITION OF WORKING CAPITAL:		
Additions to property, plant and equipment	27,454,000	29,128,000
Cash dividends on capital stock	13,866,000	9,397,000
Reduction of long-term debt — 4.50% debentures	1,875,000	1,875,000
Investments	282,000	2,206,000
	43,477,000	42,606,000
INCREASE IN WORKING CAPITAL	$20,130,000	$39,537,000

See accompanying notes.

LOCKHEED Notes to Financial Statements

Note 1

Inventories are stated at the lower of cost or estimated realizable value and are summarized as follows:

	December 29, 1963	*December 30, 1962*
Work in process	$324,115,000	$342,009,000
Materials and spare parts	64,692,000	67,515,000
Advances to subcontractors	32,928,000	37,471,000
	421,735,000	446,995,000
Less advances and progress payments	251,641,000	259,387,000
	$170,094,000	$187,608,000

Materials and spare parts are stated at average cost.

At December 29, 1963 work in process relates principally to U. S. government contracts. Work in process on such contracts includes all applicable engineering costs. As products are delivered, the estimated profit for each contract is taken into income in proportion to the sales price of the deliveries. The resultant inventory amounts are at or below estimated realizable value.

Under the contractual arrangements by which the Company receives progress payments from the U. S. government, title to inventories identified with related contracts is vested in the government.

Note 2

Property, plant and equipment stated at cost are summarized as follows:

	December 29, 1963	*December 30, 1962*
Land	$ 13,540,000	$ 12,101,000
Buildings and structures	66,352,000	62,342,000
Machinery and equipment	119,328,000	114,211,000
Leasehold improvements	23,651,000	20,095,000
Construction in progress	9,431,000	4,153,000
	$232,302,000	$212,902,000

A material portion of the plant facilities used by the Company is furnished by the U. S. government.

Note 3

The Company has noncontributory employees' retirement plans. The 1963 provision was $30,426,000, of which $28,432,000 is for current service costs and $1,994,000 for past service costs. Unfunded credits to employees for services (generally prior to 1957) are approximately $31,400,000. This amount is being funded over a period ending in 1986.

Note 4

Deferred income at December 29, 1963 includes deferred investment credits of $1,332,000. The balance of the deferred income arises from the inclusion of administrative and general expenses in the basis on which progress payments are received from the U. S. government (on other than cost reimbursement type contracts), whereas such expenses are charged off by the Company as they are incurred. This amount of deferred income will be taken into income in future years as deliveries are made under the contracts.

Note 5

The Company is required to provide sinking funds for the redemption of its 4.50% debentures of $1,875,000 annually through 1975.

The debentures impose certain restrictions on the payment of cash dividends and on the amount of funded debt. As of December 29, 1963 earnings retained for use in the business are restricted in the amount of $28,000,000.

FIG. 39. Source and Disposition of Working Capital and Notes to Financial Statement, from Lockheed Aircraft Corporation Thirty-Second Annual Report, December 29, 1963. *(Courtesy of Lockheed Aircraft Corporation)*

the current year with the year just preceding, (Fig. 37) as do the statement of consolidated earnings (profit and loss statement) and the statement of consolidated earnings retained for use in the business. (Fig. 38)

Information about the source and disposition of the company's consolidated working capital is important to those who have money invested in Lockheed. Some figures require further explanation for complete understanding. These pages from the annual report are reproduced in Fig. 39.

The financial statements are prepared by a certified public accountant after a careful audit of the accounts of the company. The audit certificate is an integral part of the financial portion of the annual report. A certificate of this nature is illustrated in Figure 40.

Auditors' Report

The Board of Directors and Stockholders

Lockheed Aircraft Corporation

We have examined the accompanying consolidated balance sheet of Lockheed Aircraft Corporation and subsidiaries at December 29, 1963, the related consolidated statements of earnings, earnings retained for use in the business and additional capital and the statement of source and disposition of consolidated working capital for the year then ended. Our examination was made in accordance with generally accepted auditing standards, and accordingly included such tests of the accounting records and such other auditing procedures as we considered necessary in the circumstances. It was not practicable to confirm certain amounts included in receivables under foreign government programs or from the U. S. government, as to which we satisfied ourselves by means of other auditing procedures. We have previously made a similar examination of the financial statements for the prior year.

In our opinion, the statements mentioned above present fairly the consolidated financial position of Lockheed Aircraft Corporation and subsidiaries at December 29, 1963 and December 30, 1962, the consolidated results of their operations and the source and disposition of their consolidated working capital for the years then ended, in conformity with generally accepted accounting principles applied on a consistent basis during the period.

ARTHUR YOUNG & COMPANY

Los Angeles, California
February 24, 1964

FIG. 40. Auditors' Report, from Lockheed Aircraft Corporation Thirty-Second Annual Report, December 29, 1963. *(Courtesy of Lockheed Aircraft Corporation)*

Financial statements are an example of a rather specialized language that is completely comprehensible only to those people who have had training and experience in its use. In order to provide stockholders with more easily understandable materials, audiovisual devices are brought into use. These devices help to explain

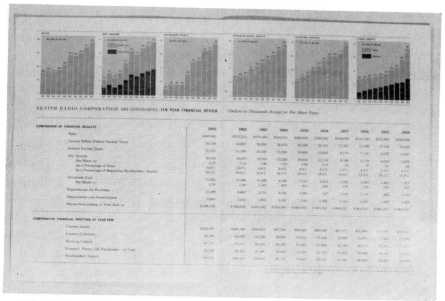

FIG. 41. Graphs in *Zenith Annual Report 1963*. *(Courtesy of Zenith Radio Corporation)*

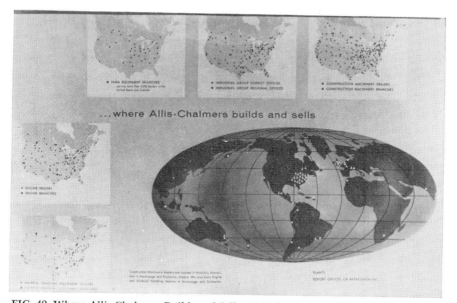

FIG. 42. Where Allis-Chalmers Builds and Sells, *1960 Annual Report, Part One,* pp. 8-9.
(Courtesy of Allis-Chalmers)

and interpret the material presented in the financial statements.

One of the methods of making the materials more meaningful is to change them into graphic form. The graphs make it possible to trace the changes that occur from year to year and to follow the company's growth over a period of time. A series of charts of this nature showing the changes in the Zenith Radio Corporation over a ten-year period is shown in Figure 41.

Geographical distribution of a company's operations can be indicated by means of maps, as in Figure 42.

Photographs of company operations, new products, new plants, and uses of the product are always interesting and informative to stockholders. The reproduction in Figure 43 of full-page, full-color

FIG. 43. Photographs from *1959 Annual Report,* Standard Oil Company (New Jersey).
(Courtesy of Standard Oil Company of New Jersey)

photographs in the Standard Oil Company (New Jersey) 1959 Annual Report interprets certain phases of the company's operations much better than the written descriptions alone could have done. Of course, only certain parts of the operation lend themselves to photographic treatment, and this sort of thing must be used with restraint. The photographs are provided for interest and for supplementary information, not to carry the main bulk of the communication.

A company whose operations are nation- or world-wide should let the stockholders know of this, as in the page from Lockheed's Annual Report (Figure 44).

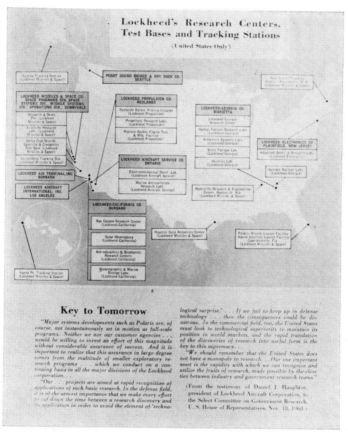

FIG. 44. Lockheed Research Centers, Test Bases and Tracking Stations, from Lockheed Aircraft Corporation Thirty-Second Annual Report.
(Courtesy of Lockheed Aircraft Corporation)

Stockholders are interested in the research and other activities that have a bearing on the future operations and profits of the company. Without divulging company secrets, the annual report can make stockholders aware of some of the fields in which the company is conducting research. A report of this nature by the Zenith Radio Corporation is illustrated in Figure 45.

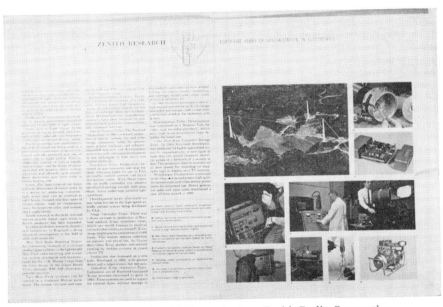

FIG. 45. Report on Zenith Research, from Zenith Radio Corporation Annual Report for 1963. *(Courtesy of Zenith Radio Corporation)*

It must not be forgotten that stockholders are also purchasers of the company's products—and often very loyal customers because, after all, they have a stake in the company. A section of the annual report devoted to the product can do double duty in showing the stockholders what the company is doing and in building a desire for the merchandise. Such a page from the Zenith Radio Corporation is shown in Figure 46.

Some companies wish to maintain closer communication with their stockholders than is possible with only the annual report. To maintain this closer liaison, these companies include stockholders in the distribution of the company publications, such as the company newspapers and house organs. The Borden Company encloses small

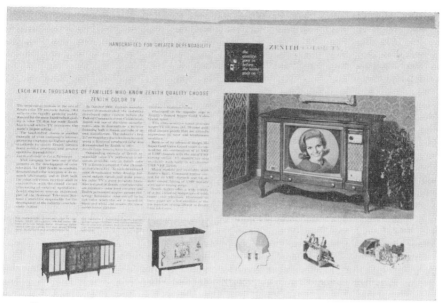

FIG. 46. Sales Pages from Zenith Radio Corporation Annual Report for 1963.
(Courtesy of Zenith Radio Corporation)

FIG. 47. *Borden Quarterly Report* Sent to Stockholders. *(Courtesy of the Borden Company)*

folders of pertinent information in the envelopes in which dividend checks are mailed. Information about the company's prospects for the future, the development of new products, and human interest stories concerning company personnel are included. One issue is pictured in Figure 47.

Summary

It is important to maintain good communication channels with company stockholders. As the owners of the company they are entitled to information regarding its operations and activities. There are limitations as to how much information they can be given without damage to the company.

Stockholders' meetings are held annually to hear reports on the company's operation and to vote on various issues with regard to company policies. Stockholders should be provided in advance with information necessary to make intelligent choices in their voting. A stockholder has as many votes as he has shares of voting stock. He may give another person authority to vote his stock for him by means of a proxy.

Most stockholders are unable to attend stockholders' meetings and so receive their information through the company's annual report and the summary of the stockholders' meeting. More frequent publications, such as quarterly memos keep the owner up-to-date on current happenings.

Interpretation of financial statements with graphs of the information and textual explanations help the stockholder who is not skilled in reading financial statements to understand the company's past operations and its aspirations for the future.

CHAPTER 8

VISUALIZATION OF INFORMATION

Purposes of Visualizing Information

Throughout our school careers we have been taught to set our thoughts, ideas, and feelings down on paper, utilizing the written language to do so. The men of letters—essayists, playwrights, and poets—are regarded as the epitomes of accomplishment in the field of communication. Largely ignored have been those who are equally outstanding in the field of communicating by visual means—artists, sculptors, photographers; and television and motion picture directors, cameramen and photographers, and editors. This latter group are the people who more and more will be affecting way we think and feel and the products we buy.

It is not easy to reverse the course of our thinking—to change from reducing thoughts to words, to expressing those thoughts visually. To visualize an abstract thought so that it can be communicated clearly to another is no mean accomplishment. It involves first an understanding of the idea and of why it is difficult for the other person to understand it. Secondly it involves a knowledge of the media for transmitting the thought. The visual and verbal language used must be intelligible to both of the persons involved in the communication. This helps to reduce the "noise" in the channel to the minimum.

Reasons for the Use of Audio or Visual Methods

A large percentage of the world's population cannot read the written word. Others have a rudimentary reading ability, and can receive only very simple ideas through this medium. Even for those proficient in written language, visual communication is often superior for transmitting certain concepts accurately. This is not to say, of course, that one could do without oral or written media. Although it may be true, as Confucius is supposed to have said, that one picture is worth ten thousand words, it is also true that a picture that is not understood is of very little value, and a few words of explanation may make the picture very valuable.

The audio-visual approach does not deny the value of any device which can help one person understand a thought or concept. For the most effective communication, one should choose the medium or combination of media that will most adequately convey the message. The choice of media will vary according to the message and the persons with whom one is communicating.

Methods of Visualizing Material

The first consideration in planning the visualization of material is the degree of knowledge and sophistication the communicatee already has of the material. One must ask:

1. How much does this person know about the subject?
2. What does he know about related fields of knowledge?
3. How much experience has he had in gaining knowledge by these methods?
4. How have his past learning experiences prepared him for this type of learning?
5. What is his purpose in learning this?
6. How much effort will he put forth to learn this material?

It might be possible to answer these questions with some degree of accuracy if they were about one person. However, they generally are for a group of people and the answers vary with each person. This means that the person planning the communication will have to estimate the typical answers.

The amount of previous knowledge about the subject determines the starting point for the communication. One would not commence a training session for a group of electronic technicians with an explanation of the theory of the vacuum tube. On the other hand, one would not start such a group out on advanced theory. The properly prepared learning situation should take the person at the point where he is in his knowledge and take him as far along as possible.

The knowledge a person has in areas related to the subject of the communication will also affect the presentation. The knowledge our electronic technicians have of electrical theory will greatly affect the method of teaching electronic theory.

As a person gains experience in learning by a certain method, his proficiency in learning by that method increases. At the beginning of a training or communications situation, some time should be spent in familiarizing all concerned with the medium by which the material is transmitted. The communicatee does not, of course, need to know how the material was prepared, recorded or transmitted; he just needs experience on the learning end of the method.

Everything a person has experienced in the past will affect the way he learns, how much he learns, and how quickly he learns. New experiences are received by the mind, compared with experiences of the past (some of which are remembered and some are subconscious), and filed in accordance with those earlier experiences. The wider background the communicatee has in the area of the communication, the more he is able to get from the message, whatever it may be.

In any transfer of a thought from one person to another, the person receiving the message must have some purpose in the receipt of it, or else the transfer to his mind will not be made. The amount and quality of the transfer depends upon the intensity of the communicatee's interest. A person training for a factory job who is interested in the job itself will learn more and faster than the person whose sole interest is to get onto the payroll.

Closely related to the communicatee's purpose is the factor of how much effort he is willing to exert in order to learn the material. Naturally, the more interest he has in the subject and the stronger his purpose in learning it, the more effort he will expend. If the interest is truly there, effort spent will not seem like work, but more like an interesting pastime.

Methods of Presentation

Why is all this significant in planning the visualization of information? By reducing information to graphic or photographic terms, certain of the difficulties involved in varying degrees of knowledge, background, purpose, and interest can be overcome. This method of presentation, if properly done, can help to provide background information, interest, and purpose for those who did not have these traits developed at the beginning.

It is hoped that the following chapters will help to determine ways for using audio or visual terms to convey information to other people quickly and accurately.

In choosing the most efficient medium, among the many available, several things must be considered.

1. Do I understand the material to be communicated and the problems involved in getting it across to my audience?
   a. Is the objective perfectly clear in my own mind?
      What are the important points?
      What is the best way to stress these points?
   b. Who will the audience be?
      How well informed are they in the field?
      How easily will they be able to grasp what I am presenting?
      How large will the audience be?
      Will the audience be friendly, hostile, or noncommittal?

2. What is my purpose in using visual presentation?
   a. Will the visuals carry the bulk of the message? or
   b. Will the visuals merely reinforce what I am saying?

3. What form should my visual presentation take?

Motion pictures	Opaque projection
Slides	Flipsheet
Filmstrip	Television
Overhead projector	Or perhaps an audio pres-
Chalkboard	entation alone or in con-
Feltboard	junction with the visual

4. What type of visualization is best suited to my own method of working, the material to be presented, and my audience?
   a. Concrete or symbolic?
   b. Arithmetic or graphic?
   c. Must it be statistically precise or can some exaggeration be brought in to make a point?
   d. Will the use of color clarify my meanings?
   e. Can some humor be brought in?
      Cartoons?

5. Have I tested the materials before I am to use them in front of an audience?
   a. Have I rehearsed using them in the auditorium where they will be presented?
   b. Is all the information legible from the most distant part of the auditorium?
   c. Is the audience's view of the materials unobstructed?
   d. Can the audience hear me and/or the audio portions of my presentation?

e. Do the visual and audio portions supplement each other, with no duplication of information and no contradictions?
6. Have I used every reasonable means to make my presentation as forceful as possible?
7. Have I planned the conclusion of my presentation well?
    a. Do I summarize the main points either visually or orally?
    b. Do I call for some action (overt or internal) on the part of the audience?
    > Vote for my proposal?
    > Buy my product?
    > Sign the contract?
    > Modify company policy?
    > Change operating methods?
8. Have I provided my audience with a means of remembering the information that I have presented?
    a. Do I have written materials for distribution? (Materials should be distributed *following* the presentation, not before or during it.)
    b. Can I provide them with pencils and paper for note-taking during the presentation?
    c. Can I mail follow-up materials to the participants?
    d. Can the formal part of the meeting be followed by informal discussion groups, led by individuals familiar with the subject? The leaders should have been chosen beforehand and provided with additional information. Someone should be delegated to take notes of points brought out during the discussion and report back on them.

What Is Good Communication?

There is no way to estimate the money lost to American business firms through improper communication or even failure to communicate at all. Descriptions of technical equipment may be perfectly clear to the person or company which wrote them but practically indecipherable to someone trying to read them, even someone be acquainted with the type of equipment. Such a situation may cause cancelled orders, unnecessary shipping expense, extensive correspondence, and even the loss of customers.

Many business people fail to realize that those with whom they are corresponding or talking, or to whom they are sending catalogs, etc., may not be as well versed in the technical language as they are. Because of this, the communication that should occur does not.

What are the indications of good communicative practices?

First, and most important, the person to whom the message is transmitted understands *exactly* what the sender means. In reality, this ideal is probably never completely attained. If the subject is at all involved, the different backgrounds, experiences, types of education, and even the dispositions of those concerned make this ideal communication very difficult. However, anyone involved in communication (and we are all in it one way or another) must strive for this ideal.

Secondly, one way to improve the quality of communication is to choose the best means for transmitting the message. Many different factors enter into this choice of the medium.

1. What is the message?
2. To how many people is it to be communicated?
3. Will they receive the message singly or in groups?
4. How much can be spent for each message received?
5. Is this a "one shot" message or will it be repeated?
6. Who are the people who should receive the message? Engineers, doctors, housewives, businessmen, etc.?
7. Is the message for people in or outside the business? the industry?
8. What do you want them to do after they have received the message? Run out and buy the product, send in a donation, improve their concept of the company, etc.?

The third factor to be considered is the over-all cost of the communication. Costs of communicating vary widely from one medium to another, and even within one medium a considerable variation can be effected by the degree of elaborateness of the communication. Should the communicator strive for low production costs? Naturally, he should try to keep them as low as possible for the communication that he is trying to accomplish. It may be necessary to utilize and elaborate form of communication to convey the message. If it is sufficiently important that certain persons be reached in a certain manner, then this will justify the additional costs. The appropriate degree of elaborateness depends upon several things.

1. How involved is the message that we want to convey?
2. To how many different people must it go?
3. What will be the return to the company from each favorable acceptance of the message?
4. Will the one communication accomplish the ends or will several repetitions be necessary?

5. Will a simple presentation accomplish the same goal as an elaborate one?
6. Might an elaborate presentation tend to turn people away from the acceptance of the message because of its ostentation?
7. Is this type of presentation forced on us by our competition?

What Are the Barriers to Good Communication?

A great deal of communication that is attempted never fulfills the goals which the originator of the message hopefully planned for it. Let us take a brief look at some reasons why the message fails to accomplish all that it is intended to.

Lack of a common language. This is perhaps the greatest barrier to communication. We all have purchased some mechanical gadget that must be assembled. It comes with so-called "easy-to-follow directions" that are supposed to make putting it together a few moments' pastime. The printed instructions describe the method of assembly, using the technical names of the parts. The only person who could read the explanations and follow them without trouble is the man who wrote them in the first place. We read the directions through several times and try to relate them to the job at hand. Finally we throw them away and put the things together in what seems to be the logical way. The failure of the communication was due to the lack of a common language. Such a shortcoming could have been largely overcome by including with the written instructions pictures of the individual parts with their names or numbers. Then the reader will at least know which of the parts the instructions are talking about. Better yet, a series of pictures can show the appearance of the device after each step in the assembly. These things would help to overcome the lack of a common language.

Vagueness of certain words. While there are many words which have very definite and precise meanings, there are others which have many meanings, or whose meanings vary among different groups of people. For instance, consider how many meanings there are for a simple word like "run." One investigator found more than four hundred. What is a dog? The definition one gets will depend upon whether he asks a hunter, a machinist, a gunsmith, a fireplace builder, a soldier, or a man-about-town. If a word is to be used in certain sense, then an illustration or other method of helping the reader to visualize that word in the intended meaning will be of value.

"Noise" in the communication channel. Noise was defined in Chapter 1 as being anything which interferes with the proper understanding of a message. One method of overcoming this noise is to convey the message in more than one way. To continue with the example of the assembly instructions, duplicating the instructions by using both words and pictures would help to overcome the noise factor. Each helps to explain the other, and what is obscure in one might be made quite clear by the other.

Lack of interest. The originator of a communication may tend to forget that the person to whom the information is directed may have little or no interest in receiving the message. Unless that interest is aroused, the person will not give the necessary attention. One excellent method of developing the necessary interest is to provide for a simultaneous visualization of the problem or the product which is being discussed verbally. Thus, advertisements in magazines seldom rely upon words alone to describe the product or its use, but include photographs intended to make that product more desirable in the mind of the reader.

Over-attention to the communication process. A person must be careful in planning his communication to take the best possible advantage of the chosen medium. At the same time, he must not get so involved in the medium that he forgets to realize that it is only a means to an end—that of conveying the message. Everything else is subordinate to and must contribute toward making that message as forceful as possible. Special effects may dazzle the viewer and make him marvel at how clever the communicator is, but this may very well cause him to miss the point of the presentation. If it does this then it is a failure, just as if it had never caught the viewer's eye. No communication should call attention to itself as a method of presentation, but should concentrate on the message.

What Constitutes Good Visualization?

Good visualization involves the best use of the means available to the communicator. This in turn implies two steps that must be taken in the process.

Proper Choice of the Medium. Many media of communication are available to the person organization with a message to convey. Some of these media are of greater value than others in their ability to help the viewer or listener understand the information being presented. In the chapters that follow, many methods of visualization are described. It is up to the person planning the communication to consider each of them in terms of the message that he wants to convey, how much money he can spend to transmit it, and the people whom he wants to react to it. With these things in mind he can choose that medium which will most effectively do the things he wants done.

Best Use of the Medium Chosen. After the medium has been decided upon, it becomes necessary to plan for its use in the way that will take the best advantage of all of its possibilities. In general, this will mean working with people who are experts in their particular types of communication. The specialist will almost invariably have a better knowledge of the possibilities, the techniques, and the possible causes of failure in his specialty than will a person in a more general field of communication. For this reason it is generally best to work with such a specialist, whether he is employed full time by the organization or is called in from outside.

What We Can Expect to Gain from Effective Visualization?

Meanings Are Conveyed More Precisely. Even the best of communication (practically speaking) fails to put across the precise shades of meaning in all of the areas of its subject. Anything which can help to pinpoint these meanings and contribute to the precision of the information conveyed is welcome. Inclusion of illustrations, motion pictures showing the movement or rhythm and the sounds made by the object or material being described or discussed can help a person understand the message more precisely.

Meanings Are Conveyed More Vividly. One of the advantages of the use of audio-visual devices in education is the fact that a child has an experience recorded in his mind in such a way that it will remain with him for a long time. Long after the things he has read have faded into the general background he will remember those things that were taught to him with the types of materials that make the subject seem to come to life—photographs, motion pictures, models, exhibits, recordings, and others. What proper visualization can do for children in school, it can also do for others with whom one wishes to communicate.

The Interest of the Communicatee is Held. It is essential that the method of conveying a message hold the attention of the person to whom that message is directed. Otherwise, no communication has taken place. Anything that will help hold that interest will contribute to the message's effectiveness, and proper visualization of the subject matter can do this.

Materials Are Remembered Longer. Materials properly visualized not only help to convey meanings more vividly: they are also remembered longer. Vivid experiences are remembered for a long time, and visually presented information is more vivid.

Communication May Be Less Expensive. There are many ways of computing the cost of communicating with others—by calculating the total cost of preparing and distributing the message, the cost per person contacted, or the ratio of the cost to the value of sales developed. If the communication is for the purpose of inducing others to purchase one's products, then the most valid criterion is the last one. An effectively visualized presentation may gain more results, thereby reducing the cost in terms of results.

Preparation for an Audio-Visual Presentation

An audio-visual presentation of data cannot be a spur-of-the-moment thing if it is to be effective. It requires much preparation and smooth presentation if it is to be of the greatest possible value.

Prior Preparation.
1. Decide upon the proper medium. As mentioned above, this will depend upon many factors.
2. Obtain or make the visuals. These may be prepared by an in-plant organization or by specialists called in.
3. Make advance preparations for the showing room, arranging for such things as light control, electrical outlets, and ventilation.
4. Arrange for projection equipment. Appropriate items of equipment must be on hand at the time of the presentation. These would include such things as the projector, screen, tape recorder or record player, etc.

Request for Audio-Visual Facilities

When an audio-visual presentation is given in the plant or other area controlled by the company, it is generally possible to have rather close control over the conditions under which the showing will occur. When a salesman or other representative leaves the company-owned premises he is more or less at the mercy of those who control the showing area.

If the material is to be shown at a trade conference or convention, advance notice about booth location, size, electrical facilities, and other pertinent information is generally available. The display can be adjusted to suit the conditions before it leaves the home office.

In many cases a hotel room or sample room is used to entertain the people to whom the company wants to tell its story. The company representative often travels by air and can take only a limited amount of luggage and materials with him. These people are relying more and more upon the hotel to provide or obtain heavy items of equipment that are not easily portable. In this case it is a good idea to notify the hotel of the equipment that will be needed when room reservations are made. Below (Fig. 48) is illustrated a postal card designed to notify a hotel of the needed facilities.

HOTEL ACCOMMODATIONS

Please reserve a (single, double) room for me at the

_____ Hotel   Arrival _____

Please confirm   □   Departure _____

Audio-Visual Equipment

Please arrange to have the following items of equipment available on the indicated dates:

	Date		Date
□ 35mm filmstrip proj.	_____	□ 16mm movie proj.	_____
□ 3¼ x 4 slide proj.	_____	□ Tape recorder	_____
□ 2 x 2 slide proj.	_____	□ Record player	_____
□ Overhead proj.	_____	□ Projection screen	_____
□ Other	_____		_____

Name	Company
	Address

FIG. 48. Hotel Accommodation and Audio-Visual Equipment Reservation Card.

Summary

Conveying information by visual means involves a different frame of reference from that which is appropriate for written communication. The communicator must consider the effect that the choice of medium and its utilization will have on those who view the materials. The choice will depend upon the message to be transmitted, the characteristics of the viewers, and the action which is desired after the viewing.

Good communication makes it possible for the communicatee to get the message exactly as it was intended and does it at the least possible cost in relation to the purpose to be accomplished. It must overcome the possible barriers of lack of a common language, vagueness of certain words, "noise," lack of interest, and over-attention to the communication process.

Good communication must be planned well in advance so that the necessary facilities and equipment will be ready when they are needed. This is especially important when the presentation is going to be away from the company premises.

BIBLIOGRAPHY

Beatts, Patrick H., *Visualizing the Abstract*, Holyoke, Massachusetts, Tecnifax Corporation, 1956.

Coffman, Joe, *The Role of Visual Communication*, Holyoke, Massachusetts, Tecnifax Corporation, 1955.

Cross, A. J. Foy, and Irene F. Cypher, *Audio-Visual Education*, New York, Thomas Y. Crowell Company, 1961, 514 pp.
    Chap. 1 Audio and Visual Aids to Learning

De Kieffer, Robert, and Lee W. Cochran, *Manual of Audio-Visual Techniques*, Englewood Cliffs, New Jersey, Prentice-Hall, Inc., 1955, 220 pp.
    Unit One. Toward More Effective Communication
        The Pattern of Development, pp. 1-4
        The Role of Communication in Modern Life, pp. 5-8
        Audio-Visual Materials and the Learning Process, pp. 14-18

Eastman Kodak Company, *Planning and Producing Visual Aids*, Pamphlet S-13, Rochester, New York, Eastman Kodak Company. (Single copy free upon request)

Kemp, Jerrold E., *Planning and Producing Audiovisual Materials*, San Francisco, California, Chandler Publishing Company, 1963, 169 pp.
    Part One Planning Your Audiovisual Materials

Kinder, James S., *Audio-Visual Materials and Techniques*, 2nd Edition, New York, American Book Company, 1959, 592 pp.
    Chap. 1 The Way of Audio-Visual Education

Sands, Lester B., *Audio-Visual Procedures in Teaching*, New York, Ronald Press Company, 1956, 670 pp.
    Chap. 1 Audio Visual Teaching

Thomas, R. Murray, and Sherwin G. Swartout, *Integrated Teaching Materials*, Longmans, Green and Company, Inc., 1963, 545 pp.
    Chap. 1 Conveying Ideas Skillfully
    Chap. 2 A Process for Selecting Methods

CHAPTER 9

PHOTOGRAPHY

Photography As a Tool of Industrial Communication

Photography, in one or another of its many forms, constitutes the basis for most of the visual communication that occurs in business and industry today. No comparable form of communication exists which can reproduce the appearance of an object as quickly, accurately, or inexpensively as can the photographic process. The possibilities and applications of this medium in recording and trans-

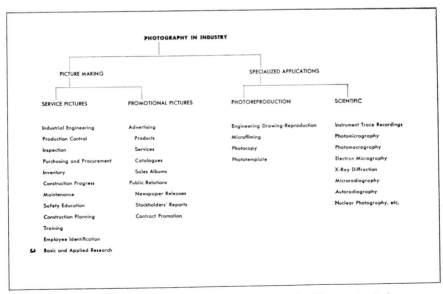

FIG. 49. Photography in Industry. *From Making Service Pictures for Industry,* Page 2, 1952. *(Courtesy of Eastman Kodak Co.)*

116

mitting information are literally without number. The only limits
are the imagination and skill of the communicator. The Eastman
Kodak Company has listed the areas shown below in Figure 49 as
the applications of photography to the needs of industry.

Photography is flexible in that it can communicate by itself or in
conjunction with other media. It is the latter that best illustrates
the wide variety of applications and forms that this medium can
fulfill. Words alone cannot communicate a full knowledge of the
appearance and characteristics of an object; photographs, likewise,
are limited in the information they can give about the object. No
one medium can give as much information as can a combination
of media. The most efficient and complete information requires a
combination of several media of communication, including verbal
descriptions, photographs, and perhaps a sound recording.

It is hoped that an appreciation of the value of photography
in communication has already been established. It is not the purpose
of this chapter to try to make a photographer of the reader. Rather,
the intent is to give him some slight acquaintance with the principles
and techniques involved so that he will have a knowledge of the
capabilities and an appreciation for the difficulties encountered in the
use of the photographic medium. A person who is in the industrial
communications field and who has this knowledge of photography
will be better able to perform his job, because he will have one
more means of portraying information.

A knowledge of the techniques and limitations of photography
will help the communications expert to convey his wishes to the
photographer, so that this photographer provides the illustration
that exactly fits the needs of the situation. At the same time, he will
know what he can and cannot expect of the photographic process.

The communicator's organization may have a photographic staff
to carry out assignments for other departments, or it may be that
a free-lance or commercial photographer is called in when there is
need for photographic services. In either event, the function of the
communicator is the same—to tell the photographer what is desired
and then to know when it has been achieved. Photography, like any
other art or science, has a language of its own and a person must
be able to speak this language in order to convey instructions and
suggestions effectively.

Photographic Theory

Light. The most common theory of light is that it is a form of radiant energy given off by certain sources such as the sun, fire, metal when heated sufficiently, and certain substances such as radium. The light travels away from the source in a straight line and at the rate of 186,300 miles a second. This rate of travel holds true in a vacuum and gases such as air, but when it enters a denser transparent material such as glass or water, it slows down, then picks up its former speed when it emerges into the air again. Objects which are not luminous have the capacity of reflecting light, which makes them visible, or absorbing it. Generally, an object will reflect part of the light which falls on it and absorb the rest. The wavelengths of the reflected light give the object its apparent color. Some substances allow certain wavelengths of light to pass through them and absorb the rest.

Light that comes from the sun or an incandescent light is called white light. Actually, this light is made up of many wavelengths of this radiant energy. Not all light has the same relative strengths in the different wavelengths. If it is stronger in the shorter wavelengths than in the longer, it is said to have a bluish cast, or if it is stronger in the longer wavelengths, it is reddish. William Thompson, Lord Kelvin, a British physicist, worked out a method of identifying the color of light. If a theoretical black mass is heated sufficiently, it will commence giving off heat, or infra-red, waves. If it is heated still further, it will give off light of a dull reddish color. As the temperature is increased, the light becomes less red and more white, and finally a bluish color. The temperature on the absolute scale (absolute zero is equal to—273° centigrade) to which the black mass is heated to give off light of an equivalent color is the color temperature, or Kelvin temperature, of the light. The color temperatures of some of the common sources of light for photography are listed in Figure 50.

The Camera. This major piece of equipment of the photographic process has four basic parts. They are the *lens, shutter, light-tight*

Sky light (excluding the sun)	10,000 K or higher
Electronic flash	7,000 K
Sunlight (noon)	6,000 K
Blue flash bulbs	6,000 K
White (clear) flash bulbs	3,400 K
Photoflood lamp	3,200 K
Ordinary incandescent lamp	2,900 K

FIG. 50. Kelvin Color Temperatures of Common Photographic Light Sources.

box, and *light-sensitive material,* or *film.* Other accessories make photographing easier and more convenient, but the four listed are essential.

Rays of light passing through the *lens* are bent, or *refracted,* as they pass from the air to the glass and back to the air again. The lens, as shown in cross section in Figure 51, is thicker in the middle than at the edges. The angle between the front and rear surfaces of the lens increases toward the edges. The greater angle at the edge causes the light to refract more than at the center. Thus, rays of

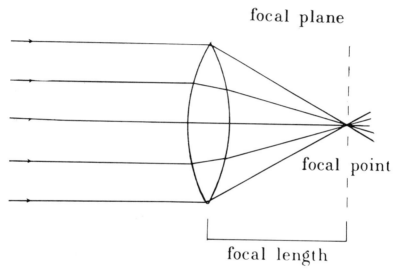

focal plane

focal point

focal length

FIG. 51. Light Rays from Infinity Passing Through a Lens.

light coming from a point a great distance away (*infinity*) will be brought together at a point behind the lens. This point is known as the *focal point.* Light coming from other distant points will form other focal points. Together, these focal points form the *focal plane.* Photographic film is placed in this plane to record an image of this distant scene. The distance from the center of the lens to the focal plane remains constant for any one lens and is known as the *focal length.* The size of the image on the focal plane is directly proportional to the focal length of the lens. If a distant tree made an image one-half inch in a camera with a two-inch focal-length lens, the image would be one inch if a four-inch focal-length lens were used.

Light rays from nearby objects are still diverging, or moving apart, as they enter the camera lens. Since they enter at an angle different from that at which the rays from the distant object enter and since the angle of refraction remains constant for any one part of the lens, they emerge at a different angle. In Figure 52, the light rays from B will meet at point b rather than at point a, causing the image of point B to be blurred, or out of focus, instead of sharp. To get a sharp image of point B, the film plane would have to be moved to the place where the rays of light from that point cross, at b. This is the purpose of the focusing device on the camera. The shorter the distance from B to the camera, the greater the distance from the lens to b must be.

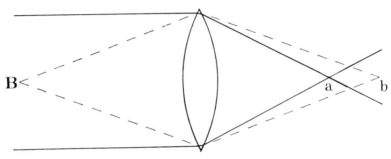

FIG. 52. Light Rays from a Nearby Source Passing Through a Lens, Compared to Rays from Infinity.

A camera can be adjusted to give a sharp image of objects a certain distance away. It is then said to be focused on that distance. As an object moves closer to or farther away from the camera than that distance, the image becomes progressively more blurred or out of focus. The distance from the near point and the far point where the image becomes too blurred for use is known as the *depth of field*. (See Fig. 53) With a particular lens, this depth of field increases as the diameter of the lens is reduced and also increases as the distance from the camera to the point focused on increases. It is also greater for a shorter focal length lens, the other conditions being equal.

The light-gathering power of a lens is determined by the ratio of its focal length to its diameter. Since a longer focal length lens casts a larger image, its light is spread over a wider area. Thus, if two lenses were of the same diameter but of differing focal lengths,

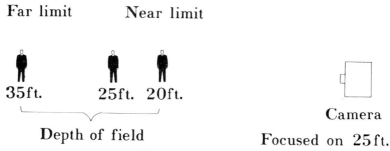

FIG. 53. Depth of Field.

the image cast by the shorter lens would be brighter because the light passing through it would cover a smaller area. The smaller the diameter is in relation to the focal length, the less light it will pass and the larger the ratio number (focal length to diameter) will be. The ratio is usually expressed with an f and a slant line—such as f/4.5 or f/8, or with a 1 (one) or a colon to indicate that it is a ratio— such as 1:4.5 or 1:8. Lens openings can be adjusted with the *iris diaphragm* which acts to reduce the lens diameter, and therefore the amount of light reaching the film. Each successively larger number indicated on the lens adjustment scale reduces the amount of light by one half.

The *shutter* performs its function by holding light away from the film except for the time when the exposure is being made, and then allowing the light to pass through for a predetermined time. The *between-the-lens shutter* is located between the elements, or glass parts, of the lens. It opens from the center outward, remains open for the specified time, then closes inward. It is a popular type of shutter, particularly for cameras which do not have interchangeable lenses. The *focal-plane shutter* consists of a curtain with a slit in it lying just in front of the film, very close to the focal plane. Exposure is made by drawing the slit across the film. Changes in exposure time are accomplished by varying the width of the slit or the speed with which it is moved. The entire lens may be removed without exposing the film behind it. A third type, the *behind-the-lens* shutter operates like the between-the-lens type but protects the film when the lenses are changed. Proper *exposure* is accomplished by the correct combination of lens opening and shutter time.

It is a function of the amount of light that is allowed to fall on the film and the amount of time that it is allowed to fall.

The *light-tight box,* or camera body, serves two major purposes. It holds the lens and film in the proper relationship to each other and protects the film from extraneous light. It also provides a place to mount many of the accessories that assist in making a good picture.

The *light-sensitive material,* or *film,* records the scene that was focused upon it by the lens and flashed to it by the shutter. Film consists of an acetate base upon which has been coated a chemical that is sensitive to light (one of the *silver halides*). The image is not visible at this time (a *latent image*), but can be made visible by development, which changes the exposed bits of silver halide to metallic silver, which forms the image. Films are available in many different degrees of sensitivity to light, and relative sensitivity to different colors of light. The degree of sensitivity to light of a film is indicated by its *exposure index,* expressed numerically. The colors of light to which films are sensitive are indicated by the names *color-blind* (or *blue-sensitive*) for films sensitive only to blue, *orthochromatic* for films sensitive to all colors except red, and *panchromatic* for films sensitive to all colors of visible light.

Processing. After exposure, *development* brings out the image, which at this stage is a *negative.* The brightest portions of the subject affect the silver halide the most, therefore are converted the most completely to metallic silver, which appears black. After development, the film is placed in the fixer, which dissolves the remaining silver halide that has not been converted to silver. The fixer then must be removed by thorough washing in order to keep the image from deteriorating. After the film has been dried, it is ready for *printing,* either *contact* or by *projection.* In printing, light is passed through the negative and onto a piece of *sensitized paper* or another piece of film. Where the negative is clear, the light passes through readily and exposes the print. Where the negative is dark, the light is held back. During development the exposed areas turn dark and the unexposed areas remain light. The print reverses the tones of the negative and the result is a *positive image* of the subject. Exposure of the positive can be made by placing the *emulsion* side of the unexposed sensitized paper or film in contact with the emulsion side negative and shining a white light through the film to the paper. This is known as *contact printing.* Projection printing involves placing the film in a *projection printer* (or *enlarger*) and shining the light through the film and a lens onto the sensitized paper. The size of the print can be varied by changing the distance from the negative to the paper. Figure 54 illustrates the methods of exposing the positive. Steps in the development of the positive are the same as those for the negative.

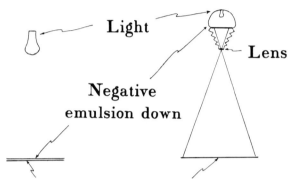

Light

Lens

Negative emulsion down

Sensitized paper emulsion up

Contact printing   Projection printing

FIG. 54. Exposing the Positive.

Accessory Equipment. These materials for use with the camera can make photography easier or more accurate, and in some cases make it possible to get a picture that otherwise would be impossible to get. In order to determine the amount of light available for a picture, a photographer uses an *exposure meter.* The meter measures the amount of light falling on the subject *(incident light meter)* or the amount being reflected by the subject toward the camera *(reflected light meter).* Either type of meter is satisfactory when properly used. A *tripod* to hold the camera steady is a requirement when making long exposures or when composing carefully. Black-and-white photography records a scene as shades of gray. Sometimes two colors will record as the same shade of gray. In order to separate them in tone, a *filter* may be used. The filter passes light of a color similar to that of the filter and holds back other colors. In a scene photographed through a filter, areas of the same color as the filter will photograph lighter and areas of other colors will photograph darker (speaking of the result in the final print). Cameras are limited in how close they can get to a subject and still have it in focus. By the use of an *auxiliary close-up lens,* the camera can move in much closer so as to get a larger image of the object.

Lighting. Control of light is an important factor in photography. Natural light from the sun is used where possible. When photographing an object that cannot be moved, it is necessary to choose the time of day when the sun is in the proper position to light the object properly. Artificial lighting makes it possible to control the light and put it where it is desired. *Flood lighting* is a continuous type of light that can be maneuvered easily while the effect on the scene is observed. *Flash lighting* is an instantaneous light that illuminates the subject for a very short time. Experience must be the guide in knowing what the effect of the flash will be. Due to the short duration of the flash, exposure is determined by the use of a *guide number* which comes with each package of *flashbulbs.* The flash of light is provided by a flashbulb which must be replaced after firing, or by an *electronic flash,* which can fire many times without having to replace a bulb each time. The electronic flash is of extremely short duration, which makes it valuable in stopping the motion for a sharp picture of a moving object.

In most artificial lighting, the attempt is made to simulate natural lighting. The main characteristics of natural lighting from the sun are that there is one main source of light casting one set of shadows and that it is usually coming from above. In artificial lighting there is usually one main source of light, the *key light.* The light is normally higher than the object being photographed and to one side of the camera. In order to lighten the shadows, one or more *fill lights* are used. These are considerably less intense than the key light so as not to set up a competing set of shadows. Another light, the *background light,* is usually used to illuminate the background and get a separation between it and the object. Other lights may be added as needed.

Color photography involves the use of a film with three emulsions instead of one. One emulsion is sensitive to each of the primary colors of light—red, green, and blue. During processing, dyes of the proper colors go to each of the color-sensitive layers. There are two main types of color films. The *reversal* color film yields a transparency in the natural colors of the original. *Color negative* film yields a negative in which the colors as well as the tonal qualities are the complements of the original. The color negative is printed onto a positive print or transparency material. The second step produces colors which correspond to those of the original ob-

FIG. 55. Effect of Change in the Depth of Field.

ject. Reversal color film must be exposed under light of the color temperature for which it was made; otherwise it will have a reddish or bluish color cast (see Fig. 50). Color negative film can be exposed under either sunlight, photoflood, or flash, and color differences are compensated for in the printing. Reversal color films can be adapted for use in light other than that for which they were designed by means of color filters. Care must be used not to mix light from sources having different color temperatures.

Composing the Picture. Photographs to be used in business communication do not need to be composed according to the classic rules for paintings, but they do need to be made in such a way that the viewer can determine quickly and accurately what they are meant to convey. Some methods of directing the viewer's attention to the important part of the picture are described below.

Selective focus makes the important object stand out because only that part of the picture is in sharp focus. The eye naturally spends the most time looking at the sharp part of the picture and less time where detail cannot be seen. The effect of the use of selective focus can be seen in Figure 55, which shows the same scene photographed using different depths of field.

Contrast between the important object in the picture and the background calls attention to the object that is different. Contrasts can be in light and dark, colors, textures, or any other way which differentiates the object from the background (see Fig. 56).

All lines of the photograph should lead to the *center of interest.* This includes both physical lines and lines of attention. For instance if a photo includes people, their attention should be directed at the center of interest. Even one person looking at the camera or away from the center of interest can destroy the whole mood of the picture (see Fig. 57).

Placement of the center of interest is important. Probably the poorest placement is in the dead center of the picture area. An appropriate off-center placement gives more of a feeling of movement and action, and vitality to the picture. The *"rule of thirds"* is a device to help in this placement. Mentally divide the picture area into thirds vertically and horizontally. The two vertical and two horizontal lines intersect in four places. Location of the point of interest at one of these intersections will result in a balanced yet dynamic arrangement (see Fig. 58).

Motion or implied motion should be toward the center of the picture rather than away from it. Movement off the edge of the

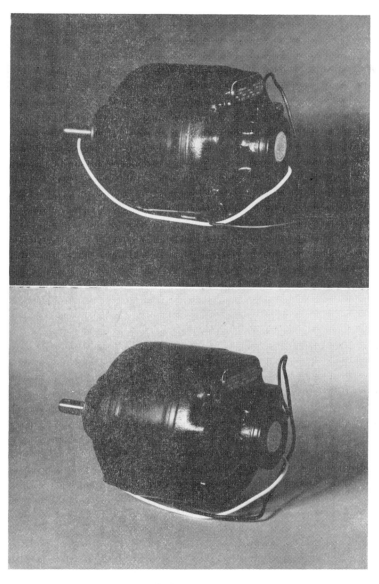

FIG. 56. Contrast.

FIG. 57. Lines Leading to the Center of Interest.

picture when the viewer cannot see where the object is going gives a vague feeling of uneasiness (see Fig. 59).

Elimination of distractions helps to concentrate the interest on the important object. This can be done by choice of camera angle, lighting, blocking off the background with a card or sheet, or retouching the negative or print. Figure 60 shows an industrial photo before and after retouching. In this case the procedure was to cover the main point of interest with protective paper and then airbrush the rest of the photo with white watercolor to subdue the detail.

Persons who have been reared in Western culture are used to reading from left to right. They naturally expect that the beginning of a subject will appear at the left and proceed logically to the right. For this reason, a photograph showing stages in an operation or other development should "read" from left to right. Any other arrangement would be more difficult to understand.

Working with the Photographer

The photographer with whom the communicator is working may

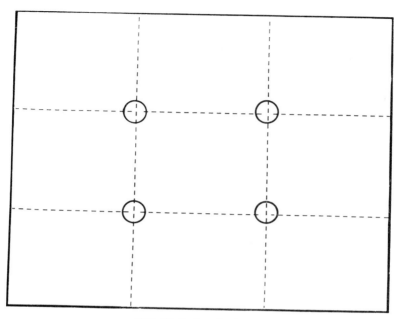

FIG. 58. Rules of Thirds.

be a part of the permanent organization of the company or he may be someone brought in from the outside to fill just the one assignment. In either case, the person who has the message to disseminate must first tell the photographer just exactly what he is trying to say and to whom he is trying to say it. He must also know what part he expects photographs to play in carrying the message. The more information he can give to the photographer the better the chance will be of getting useful photographs.

While it is necessary to give rather detailed instructions to the photographer, it is an error to make the directions *too* explicit. A professional photographer has had experience in solving photographic problems in the past. The solutions to those problems may very well hold clues to the easier working out of those that are now awaiting solving. The nature of the problem and the experience of the photographer will determine the degree of autonomy which he can be given. In general, a photographer who is a permanent employee and who thus knows the philosophy and policies of the company can be given a freer rein than can the outside photographer. Another factor involved is the fact that some people in the plant

FIG. 59. Motion Into and Out of the Picture Area.
(Courtesy of California State Polytechnic College)

might have a certain reticence about giving an outsider their complete cooperation. If a security problem is involved, it might be
simpler to use an in-plant photographic unit than bring in outsiders
who would require clearance. The in-plant photographer will have

FIG. 60. Effect of Retouching.

a better knowledge of what can and cannot be photographed for security reasons. Within whatever limits it is necessary to work, the photographer should be encouraged to come up with ideas of his own as to how some of the problems of conmunicating the ideas might be solved.

The photographer should be allowed sufficient time to work out his end of the communication problem. It often happens that he is called in at the last moment, after all of the planning has been done. Doing this fails to take advantage of the experience that a specialist in this form of communication can bring to bear on the problem. By giving the photographer sufficient time to work without the pressures of impending deadlines, he can provide the company with better organized and thought-out pictures which will be more successful in telling the story.

Summary

Photography is perhaps the best means of preserving the appearance of an object, situation, or a relationship. The person who is responsible for communication activities for an organization should have some knowledge of the photographic process, its capabilities and limitations, and its vocabulary. He should know photographic terminology so that he can tell the photographer precisely what is wanted in the picture. He should be a qualified judge of photographs.

The photographer should be given the information he needs to do his job and then be permitted to do it in his own way. Also, he should be allowed sufficient time to do his best work and not be under the pressure of a short deadline.

The choice of using the in-plant photographer or calling in an outside specialist must be based upon the capabilities of the company personnel and the job to be done. The person responsible for the communication must determine the best solution for each problem.

GLOSSARY OF PHOTOGRAPHIC TERMS

The purpose of this glossary is to assist the communications person who is not versed in photography in working with photographers.

adapter ring: a ring which fits over the lens mount and holds filters, auxiliary lenses, sunshades, etc., in place.

airbrush: a device utilizing compressed air to spray color; also the technique of using this device.

aperture: lens opening controlled by the iris diaphragm.

art work: retouching and lettering added to a picture or group of pictures to prepare them for publication.

auxiliary lens: a supplemental lens added to the regular lens to modify its effective focal length.

back lighting: directing the main light for a picture onto the side of the subject away from the camera.

between-the-lens shutter: a shutter situated between the front and rear elements of a lens.

black-and-white: the photographic process in which objects are rendered monochromatically in shades of gray.

bleach: to remove part or all of the silver in a photograph to reduce its density.

blocked up: said of a highlight so overexposed that details are not visible.

burning in: giving a part of a projection print more exposure than the balance of the print, making that portion darker.

cable release: a flexible device to release a camera shutter without jarring the camera.

candid: a photograph taken without the knowledge of the subject.

cartridge: a light-tight container for film; used primarily for 35mm.

changing bag: a lightproof fabric bag with elastic-closed openings for inserting the hands; used to change film, etc., when outside the darkroom.

close-up: a photograph taken very near to the subject.

close-up lens: an auxiliary lens which allows the camera to be moved closer to the subject than would ordinarily be possible.

color: the visual sensation caused by light waves of a given length.

colorblind: a type of film sensitive only to the extreme blue and ultra-violet end of the spectrum.

color negative: a color rendition of a subject in which the tones are reversed and the colors are complementary to those of the subject.

color reversal: a color system which produces a rendition of the subject in which the tones and colors are those of the original.

color temperature: the method of specifying the color of light; expressed in degrees Kelvin.

complementary colors: colors of light which added together produce white light.

contact print: a positive print exposed with the negative and sensitized paper emulsion to emulsion.

contact printer: a device for exposing contact prints.

contrast: the difference between the lightest and darkest portions of a photograph.

contrasty: a great difference between the lightest and darkest portions of a photograph.

crop: eliminate part of a negative in making a print .

cut film: film prepared in individual sheets.

darkroom: the laboratory for the loading and processing of photographs.

daylight loading: capable of being loaded without damage to the film when outside of the darkroom.

dense: a very dark negative or transparency.

density: the degree of opacity of a negative.

depth of field: distance from the nearest to the farthest points from the camera where the image is sufficiently sharp.

developer: the chemical used to change exposed silver halides to metallic silver.

development: the chemical process which makes the latent image visible.

dodging: giving part of a projection print less exposure than the balance of the print, making that portion of the print lighter.

double exposure: making two exposures on one piece of film or paper.

dry mount: mounting a photo to a backing with the use of a tissue impregnated with material that melts when heat is applied.

easel: a device to hold sensitized paper while exposing with an enlarger.

electronic flash: a device which gives a very brief, brilliant flash by sending a high-voltage charge of electricity through a gas-filled tube.

emulsion: light-sensitive chemical, usually a silver halide, mixed with gelatin and coated on the base.

enlargement: a print made by projection to a size larger than the negative.

enlarger: a device for projecting the negative image onto sensitized paper.

exposure: the amount of light falling onto a film or print; a function of the light intensity and the length of time it is allowed to operate.

exposure index: a numerical indication of the sensitivity of a photographic emulsion.

exposure meter: a device for determining the intensity of light for photography.

f/: the ratio of the focal length to the diameter of a lens. Used to indicate the light-gathering-power of the lens.

ferrotype plate: a chromium or enameled surface used to impart a high gloss to prints.

fill light: a light used to decrease the density of the shadows cast by the key light.

film: a flexible, transparent sheet of acetate coated with a photographic emulsion.

filter: glass or gelatin used to remove certain wavelengths of light from that passing to the film.

filter factor: the change in exposure necessary to compensate for light removed by the filter.

finder: the device on a camera which shows the coverage of the lens.

fixer: a chemical used after development to remove unconverted silver halides from the emulsion.

flashbulb: a glass bulb filled with magnesium wire in oxygen; burns very rapidly, giving intense light.

flat: said of a picture in which the difference between the lightest and darkest portions is not great.

floodlight: a continuously burning light covering a large area.

focal length: the distance from the optical center of a lens to the focal plane.

focal plane: the plane on which objects at infinity are in focus.

focal plane shutter: a curtain with a slit in it that is drawn across just in front of the film to make the exposure.

focus: the point at which rays of light from a certain source come together after they have passed through a lens, to form a sharp image of that source; the act of adjusting a camera to obtain a sharp image.

grain: individual clumps of silver forming the photographic image; may be visible as a sandpapery effect when a negative is enlarged many diameters.

guide number: a number to be used in determining the lens opening for flash photographs. A guide number is published for each type of flashbulb and film speed. The guide number is divided by the distance from the flash to the subject in feet. The quotient is the lens opening.

halftones: intermediate shades of gray.

hardener: a chemical added to the fixer which makes the emulsion less liable to scratching.

high-key: a print very light in tone with very few dark areas.

hypo: sodium thiosulphate, used in the fixer; also the fixer itself.

image: the likeness of an object formed by a lens; also the preservation of the likeness by photographic means.

infinity: a distance great enough so that light rays coming from a source at that distance are considered to be traveling parallel.

infrared: light rays beyond the red end of the visible spectrum.

intensify: increase the density of a negative by chemical means.

iris diaphragm: an adjustable device used to regulate the effective diameter of a lens by covering the outer portion with metal plates.

key light: the main light source in a photograph, establishing the shadows and delineating the shape of the object.

latent image: the image formed by exposure of film or sensitized paper but which is not visible until developed.

latitude: the degree to which a particular photographic emulsion can be over- or under-exposed and still yield a satisfactory image.

lens: a device to form an image, usually composed of one or more pieces of glass.

light meter: same as exposure meter.

low-key: a print very dark in tone with few light areas.

modeling: bringing out the shape of an object by the proper placement of the lights.

normal focal length lens: one whose focal length is approximately equal to the diagonal of the picture area.

orthochromatic film: an emulsion which is sensitive to all colors but red.

overexpose: allow too much light to strike the emulsion, resulting in too much density when developed.

panchromatic film: an emulsion sensitive to all colors of the visible spectrum.

parallax: the difference in the field of coverage of a view-finder and the lens of a camera.

photoflood: a high intensity, shortlived electric light for photography.

photomontage: a photographic print composed of parts of several different negatives.

photosensitive: capable of being chemically changed by the action of light.

portrait attachment: see close-up lens.

positive: a photographic image in which the tones correspond to those of the original.

print: a positive photographic image, usually on paper.

printing: making a positive from a negative.

projection print: a print made with an enlarger, either larger or smaller than the negative.

reduce: make a print smaller than the negative; decrease the density of a photographic image.

refraction: the bending of a ray of light as it passes from one medium to another at other than a right angle to the surface.

retouching: changing the appearance of a negative or positive by mechanical means.

rising front: an adjustment found on some cameras for correcting distortion.

safelight: a darkroom light of low intensity and of a color to which the photographic emulsion is not sensitive.

sensitized paper: paper which upon exposure and development is capable of producing a photographic image.

sheet film: see cut film.

shutter: a device to allow light to pass through the lens to the film for the time of the exposure and to prevent it from passing at other times.

silver halide: any of the salts of silver, including silver bromide, silver chloride, and silver iodide.

slide: an individual positive transparency mounted in cardboard or glass for projection.

snap: the quality of a print having good graduation and tone.

soft: little contrast; the opposite of contrasty.

spectrum: all of the colors of light comprising white light.

spot: a spotlight.

spotting: removing white and black spots from a print.

still: a single photograph.

stop: the distance from one marked setting to another on a lens.

stop bath: an acid solution used between developing and fixing to stop development immediately and reduce the dilution of the fixer.

stop down: reduce the size of the lens aperture.

studio: the room where photographic exposure takes place.

supplementary lens: an auxiliary lens used to modify the effective focal length of a lens.

swing back: a construction feature on some cameras permitting the back to be placed in a position other than at right angles to the lens, used to correct certain distortions.

swing front: a construction feature on some cameras permitting the lens to be placed so that the axis is in other than the normal position.

telephoto lens: a lens in which the effective focal length is greater than the lens-to-film distance; sometimes used to indicate any lens of longer than normal focal length.

thin: said of a negative of little density.

time exposure: a relatively long exposure in which the shutter is opened and closed manually.

ultraviolet: light rays beyond the blue end of the spectrum.

underdevelopment: insuffcient development of the image, usually resulting in a thin and flat image.

underexposure: not allowing sufficient light to strike the emulsion.

view camera: a camera with many adjustments of back and lens to correct for various sorts of distortion.

wide angle: a lens of shorter than normal focal length.

BIBLIOGRAPHY

The American Society of Mechanical Engineers, *A Guide for Preparing Technical Illustrations for Publication and Projection,* New York, The American Society of Engineers.

Ansco, *How to Make Better Pictures with Anscochrome and Super Anscochrome Film,* Binghamton, New York, Ansco, 1961.

Brown, James W., Richard B. Lewis, and Fred F. Harcleroad, *AV Instruction Materials and Methods,* Second Edition, New York, McGraw-Hill Book Company, Inc., 1964, 592 pp.
      Chap. 20 Using Still Pictures
      Chap. 21 Photographing

Brown, James W., and Richard B. Lewis (Ed), *AV Instructional Materials*

Manual, Second Edition, New York, McGraw-Hill Book Company, 1964, 188 pp.

      Exercise Twelve Mounting Flat Pictures
      Exercise Twenty-One Making Still Pictures
      Exercise Twenty-Nine Flat Pictures

Cross, A. J. Foy, and Irene F. Cypher, *Audio-Visual Education,* New York, Thomas Y. Crowell Company, 1961, 415 pp.

      Chap. 5 Flat Pictures

Eastman Kodak Company Publications

      Kodak Films, 70 pp. 50¢
      Filters and Pola-Screens, 52 pp, 50¢
      Enlarging with Kodak Materials and Equipment, 56 pp, 50¢
      Copying, 48 pp. 50¢
      Color as Seen and Photographed, 68 pp, 75¢
      Color Photography Outdoors, 56 pp, 75¢
      Color Photography in the Studio, 64 pp, 75¢
      Kodak Color Films, 72 pp, 75¢
      Camera Techniques for Professional Photographers, 64 pp. 50¢
      Studio Lighting for Product Photography, 64 pp, 50¢
      How to Organize and Operate Photographic Service Departments, 60 pp. 50¢
      Photographic Production of Slides and Filmstrips, 52 pp, 50¢
      How-to-do-it Pictures, 60 pp, 50¢
      Making Service Pictures for Industry, 72 pp, 50¢
      Kodak Master Photoguide, 32 pp, $1.75

Foldes, Joseph, "Your Camera's Parts and What They Do," *Popular Photography,* 1956

Haas, Kenneth B., and Harry Q. Packer, *Preparation and Use of Audio-Visual Aids,* Englewood Cliffs, New Jersey, Prentice-Hall, Inc., 1955, 381 pp.

      Chap. 8 Pictures and Photographs

Jones, B. A., *Slides: Confusing or Clear?,* Detroit, Michigan, The Ethyl Corporation, 1952

Kemp, Jerrold E., *Planning and Producing Audiovisual Materials,* San Francisco, California, Chandler Publishing Company, 1963, 169 pp.

      Part Two Fundamental Skills
        1. Photography
      Part Three Producing Your Audiovisual Materials
        1. Picture Series

Kinder, James S., *Audio-Visual Materials and Techniques,* 2nd Edition, New York, American Book Company, 1959, 592 pp.

      Chap. 4 The Camera and Photography

Sands, Lester B., *Audio-Visual Procedures in Teaching,* New York, The Ronald Press Company, 1956, 670 pp.

      Chap. 15 Photography in Teaching

Thomas, R. Murray, and Sherwin G. Swartout, *Integrated Teaching Materials,* New York, Longmans, Green, and Company, 1960, 545 pp.

      Chap. 10 Taking Photographs

CHAPTER 10

MOTION PICTURES

Motion pictures are becoming increasingly important in all areas of communication. Schools, religious groups, governments, the armed services, youth groups, adult organizations, and industry are but a few of the diversified types of groups which regularly take advantage of the many potentialities of this medium. People in industry are involved in motion pictures in both the utilization and production ends.

Utilization of Motion Pictures

Business and industrial utilization of motion pictures for many different types of communication situations was discussed earlier in this book. As a review, some of the applications are as follows:

Employee recruitment involves presenting to the prospective employee an idea of the company, its products, its manufacturing facilities, and its philosophies. In many instances the motion picture can communicate these things more efficiently than any other method or combination of methods. Distances may be too far, dangers may prohibit taking groups to view the facilities or products, or direct viewing may not convey the message well. At any rate, the motion picture may do these things best.

Employee training must prepare new employees to become well adjusted, producing members of the corporation. Types of information to be transmitted will vary greatly, but in many instances the motion picture medium accomplishes the best results and in the least amount of time. Employee advancement also calls for training and help to understand the new responsibilities, particularly when a man moves into a position where he has charge of subordinates for the first time. Motion pictures can present to the employee certain problems for discussion and solving.

Public relations films are used by an industrial organization to familiarize that company's personnel with the products and suppliers of raw materials and processing machinery.

Sales and promotion are greatly aided by the use of motion pictures which make it possible to show the product in use, whereas direct observation of the product might be impossible or impractical.

Reporting to the company's own management group by means of films makes it possible for the company officials to see certain activities without expensive and time-consuming travel to the sites of these activities. Research activities can be documented on film and presented to executive meetings. Activities which may have occurred over a period of months or years can be summarized and evaluated in a few moments through motion pictures.

Stockholders' meetings can gain much from films of the major activities and accomplishments of the company during the year. Such presentations might be of the newsreel type presented in chronological or some other logical order.

Advantages of Motion Pictures. In all of these situations, the motion picture has certain advantages over other forms of communication.

1. The motion picture, with its combination of movement, color, and sound, creates the nearest approach to being at the place where the event occurred.

2. Showing in a darkened room eliminates distracting elements that otherwise compete for one's attention.

3. It is possible to recreate an event, action, or sales presentation in exactly the same way, time after time.

4. Processes and actions that are not normally visible to the human eye or understandable in their natural situation can be made understandable or visible through:

   a. Cinephotomicrography, taking motion pictures through a microscope.

   b. High speed cinematography, photographing actions that occur extremely rapidly. By photographing at the rate of hundreds or even thousands of frames a second and projecting them at the normal rate, actions are spread out over a much longer period of time for study and analysis.

   c. Time lapse photography, a method of exposing a single frame of the film at a time and separated by whatever length of time is desired. Action which takes days to complete can be shown in a few seconds on the screen.

    d. Animation, which makes it possible to show internal parts of machines in operation or even to show in concrete form actions of a theoretical or intangible nature.

5. Events that take place only once can be repeated as often as wished, and at any time desired.

6. Only relevant information which advances the company's interests need to be included.

7. Since most people associate motion pictures with entertainment, they view the presentation with interest and the expectation of being amused.

8. Showing material on the screen somehow adds more authority than the same material would have if conveyed by the spoken or written word.

9. Editing eliminates distracting elements and any other factors that could impair the impact of the film.

10. The information presented and the method of presentation can be adjusted to suit the age and level of experience of the audience.

If we are to get the full value out of a motion picture, we must keep in mind certain facts about effective utilization. Not all of these suggestions will apply in every projection situation, but they will fit in to a greater or lesser degree.

Projection Room. See Chapter 19, Facilities for Audio-Visual Presentation, for details about efficient utilization of motion pictures and other audio-visual devices.

Before Projection. The projector should be ready for operation before the audience comes into the room. This means that the following steps should have been taken:

1. Darken the room and make whatever adjustments are possible for optimum ventilation and temperature.

2. Set up the screen at the front of the room, with the bottom edge slightly higher than the heads of the viewers.

3. Set up the projector on a stand at the estimated proper distance from the screen and plug it into a suitable electric outlet. It must be directly in front of the screen and the lens should be the same height as the middle of the screen.

4. If the speaker can be separated from the projector, place it next to the screen and off the floor, preferably on a chair or desk.

5. Turn on the projector motor and lamp and focus the light on the screen until the edges appear sharp. If the image is too large, move the projector closer to the screen. If it is too small, move the projector farther away. Some projectors are provided with zoom

lenses which make it possible to adjust the size of the image without moving the projector.

6. Turn on the sound system. On most projectors a hum or hissing sound coming from the speaker will tell when the sound system is warmed up and ready to operate.

7. Place the reel with the film on it onto the supply arm of the projector, square hole first. (The reel will have a square hole on one side and a round one on the other.) Pulling the end of the film should cause the reel to turn in a clockwise direction as you face it from the right hand side of the machine. If it goes the other direction, the film needs rewinding, or else has been rewound improperly.

8. Pull off about five feet of the leader and thread the machine according to the instructions printed on the projector.

9. Start the machine and focus it sharply when the first titles appear. Adjust the level of the sound.

10. Reverse the machine to back up to the beginning of the titles. Turn off lamp and motor, but leave the amplifier system turned on.

Preparation of the audience is even more important than preparation of the machine. The type of preparation will depend upon the nature of the audience and the nature of the motion picture they are going to see.

1. Tell the audience something of the film, the reasons for showing it, the general subject, etc.

2. Outline what the audience should look for and what it is hoped they will gain from it.

Projection. Any presentation can be enhanced by good showmanship techniques. Good preparation beforehand and smooth movement into and out of the film are elements of showmanship.

1. Turn on the projector motor and let it run until the first titles arrive at the film gate, where the projection takes place.

2. Turn on the projection lamp.

3. When the titles can be seen on the screen, turn off the room lights.

4. Adjust the volume to give a pleasing level of sound.

5. Stay by the projector in case the machine needs attention.

6. When the end titles come on the screen, turn on the room lights.

7. Turn off the projection lamp.

8. When the end of the sound track is reached, turn the volume down and switch the amplifier off.

9. Allow the projector to run 30 seconds or so after turning off the projection lamp, then turn the motor off. This will cool the lamp and housing and add greatly to the life of the lamp.

The above procedure gets the audience smoothly into and out of the film. It does not plunge them into darkness at the beginning or end or allow the bright light of the clear screen to blind them.

If it is necessary to stop and start the projector during the showing, the volume should be turned down first. This avoids a wow, or unpleasant change in the pitch of the sound track, as the film slows down or speeds up.

After Projection. The audience will undoubtedly have questions arising from the films and this is the time to answer them, or to make comments about the film.

Appropriate follow-up activities can be conducted while the film is still fresh in the audience's minds and the emotional impact is still at its height. If it is a selling film, salesmen might be available to take orders. A training film might be followed by experience in the activity described. Whatever the audience, proper follow-up activities can make the impact greater, longer-lasting, and of more value.

Availability of Materials. Motion pictures suitable for business or industrial use are often available through the suppliers of materials or equipment used by the company. The companies are glad to supply the films, which are their sales materials, on a loan or gift basis.

Other films are available for purchase or rental from commercial film libraries, universities, governmental sources, and educational film producers. These materials are often quite well adapted, or can be easily adapted, to the company's needs.

Specialized films not available elsewhere may have to be produced by the company itself, or in conjunction with an independent film producing organization.

Production of Motion Pictures

The production of a motion picture, whether for use within the organization or elsewhere, is generally a major undertaking. It will involve large amounts of money, occupy the time and energies of one or more company executives, and disrupt the activities of one or more departments during filming.

Organization. The position of the film unit within the company

organization has an effect on its operating efficiency. A good supervisor and willing personnel can often overcome an unfortunate
placement in the organization, but the group should not have to
work under this handicap when proper placement can make the task
much easier.

Whatever the final choice for its location, the film unit should
be placed under the direct control of one of the top executives. The
success of a film program is directly dependent upon the whole-
hearted cooperation of top management and a member of this group
who is vitally concerned with the success of the program will help
to maintain that spirit of cooperation. A film group that does not
have this direct representation at the policy-making level must rely
upon reports and memoranda to carry its needs and information to
management. A direct line to the top can help to smooth relationships with other departments. The member of the management
group will not generally participate directly in the planning, production, or distribution of the films. The production unit will report
directly to him, however, and he in turn will be responsible for
the quality of the finished material.

Which of the top echelon personnel will have the duty of administering the film unit? If one executive has a personal interest
in this sort of thing because of prior experience or training, he
would be the logical person to assign. The danger must be avoided,
however, of letting someone ride his hobby. A person who is an avid
motion picture amateur, for instance, might not be the best choice.
He may tend to try to force his ideas and methods onto someone
who is more expert than himself.

If the major use of motion pictures produced by the company
will be to assist in the selling activities, the film unit might very
well be made a responsibility of the sales manager. If most of the
production would be for internal use in the training of new employees, the motion picture unit would logically fall under the control of the personnel director. Public relations is another department
which might take over the work. One rather common choice is to
place the motion picture unit under the executive who adminsters
the photographic unit.

Whichever executive has charge of the program, the following
should be kept in mind.

  1. The department is a service department and as such its services
     are available to all departments.

2. Formal channels of communication between this and other departments should be dispensed with as much as possible.

3. Budgeting for this department should be sufficient to cover its expenses. Charges for services to other departments should *not* be made, as this tends to discourage them from making use of the facilities.

Organization within the department depends upon several factors. Most important is, to what extent will company personnel be utilized, as opposed to contracting for the services of an outside motion picture producer. Production companies can provide any sort of services, from preparing the entire production to doing any part of the job.

The functions described below comprise the types of activities that must be done, not the personnel. In small units one person might perform several of the functions, while in larger groups performing a larger quantity of work, each function might need one person or a staff. This listing assumes that the company is doing all of the work itself, without any outside help.

The *supervisor* of the motion picture unit is responsible to those above him for the over-all operation and production of the organization. He sets up the organization within the department, makes arrangements for the scheduling of photographic activities with a minimum of disruption to the company's normal activities, arranges for coverage of unusual events or activities, follows a production through to completion, and maintains quality standards, time schedules, and cost records.

The *writer* works directly with the people whose message is to be transmitted by the motion picture. He must gather such information as:

1. The age and experience level of the audience for whom the material is being prepared.

2. The magnitude of the production. How much money has been set aside for producing the film?

3. Technical considerations that will affect the organization and writing of the material;
   Length in minutes.
   Whether it is to be photographed in black-and-white or color.

4. The treatment to be used—whether it is to be straight-forward, humorous, technical, or basic.

Having gathered the pertinent data, he uses this information to prepare the script, which contains the detailed instructions to be followed in making the film.

The *director* takes the script provided by the writer and transforms it into the visual medium of motion picture film. He works with the motion picture unit to accomplish these things:

1. Make the scenes follow the intent of the script.
2. Determine the composition and lighting.
3. Make arrangements for shooting, including the schedules and the sets and properties.
4. Determine how each scene should be photographed so that it will fit with the ones before and after it to make a unified whole.
5. Be aware of and ready to take advantage of the possibilities of situations that the script does not cover.
6. Communicate to the actors, cameramen, and others just exactly what he wants to accomplish in a particular scene and how he wants to do it, and rehearse the action until it is ready.
7. Direct the starting and stopping of the scene and the action that takes place during the photographing.
8. Determine when the scene has been properly recorded and keep redoing it until it is satisfactory.
9. Assume complete charge of the actual photographic activity.

The *cameraman* is responsible for getting the action recorded on motion picture film, working under the director and following his intent. He is responsible for the following:

1. Overseeing the placement of the lights for proper illumination of the set.
2. Correct exposure of the film for the effect desired.
3. Loading and unloading of the camera, always checking to avoid the possibility of running out of film in the middle of a scene.
4. Choice of the best camera angles (working in conjunction with the director).
5. Choice of the proper lenses to record the scene.
6. Photographing the scene, starting and stopping the camera on cue from the director.

The *sound engineer* is responsible for the optimum recording of dialogue, sounds, music, and narration. His responsibilities are;

1. In recording dialogue, insuring that the movement and sound are in synchronization.

2. Proper placement of microphones so that they will not be photographed, but will record the sound properly.
3. Determining the level and tone of the sound recording.
4. Operating the sound recording equipment on cue from the director.
5. Indicating to the director at the end of the take whether the sound recording was satisfactory.
6. Playing back the previously recorded sound track for the actors to follow when a scene is using pre-recorded sound.
7. Recording indigenous sounds for later dubbing onto the sound track.
8. When a scene uses post-recorded sound, operating the sound equipment as the sound is recorded to match the action.

The *actors*, whether plant personnel or outside talent, take their orders from the director. They perform the actions and speak the dialogue as they are directed.

The *script girl* is the person responsible for keeping the records of the operation of the unit while it is photographing the scenes. The duties of this person include:

1. Reading aloud the description of the scene about to be photographed.
2. Recording the technical data about the take after it is photographed, including the light level, frames per second, lens focal length, lens aperture, length of scene in seconds or feet of film, whether or not it was a good take, and any remarks pertinent to the take.
3. Making note of placement of properties, clothing worn by the actors, and other details so that the scene will tie in with others and so that it can be reconstructed if necessary. A still photograph may be taken at the beginning and end of the scene to assist in this.

After each of the scenes of the motion picture has been taken to the satisfaction of the director, the work of the *editor* begins. His job is to take these short scenes and arrange them into a coherent, properly paced motion picture that tells the story it is intended to tell. His functions are as follows:

1. Views the workprint and reads the comments of the director on each take.
2. Arranges the scenes in the proper order to determine their flow and to see how well they fit together. He must watch to see how they can be assembled to match the action from one scene to

another. He watches for transition shots to smooth the movement from scene to scene or from sequence to sequence.

3. Adjusts the length of scenes to give proper rhythm and pacing to the film and to provide for a smooth flow of action.

4. Edits the sound track to correspond with the edited workprint. Adds musical background and any other sounds which have been prepared for him by the sound engineer.

5. Works with the director before and during the shooting phase of the production to decide upon the effects they want and to arrange to get the film footage and sound track needed to permit those effects.

6. Returns the finalized work print to the processing laboratory where the original film is cut to conform to the work print, the sound is combined with the film, and the answer print is prepared.

7. Assumes responsibility, along with the director, for the over-all artistic and communicative quality of the completed motion picture.

Processing of the film is generally performed by an independent *laboratory,* but it can be handled internally if volume or security needs justify it. These laboratories will provide just about any services which the customer may want after the film has been exposed. In general, the services of a laboratory include the following:

1. Processing of the exposed film, either black-and-white or color, including edge-numbering the film every foot.

2. Printing the workprint. The original footage may be returned to the company for examination before the workprint is made. The customer may examine it for exposure and color quality, but does not usually project it. Obviously unsuitable sequences can be removed before the workprint is prepared. The numbers on the edge of the original are printed onto the workprint.

3. After the customer has edited the workprint, he returns it to the processing laboratory. There the original film is edited to match the workprint. It can be matched to the frame because of the edge numbers that appear on each.

4. The sound track is added. If proper synchronization has been attained between the sound track and the workprint, the same synchronization will hold when applied to the original film footage.

5. The answer print is prepared and sent to the client. This is done to get his approval on the completed job, including such things as synchronization of sound and picture and the density and/or

color balance of the final result. The client can specify changes in these things, but any other changes at this time will be very costly.

6. After the answer print has been approved by the client, the release prints are prepared in whatever number the client requires.

7. The original is kept for the client so that additional release prints can be made whenever needed.

In addition to the services outlined above, the independent laboratories will also rent certain parts of their facilities, such as cutting rooms and editing equipment, to clients who do not have these facilities.

In-Plant Production vs. Outside Production. The above listed functions must all be performed, regardless of who does them. The sponsoring company may provide for all of the production activities within its organization as a regular and continuing function of the department which has been assigned this duty, or it may subcontract any of the individual phases for which it lacks either the personnel or the equipment to handle according to professional standards. A third method is to contract with a producer to make the film, beginning at any desired point and carrying the production through to completion.

Some of the advantages of utilizing company facilities for the production of the films are listed in the AR Adman's Handbook:

1. Convenience . . . It is simpler to maintain control when all who are working on a film are part of the sponsoring organization.

2. Economy . . . This is the main argument put forward, although it is difficult to obtain a realistic cost picture on an internal production, and outside producers insist no savings exist.

3. Education . . . The very process of film making seems to lend new perspective to an executive's view of his company.

4. Simplicity . . . It is too difficult to give outsiders the intimate feeling of how a company thinks and operates.

5. Security . . . What with government restrictions on access, it is simpler to get one crew cleared for everything once and for all, rather than having to clear outside personnel for each filming assignment.

6. Availability . . . A staff photographic unit can pick up shots as they occur, and on short notice, making it easier to build up a library of useful footage.[1]

---

1. "A Guide to Business Films," *Advertising Requirements* (Now *Advertising and Sales Promotion*) .

Arguments for the opposite viewpoint—that of the independent producers—were given to AR in the following ten categories:

1. Equipment . . . An outside film source invariably is better equipped to handle every phase of a film job than is an inside source. No matter what the size, an industrial user of films has a difficult time justifying the cost of top quality equipment, simply because the number of jobs going through the shop makes it difficult to amortize the cost of this equipment. Furthermore, most studios maintain a surplus of equipment beyond the minimal needs for one job. This again is a difficult thing for an industrial user to achieve, without getting involved in a considerable amount of money.

2. Personnel . . . Production of films requires a combination of many arts and crafts. It requires special skills and talent born only of experience. Films are only as good as the combined experience of the specialists and craftsmen who work on them.

   A professional film producer maintains a permanent staff of experts trained in all phases of film production. These include men trained to assist in the planning of a film, expert scenario writers, directors, animators, cameramen, sound recording engineers, makeup men, artists, film editors and laboratory technicians.

   Naturally, staffing a department this extensively involves considerable expense. The usual alternative is to expect a small staff to perform several of these specialized functions—or to job out various elements of production. Either way, the necessary close coordination is lacking and the end result on the screen usually reflects it.

   The professional film studio allows for specialization, advancement and diversification of projects, and normally the studio can afford better salaries than can industrial units.

   In addition to motion pictures, the professional studio is in a position to make stills and do slide films as part of its normal operation. An industrial user would have to have different people for these jobs, since few individuals can do stills, know slide films, take movies, and supervise script and production as well.

   Film specialists who will take an assignment for permanent employment with a company, generally speaking, are not the top personnel in the field. A company is limited, then, in its creativeness, to the minds of one or two men in the department.

3. Sources of supply . . . Professional film producers have instant access to the sources of supply and talent. They have at their fingertips material which they use frequently—items that are

everyday occurrences to the professional film producer, but which would be so rare as to be unknown to an industrial user of films running an internal unit.

In addition, since technical advances in equipment are made constantly, virtually daily, in the motion picture business, it is difficult even for a large producer to maintain modern equipment—even difficult to keep informed about it. For an individual company to undertake the job of keeping completely informed is far more difficult—and to replace equipment with more modern developments is economically impossible in most cases.

4. Facilities . . . The making of good, quality motion pictures involves the use of specially designed facilities. A professional producer has full shooting facilities, sound stages, recording equipment and laboratory facilities. Just the space requirements alone frequently make such an advantage impossible for the internal film unit.

The professional is equipped to shoot film in either 35mm or 16 mm, on location or in specially designed sets in the studio, with professional talent and with a carefully selected musical score, using special effects, and employing either "voice-over" narration or dialogue.

Accordingly, the professional producer is staffed and equipped to deliver the best picture possible. All facilities necessary for planning and production are contained within his one organization. He is thus geared to meet every requirement for making the film effective, and to make certain the client gets full value for every dollar spent.

5. Control . . . A professional film producer has greater control over the various elements of production—thus enabling him to guarantee and deliver the best professional screen quality.

The making of professional and successful motion pictures with the standards set by Hollywood in the American mind is a full professional job. Audiences today have come to recognize and expect good screen quality because of their exposure to the better theatrical pictures, tv programs and the increasing number of quality commercial motion pictures now available.

Should a picture lack this expected quality, it often creates an adverse reaction that defeats the entire film program.

6. Experience . . . The professional producer brings to the client a wealth of diversified experience in the production of films of all kinds—films designed for many purposes and for many types of audiences.

Through his team of specialists he is ready to advise on all phases of film planning and production—as well as the best ways for getting maximum use of finished film.

His staff of experts combines a background of experience in selling, training, merchandising, public relations and advertising. He offers, then, not only production experience but in addition a knowledge of how the film medium can be adapted to perform a specific function.

What might motivate one audience will leave another untouched, and a producer is capable of selecting an effective approach, regardless of the film problem.

Significantly, he also can bring to a client a fresh—and unbiased —viewpoint which the internal film department may have difficulty in doing because of its closeness to the subject.

7. Psychological Factors . . . Experience of professional film producers has indicated that workers within a plant respect and cooperate with an outside production unit far more than they will with an internal unit, with whom they may have daily contact.

Another psychological factor of importance is that a film specialist, whose income source is the company for which a picture is being shot, is far less likely to speak up and demand necessities than is an outsider whose thought is a good film job. Responsibility always should be toward the individual picture in progress, not toward the boss.

8. Use of Facilities . . . In the employment of an outside film producer, the client utilizes as much or as little of that facility as he needs at the moment. There definitely is an economy available in this situation. In addition, should there be a necessity of shooting two jobs at one time, or perhaps doubling up, the professional film producer is in a far better position to effect this.

Few companies will stand by and let internal facilities stand idle. The natural tendency is to dream up projects to keep men and equipment busy—frequently without giving sufficient thought to the real need for what is produced.

9. Using Specialists . . . When a company has an internal film unit, it is natural to try to use this unit for all films. A company not impeded by its own film department is more likely to buy films from companies which are specialists in certain fields of film production —notably animation, color photography, stop action, etc.

10. Responsibility . . . The professional film producer is a business man with financial responsibility. He must have the faith and good will of previous clients to get repeat business. Similarly he must be able to guarantee production quality—as well as the ability to produce a client's picture, as planned, and on time.

Every time a producer's film is shown, his reputation is at stake. Each film has to stand on its own merits. He must be able to guarantee production quality.

This same concern and careful attention to the multitude of details involved in the production of a good film do not necessarily apply to an internal film department. If its film turns out badly, it can always find ample reasons to justify it. The professional producer in contrast has to deliver in order to stay in business.[1]

These points are naturally biased toward the point of view of the independent producer, since they were prepared from replies of producers when asked to give reasons why companies should use their services. There are, however, some good arguments in the list.

Some companies find that they can keep both internal and outside groups busy. The internal crews prepare films for use within the company and independent producers make films for distribution to the general public.

A company must consider very carefully the arguments for both sides when it is determining whether its films should be made by an internal unit or an independent producer. The job to be done is the same; the only difference is who does it.

The general trend is that in-plant production is increasing at a faster rate than external production. For some purposes the less elaborate and less expensive films suit the needs just as well as the more ambitious efforts of the professional producers. Some of the prime aims of films created by the plant personnel are:

To create a favorable corporate image.
To move products.
To make the results of research activities available for repeated study.
To maintain a record of events in the company.
Dealer and distributor training.
Personnel training.
 Safety training.
 Sales training.
 Supervisory training.

The growth of the business of business movies is due primarily to the strength they have shown as an expository media for the communication of ideas. That strength is drawn from their ability to depict motion as it appeared to persons viewing the original movement firsthand. There are additional motion-picture attributes which recommend films as instructional, analytical and recording aids, but in the final analysis, their reproduction of motion is the essence of

1. "A Guide to Business Films," *Advertising Requirements* (now *Advertising and Sales Promotion*) .

their effectiveness. Still picture techniques can imply motion, break it down into its components and freeze it for convenient study; but where a movement or series of movements is important as an integrated operation, only motion pictures can completely and adequately describe the sequence.[1]

Equipment. It is not the purpose here to attempt to set out a detailed list of equipment that should be obtained for the in-plant photographic unit. For one thing, the equipment would vary in quantity and type, depending upon the envisioned use and purpose of the ultimate product.

If the motion picture unit is to be added to a previously existing photographic unit, the investment in additional equipment should not be heavy. Many of the necessary items will already have been purchased. Besides the lighting equipment and cameras and lenses that will be needed, the chief purchases should be for editing equipment. A viewer and a splicer are the main items, plus rewinds and film reels and cans. Other equipment will probably not be used enough of the time to justify its purchase. Camera equipment companies will lease any items of equipment that may be needed. Also, film processors have facilities such as completely equipped editing rooms that can be rented on an hourly or daily basis.

What Width Film? Thirty years ago an argument was raging among the producers of professional motion pictures as to whether the 16mm size of film would ever by anything more than a toy for amateurs to play around with. Today, because of developments in the quality of equipment and materials, that argument is no longer heard. Instead, another has come up to take its place. It is, "Is the 8mm motion picture film suitable for business and industrial motion pictures?" Increasing quality of equipment has brought the picture up to the point where it is of acceptable quality for small screen projection. Now the introduction of magnetic sound tracks for this size of film and projectors to use it brings new possibilities for this small film.

> Without much fanfare, 8mm motion pictures have created a new role for themselves. No longer just an amateur movie-maker's toy, they are now also a professional audio-visual tool. The reason is simple: New equipment and techniques have elevated 8mm to the point where it offers business results that were previously impossible except with top-budget film productions.

1. "Industrial Motion Picture Survey," *Industrial Photography,* March, 1961, pp. 24, 25.

Automatic cameras and easy to operate viewing devices allow salesmen, engineers and other non-photographic personnel to make and/or utilize 8mm films effectively. Particularly significant has been the advent of magnetic sound which adds the "professional touch" long missing in 8mm efforts.[1]

Will 8mm motion pictures replace the more costly 16mm films in future productions? The general feeling is that it is very unlikely.

It's safe to bet that 8mm sound will supplement, not supplant 16-mm sound. In other words, 8mm sound promises to become an "added plus."

Ultimately, here are advantages predicted for 8mm sound films:

1. Economy of release prints.
2. Lower-cost projectors.
3. Less bulky prints (an advantage when carrying, storing, shipping).
4. Smaller sized projectors.
5. Lighter weight release prints (an advantage in an age of air transportation).
6. More portable projection equipment.
7. Improvement in looping performance (or motion pictures in connection with continuous-running or repetitive projectors).
8. Self-threading, or cartridge-load mechanisms, now become more feasible.
9. A self-contained, "suitcase theater," for salesmen to deposit on the prospect's desk now nearer to realization.

For the next year or two:

1. Savings in release prints (up to 37% based on one laboratory's current prices).
2. Lower-cost projectors. (Not a lot, but significant if you're equipping a fleet of dealers).
3. Suitcase-type repetitive projectors more feasible—good for lighted rooms or display work. (Apparently, 8mm means less servicing than 16mm).
4. Low-cost, "home-made" films of the in-plant type are more feasible. (Where the 8mm original is all you need, or where you can shoot a spare version or two).

In a few years:

1. By then, laboratories will have perfected gang-printing methods

1. Mitchell M. Badler, "8mm Turns Pro," *Industrial Photography*, May, 1960, Sec. 2, p. 20.

of making high-quality, low-cost 8mm sound-and-color release prints.

2. By then, several million "audiences" will have access to convenient, inexpensive 8mm sound-on-film projectors; they will be owned, like typewriters, throughout leading business establishments.

3. Technical problems still holding back direct, single-system 8mm color movie-making on fool-proof pre-striped 8mm film will probably have been resolved. You'll be able to record business conferences and sales meetings in movies as you now do with your quarter-inch sound tape recorder.

By the year 1976:

1. It's predicted that there may be as many as 10,500,000 8mm sound-on-film projectors in use in the USA—with another 5,000,000 in other parts of the world.

2. The sale, rental and loan of 8mm sound-and-color release prints will be big business. Hollywood, industry, everybody and his cousin, will be supplying professionally-made moves that can be run on the millions and millions of screens of this new medium.

3. Motion pictures, distributed through super-markets, drugstores, phonograph record and sporting goods shops, as well as by means of aggressive direct-mail merchandisers, will be well on the way to supplanting the printed word as man's most popular form of recorded information.

4. Documentary films, sponsored films of all types, will be seen—through 8mm channels—by that prime target for most US consumer advertising: Mrs. Housewife, purchasing agent for the typical American family.

5. Business and industry will be making automatic use of sound-and.color motion pictures as a means of screen communication at every level of corporate activity and in nearly every department.

6. Young people in high school and college will acquire, as a matter of course, at least the rudiments of movie-making know-how. The mark of an educated citizen of tomorrow will not be how proficient he is in the use of spoken and written forms of his language but also the degree to which he can also express himself effectively in the international language of the film and the moving image.[1]

The preceding forecast predicts a tremendous future market and use for the 8mm sound film. For the present, however, films for

---

1. John Flory, "8mm in the Crystal Ball," *Industrial Film and Audio-Visual Annual*, May, 1961, p. 36.

general distribution will continue to be made in the 16mm format. For one thing, practically all projectors now in use by groups that would be utilizing the films are of the 16mm size. Until the 8mm sound-on-film projectors have gained more widespread use, the industrial producer of such films will probably have to lend the projector as well as the film. This, of course, will limit the possible circulation of the films.

A second limitation of the 8mm film is the size to which it can be projected. The original picture is so small that the practical limit for the size of the projected image is about four feet. Because of this small size, the number of people who can be accommodated within the optimum viewing distance (2 to 6 screen widths, or 8 to 24 feet) is limited. Screenings for larger groups would have to be done on 16mm film. The small screen size is not a limitation when projecting for a prospective customer, a board of director's meeting, a small training class, or a single class in a school situation.

A third drawback is the quality of the sound reproduced from the magnetic sound track. Magnetic recording has a very high potential quality, but this is obtained only when the recording and playback are accomplished with the tape or other magnetic surface moving at a rather rapid rate (see p. 256) through the machine. At 16 frames per second, the standard speed for 8mm motion pictures, the film is moving at less than $2\frac{1}{2}$ inches per second. Compared to the standard speeds of tape recorders of $7\frac{1}{2}$ or $3\frac{3}{4}$ inches per second, this is quite slow. Even a speed of 24 frames per second, is barely up to the $3\frac{3}{4}$ inches per second of the slower standard for tape.

A fourth limitation to the widespread use of 8mm sound motion pictures where they are distributed to various users is that at the time of this writing the various manufacturers of this equipment have not agreed on the speed of projection or the location of the sound in relation to the corresponding picture. Thus a sound film made for use on one brand of projector would be out of synchronization and perhaps run too fast or too slowly on another machine. The manufacturers will have to get together and decide on some standards before this new film size will reach its ultimate degree of usefulness.

In situations where the above limitations are not factors, the 8mm film will have increasing acceptance in the business world.

Eventually—as schools, churches, clubs, and other groups acquire 8mm equipment for their average-sized classes and audiences—advertising and public relations films can be released on 8mm film.

Whereas there are some 630,000 16mm sound projectors in the United States today, within a few years there could well be several million 8mm sound projectors. Motion pictures would then become one of the mass media.

The motion picture has played a big role in selling. Now it will be even easier and less expensive to use films in all forms of sales work. A sales manager can equip his entire sales force with low-cost 8mm projectors that are quite portable, and release prints that are in line with the cost of other selling aids. With little preparation or wasted time, a salesman can walk into a prospect's office and run a short film for an individual or a group. Special applications lend themselves well to 8mm presentation. For instance, companies that sell large, bulky equipment may use films extensively to demonstrate their products.

Visual aids play an important part in sales training. Usually, few sales groups are larger than 50 or 60 persons. When a training program is to be taken to distributors, jobbers, and retail outlets, 8mm prints will be economical and 8mm equipment easy to transport.

In the field of advertising, 8mm sound films will prove popular for exhibits at trade shows. The motion picture is already found in booths as well as in the company suite (where important customers can watch a filmed message).

There are approximately 4,000,000 silent 8mm projectors in homes across the country. As these are gradually replaced with sound machines, advertisers will want to consider having films made for home use. Heretofore, the only sound movies available were 16mm, and many sponsors shied away from having their prints booked for use in homes. This restriction has usually been necessary because only about 100 prints are made of the average sponsored film. With 8mm, a sponsor will soon be able to purchase 300 to 400 sound 8mm prints for the money previously spent on 100 16mm copies. More ambitious film programs will now run into thousands of copies, thus allowing businesses to make prints available for home consumer use.

Along with advertising films, public relations films will also be printed on 8mm, as schools, churches, clubs, and other institutions invest in 8mm projectors. As more and more amateurs purchase 8mm sound equipment and buy or rent entertainment films, they, too, will be interested in free film of this type.

Distributors of Hollywood entertainment films already enjoy a good business in 8mm silent films. They will soon have full catalogs of sound cartoons and short subjects at prices that will appeal to the home market.

In the field of industrial relations, many audiences, including training groups, are composed of 50 persons or less. When a company has numerous plants spread across the country, savings can be effected by releasing low-cost 8mm prints, where the situation calls for this type of graphic presentation. Ultimately, it will be natural for such a company to produce its own films with its own facilities.[1]

Shooting for 8mm. 8mm motion pictures may be shot originally on 8mm stock and reproduced in that size for release prints or it may be photographed on 16mm or 35mm film and optically reduced to the smaller size. Original shooting in the larger format results in better quality 8mm than reproduction from 8mm original footage. Also, having the original in one of the larger sizes makes it possible to release the film in the other sizes for theatrical or larger group showings.

Planning of 8mm motion pictures involves certain camera techniques that are not as important when working with the larger film sizes. If these limitations inherent in the small size of the frame are kept in mind, 8mm films can do an excellent job. This is the feeling of J. C. Frandsen, owner and executive producer of Unit One Productions. He goes on to say:

> Shooting in 16 or 35 with 8mm in mind is important, Mr. Frandsen reminds, because as a medium 8mm is not merely half of 16mm. It's a smaller world on screen that cannot be crowded or pushed to great distance. For this reason, many of the films in the great stockpile of 16mm product will lose much in quality and suffer greatly in effectiveness when reduced to 8mm, Fr. Frandsen explains. This can be likened to the ex-fat man and his loose clothing.[2]

Many factors are involved in obtaining the best quality and view impact, Mr. Frandsen reports. Unit One has taken these factors and incroporated them into the following brief approach:

1. Because of some loss in definition, a camera technique keeping this in mind is an absolute need.
2. Backgrounds and makeup should be carefully considered to heighten color separation.
3. As the projected image is somewhat smaller than that of 16mm. close camera work is used, as well as cuts to individuals instead of scenes with many persons.
4. Color choice for art work and graphs is important for clarity.
5. Sound quality on 8mm is excellent, but considering the still pos-

---

1. Courtesy Eastman Kodak Company.

2. "Need New Camera Techniques in Use of 8mm," *Film World and A-V News,* September, 1961.

sible slight amount of "wow," music should be used carefully. This is a mass copy problem that should be corrected in the near future.[1]

The smaller frame size of the 8mm film calls for more knowledge and better technique on the part of the photographer, regardless of whether he is shooting original 8mm footage or shooting 16mm or 35mm with planned reduction to 8mm in mind. Some of the rules that will help to govern this shooting are listed below:

Tighten up on composition and condense wherever possible. Eliminate non-contributing elements. Rather than seating two speakers at opposite sides of a table move them in until their elbows touch.

When shooting a room setting or even a big machine take a few feet of the overall scene and then close in tight on the significant points. This not only gives unusually good resolution on the screen but allows for creative, dramatic effects.

Close cropping requires careful positioning in the viewfinder. The reflex viewing offered by zoom lenses avoids any chance of parallax error. The lens gives precise framing and allows the quick selection of any needed focal length without moving the camera or subject. This is helpful in framing titles, charts and graphs.

Zoom effects should be done within a very shallow field, changing from medium close-up to close-up at a very slow speed. Long zooms from 10 to 40mm are dramatic but serve little purpose in a business film. *Never zoom in or pan to a chart.* Any image movement makes reading at least ten times tougher for the viewer and image resolution is seriously impaired.

Edge definition should be forced. One logical way to achieve this is by illumination of the background or backdrop, or direct or indirect backlighting of the subject. Stronger than usual color contrasts are also helpful.[2]

Just as 16mm film is not expected to compete on an even basis with 35mm film in projection to the large, theater size screen, 8mm film should not be expected to compete with 16mm for large group showings. However, for groups of up to 50 people, which includes most school and selling situations, the smaller size of film provides an excellent, inexpensive method of conveying a visual message.

Introduced in 1965 was a variation of 8mm film which may largely displace the original type. This format, called "Super 8", provides a picture area that is 50% larger than the regular 8mm, with a re-

---

1. *Ibid.*
2. "Tips on Shooting 8mm Sound Movies," *Industrial Photography*, August, 1959.

sulting increase in projected size and brilliance. Fig. 61 illustrates the differences in size and appearance between these two types of 8mm film.

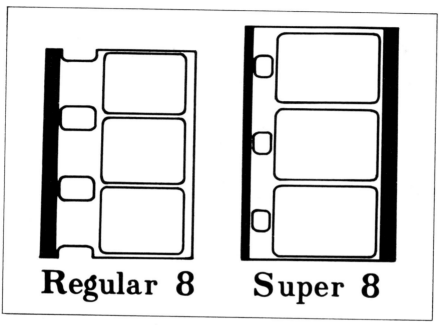

Regular 8   Super 8

FIG. 61. Comparison of Regular and Super 8mm Film.

The wide, black lines indicate the locations of the magnetic sound stripes. On regular 8mm, the sound stripe is between the sprocket holes and the edge of the film. On super 8, the sound track is on the side opposite the sprocket holes and between the picture and the edge of the film.

As can be seen in the illustration, the two types of film are not compatible in either camera or projector. In the older format, the sprocket holes are at the frame line, while in the newer type, the holes are opposite the middle of the frame. Also, the width of the sprocket hole has been reduced to permit a larger picture area.

Because of the investment that has already been made in equipment and films of the original 8mm format, there is some question as to how quickly the new film will catch on. People with money invested in regular 8mm cameras, projectors, editing equipment, and film are not likely to discard it all in favor of the new size in order to gain the additional picture area. Those, however, who are just beginning to assemble equipment and make films will want to use the newer format. Perhaps a manufacturer will solve the dilemma by introducing a projector which will handle either type of film.

A business organization considering 8mm motion pictures as a suitable medium for carrying its communications should choose between regular and Super 8 based upon the type of equipment that will be available where the material is to be projected. If the films are intended primarily for internal use—training, sales, etc.— the type of projection equipment available will be known. If they are to be loaned to individuals and organizations outside the company, some complications might arise in knowing which type of 8mm print to send. A space might be included on the film booking request form to indicate the type of projector which the borrower has available. Failure on the part of the borrower to indicate this information would require additional correspondence to make sure that the print sent would be compatible with the projection equipment.

8mm motion pictures as a personal sales tool requires a self-contained projection unit that is light enough and compact enough to be carried like a briefcase and capable of being set up on the prospect's desk quickly and without undue disturbance of the surroundings. The unit should utilize rear-screen projection so that darkening of the room is unnecessary. A continuous loop magazine will make it possible to leave the film in the projector, making it unnecessary to thread the machine each time. As 8mm sound becomes more widespread in its use many such projectors will undoubtedly come onto the market. One such projector is the Fairchild Mark IV (See Fig. 62). About the size of a briefcase and easily portable, this machine needs only to be placed in position and turned on. The continuous loop film does not have to be rethreaded or rewound and is ready to repeat the message as many times as necessary.

Consider Your Audience. On page 1 reference was made to the communication process. It was brought out that if the message is to be transmitted to the intended recipient, a language must be chosen that both understand. Nowhere is this more true than in the case of motion pictures. Excellent as they are for the communication of information and ideas, they must be planned intelligently for the comprehension level of the viewer. One would not, for instance, use the same film for a report to management and for new employee training. The level of the audiences and the purposes of the film

FIG. 62. Fairchild Mark IV Desk-top Projector.
(Courtesy of Fairchild Instrument Corporation)

are too widely different in the two cases. It is important that you neither talk over the heads of your audience nor talk down to them.

If the film is intended for distribution to schools, it should meet certain requirements in addition to that of being designed for as specific age level. Some of these necessities are listed below:

The more than 45 million children in our nation's schools represent a tremendous audience for business-sponsored films. These movies offer companies a way to achieve identification among youngsters, create a corporate image and build future good will.

School administrators, although aware of the educational value of company films, have become increasingly selective with respect to these films. They won't accept them unless they meet certain standards. Here are some of the criteria which these educators have set up:

Basic Educational Approach

1. *Fits into curriculum.* Is the film designed so that it can be readily used in the curriculum?

2. *Constructive.* The film should make a significant contribution toward educational goals.

3. *Educational scope.* Is the film sound in terms of educational standards?

4. *Graded material.* The film should be suited to its intended age level in regard to vocabulary, diction, literary quality, depth, and pace.

5. *Best available.* To what extent does this film promote the educational program better than any other film generally available at this time?

6. *Packaged program (or kit).* The film is usually more desirable if part of a packaged kit, including a teacher's guide and other items.

7. *Unity of theme.* The film should have a few basic points and not be cluttered with too many objectives or ideas.

Subject Matter

8. *Authentic.* The film should be authentic and accurate as to facts.

9. *Unbiased and objective.* The film should be representative in its selection of facts. It should present general understanding, processes, or methods rather than a point of view. It should not obviously promote a specific brand.

10. *No excessive commercialism.* Where the sponsor's interest or product is shown as an integral part of the film it should be handled without emphasizing a specific brand or trade name to a point where such product information is the focal point of the scene.

11. *Avoid prejudice.* The film should be free from any uncomplimentary reflections on the dignity and status of any group, race, or religion, whether expressed or implied, by statement or omission.

Production

12. *Proper identification.* The sponsor should always be clearly identified in the title of the film.

13. *Type of audience.* The sponsor must decide whether his film is to be used only for a specific type of class or will have more general use for assemblies and outside organizations.

14. *Age of actors.* Youngsters are sensitive to proper age of children in films. Maximum empathy results where child actors are the same age of the target audience or slightly older.

15. *Running time.* Teachers require a film which fits school scheduling and does not run over 20 to 27 minutes. Actually 10 to 15 minutes is a more acceptable length, leaving time for discussion and class participation.

16. *Avoid obsolescence.* Women's hair styles and dress lengths, auto-

mobile models and sponsor's products are the chief factors which outdate a film.

17. *Availability of films.* The company should set up the distribution program so that enough prints are readily available to educational users when and where needed.

18. *Purchase policy.* If a film is well received by teachers, schools and libraries the company should be ready to lease or sell prints.[1]

(With regard to the last mentioned suggestion, the more common method is to donate the print or issue it on a long-term load.)

Distribution of Business Films

Motion pictures produced by business organizations are of no value sitting on the shelf. They can fulfill the purpose for which they were made only if the people for whom they were designed get to see them. This means that some system for distributing them must be developed.

Distribution within the company can be handled by the division of the company for which the film was made and to which it is applicable. Thus training films would be booked by and returned to the employee training division. Regulating the sales films would be a function of the sales manager's office. Another methods is to have the audio-visual department store, book, and maintain all of the motion pictures that were made for use within the company.

Films which go to distributors and dealers are still, in a sense, within the company, since the audience is rather carefully controlled. The booking of these films should be handled by whichever department distributes informational and sales literature.

Public relations and other sponsored films that are to be made available to schools, clubs, and other groups of the general public are more of a problem. Two difficulties are involved here. First, teachers and other potential users of the films must be made aware of the films and their contents so that they can decide whether they wish to use them with their groups. Second, the mechanics of getting the material out and back again, inspected, maintained, and stored must be provided for.

Several methods are used to inform potential users of the films about their availability and their contents. Perhaps the most commonly used is listing in either a general or a specialized publication

---

1. "Give It the School-Kid Slant," *Industrial Film and A-V Annual,* May, 1961, p. 82.

which describes materials of this sort. The following list is extracted from the Eastman Kodak pamphlet, *Sources of Motion Pictures and Filmstrips.*[1]

General Catalogs of Films

The Blue Book of Audio-Visual Materials
    Educational Screen & Audio-Visual Guide
    200 Lincoln Park West
    Chicago 14, Illinois

The Blue Book of 16mm Films
    Educational Screen & Audio-Visual Guide
    200 Lincoln Park West
    Chicago 14, Illinois

Educational Film Guide
    The H. W. Wilson Company
    850 University Avenue
    New York 51, New York

Educators Guide to Free Films (annual)
    Educators Progress Service
    Randolph, Wisconsin

Library of Congress Printed Cards for Motion Pictures and Filmstrips
    Card Division
    Library of Congress
    Washington 25, D. C.

Business and Industry

Annotated Bibliography of Audio-Visual Aids for Management Development programs
    Research Service
    353 West 57th Street
    New York 19, New York

Business Education Films
    Business Education Films
    4607 16th Avenue
    Brooklyn 4, New York

Catalog of Business and Professional Films
    Modern Talking Picture Service, Inc.
    3 East 54th Street
    New York 22, New York

---

1. *Sources of Motion Pictures and Filmstrips,* Eastman Kodak Company Pamphlet No. S-9, Sales Service Division, Eastman Kodak Company, Rochester 4, New York.

Catalogue of Films
 American Marketing Association
 27 East Monroe Street
 Chicago 3, Illinois

Dartnell Sales Training Films
 Dartnell Corporation
 4460 Ravenswood Avenue
 Chicago 40, Illinois

Directory of Journalism Films
 Association for Education in Journalism
 State University of Iowa
 Ames, Iowa

Film Guide for Industrial Training
 National Metal Trades Association
 337 West Madison Street
 Chicago 6, Illinois

Film Guide on Production and Management Methods
 Film Research Associates
 304 Pinebrook Boulevard
 New Rochelle, New York

Films for Labor
 American Federation of Labor and Congress of Industrial
 Organizations
 815 Sixteenth Street, N. W.
 Washington 6, D. C.

Films Relating to Printing and Graphic Arts
 Michigan Industrial Education Society, Inc.
 4628 Flajole Road
 Midland, Michigan

Films to Explain American Business
 Chamber of Commerce of the United States
 1615 H Street N. W.
 Washington 6, D. C.

Guide to Films, Periodicals, and Books in Printing, Paper, Publishing,
Printed Advertising and Their Closely Related Industries
 School of Printing Management
 Carnegie Institute of Technology
 Pittsburgh 13, Pennsylvania

Guide to Motion Pictures and Filmstrips of Interest to Management
 American Management Association
 1515 Broadway
 New York 36, New York

IMS Film Rental Library
    Industrial Management Society
    330 South Wells Street
    Chicago 6, Illinois
NARGUS Better Stores Program
    National Association of Retail Grocers of the United States
    360 North Michigan Avenue
    Chicago 1, Illinois
Railroad Film Directory
    Association of American Railroads
    Transportation Building
    Washington 6, D. C.
See . . . Hear . . . Mr. Businessman 1958-59
    Audio Visual Center
    The City College
    Bernard M. Baruch School of Business and Public Administration
    17 Lexington Avenue
    New York 10, New York
Selected Guide to Films on Public Relations Practice
    Public Relations Society of America, Inc.
    375 Park Avenue
    New York 22, New York
U. S. Government Films for Industry
    United World Films, Inc.
    1445 Park Avenue
    New York 29, New York

The preceding lists were concerned with listings of films in general and those that were related to some phase or other of business. Most of these associations and libraries welcome listings of additional films of their special type for their catalogs.

Periodicals that concern themselves with the uses of motion picture films in their various aspects carry advertisements in which producers can announce the availability of films to the public. Some of these periodicals are listed below (continuing with information from the Eastman Kodak Pamphlet, *Sources of Motion Pictures and Filmstrips*).[1]

Periodicals

Advertising Requirements
    200 E. Illinois Street
    Chicago 11, Illinois

_____

1. *Ibid.*

Business Screen
  Business Screen Magazines, Inc.
  7064 Sheridan Road
  Chicago 26, Illinois
Film Media
  Photography in Business, Inc.
  10 East 40th Street
  New York 16, New York
Film World and A-V World News Magazine
  Sidale Publishing Company
  672 So. Lafayette Park Place
  Los Angeles 57, California
Industrial Photography
  Photography in Business, Inc.
  10 East 40th Street
  New York 16, New York
Industrial Screen
  Fountain Press
  46-47 Chancery Lane
  London W. C. 2, England
Photo Methods for Industry
  NPD Corp.
  33 West 60th Street
  New York 23, New York

As the company completes sponsored films and announces them to the public, it is necessary to make provision for the physical handling and distribution of these films. There are several alternative ways of performing this.

The company may wish to handle its own bookings. This will involve a considerable amount of work for the audio-visual organization or whatever other department is assigned the responsibility. Some of the problems involved are;

1. Providing space for the storage and handling of the films.
2. Keeping reservation records so that a user of the film will have it when scheduled.
3. Shipping the films so that they will arrive a day or so before the scheduled use, but no so long that it ties up the print unnecessarily.
4. Paying postage costs for the films.
5. Inspecting the films after each showing, including repair or replacement where necessary.
6. Maintaining records so that reports can be made to management

as to the number of bookings, where they were, and the numbers of men, women, boys, and girls who see the films.

The activities listed above will increase the work load of the department considerably, but the degree of control and the accurate knowledge of the bookings and the numbers of people who see the film may be worth it. The company will handle its own promotional publicity and has the additional public relations advantage of being in correspondence with the users directly rather than working through an intermediary.

Located in cities throughout the country are commercial lending libraries for motion picture films. The company can place the appropriate prints on deposit with these film libraries. When a request for a film comes in to the company a shipping label is made up and sent to the local library. The library attaches the label to the film shipping case, ships it out and receives it, inspects it, and returns it to the shelf. Reimbursement to the library would be on the basis of the number of bookings received. Generally any promotion of the film is up to the sponsor, except for the incidental notice that is a result of being included in the library's catalog.

Some booking companies handle distribution for business films on a nationwide basis. The company can contract with the distributor for as much of his service as is desired. The prints are placed on deposit and held for requests. Announcements and brochures are sent out by the distributor to the mailing list which he maintains. As the distributor receives a request for a film for a certain date he notifies the company of the booking so that the company can send a representative to the showing to help follow up the film. Users are requested to complete cards which indicate the number of showings and the number of people in attendance. Information from these cards is punched onto IBM cards and is the basis of monthly reports of utilization. The billing to the sponsor is based on the number of showings or on a flat charge per print each month. Some of the leading companies performing this service are listed below:

Association Films
    347 Madison Avenue
    New York 17, New York

Farm Film Foundation
    1731 Eye Street, N. W.
    Washington, D. C.

Ideal Pictures
  58 South Water Street
  Chicago 1, Illinois

Institute for Visual Training
  40 East 49th Street
  New York, New York

Modern Talking Picture Service
  3 East 54th Street
  New York 22, New York

Princeton Film Center
  Princeton, New Jersey

Sterling-Movies U. S. A.
  6 East 39th Street
  New York 16, New York

United World Films
  1445 Park Avenue
  New York 29, New York[1]

Sponsored films may be deposited with libraries operated by universities and by city or county school systems. Reimbursement by the sponsor may be on the basis of a yearly report of bookings. Alternatively, the library may make a charge to the borrower to cover the cost of postage and handling. Some of the major university film libraries are listed below:

Florida State University
  Audio-Visual Center
  Tallahassee, Florida

Indiana University
  Audio-Visual Center
  Bloomington, Indiana

Michigan State University
  Audio-Visual Center
  East Lansing, Michigan

Pennsylvania State University
  Audio-Visual Aids Library
  University Park, Pennsylvania

University of California Extension
  Department of Visual Education
  Berkeley, California

---

1. "A Guide to Business Films," *Advertising Requirements* (now *Advertising and Sales Promotion*).

University of Colorado
    Bureau of Audio-Visual Instruction
    Boulder, Colorado
University of Michigan
    Audio-Visual Education Center
    Ann Arbor, Michigan
University of Missouri
    Adult Education and Extension Service
    Visual Education Department
    Columbia, Missouri
University of Wisconsin
    Extension Division
    Bureau of Audio-Visual Instruction
    Madison, Wisconsin[1]

Summary

Motion pictures can help to solve many of a business organization's communication problem, because of their ability to recreate reality through the combination of movement, color, and sound. They can present an event many times in an identical manner and can be designed so as to present just the information desired in the way calculated to give the best results.

Proper utilization of motion pictures requires the application of a certain amount of showmanship. The projector should be set up and adjusted for showing before the audience is present. The machine should be started while the room lights are still on and allowed to run until the titles come into position. The projection lamp is then turned on and the room lights turned out. At the end of the film the room lights are turned on while the end titles are still showing. The projection lamp is then turned off and the motor allowed to run until the film end has passed through the machine.

The effectiveness of a motion picture can be greatly enhanced by proper preparation of the audience beforehand and followup after the showing.

Production of a film may be undertaken by the company or an outside producer may be called in to do it. Each method has its advantages and disadvantages which must be considered carefully before a decision is reached. Regardless of who does them, there are certain activities which must be performed in connection with

---

1. *Ibid.*

the production of a film. The person in charge of the production (the supervisor) oversees the activities of the writer, director, cameraman, sound engineer, actors, script girl, editor, and the laboratory.

Most business productions are made on 16mm film, but with the introduction of magnetic sound to the 8mm film, this smaller size is gaining popularity. Equipment, film, shipping, and storage costs are less and the results are quite satisfactory for smaller audiences. The equipment is also more portable.

Motion pictures must be designed and produced with a specific audience in mind. Otherwise their success is likely to be very limited.

A sponsored film may be distributed directly by the company or through a commercial library.

GLOSSARY OF MOTION PICTURE TERMS

The purpose of this glossary is to assist the communications person who is not versed in cinematography in working with motion picture photographers. Photographic words defined in Chapter 9 are not repeated.

A and B rolls: a method of providing overlapping footage for dissolves.

abrasions: scratches running lengthwise on the film from rubbing or scraping.

acetate base: film base composed of nonflammable cellulose acetate; used for 16mm and 8mm motion picture film.

action: the signal to commence the acting of the scene.

amplifier: a device to increase the volume of an electric current; used in a motion picture sound system to build up the current from the photoelectric cell to the point where it can operate the speaker.

animation: illusion of continuous movement obtained by photographing a series of drawings or objects one frame at a time, moving the object slightly before each shot.

answer print: first print of the completed motion picture sent to the client for approval before the release prints are run off.

assembly: putting the scenes together in the proper order, before adjusting for pacing and mood.

barn doors: hinged plates on the sides of lights that may be placed so as to control the light.

base: the flexible, transparent material to support the emulsion where the picture is located.

blimp: a soundproof housing for a motion picture camera.

boom, camera: a mobile camera mount, movable through all three dimensions.

boom, microphone: a device for suspending a microphone over the set so that dialogue may be picked up without the microphone being visible.

camera angle: the point of view from which the scene is being photographed.

camera log (or sheet): a record of technical information about each scene that is shot.

cell: a sheet of acetate on which one of a series of drawings is made in animation.

changeover: switching from one projector at the end of a reel to another which is loaded and ready to operate.

changeover marks: the signal to change over; usually a flash of light at the upper right-hand corner of the frame.

cinch marks: parallel scratches made by tightening a reel of film by pulling on the end.

clap-sticks: a device to insure synchronization between sound and picture; sticks are attached to the top of the slate and are clapped together at the beginning of a scene; the frame showing them meeting is matched with the sound track sound, putting the two "in sync."

claw: the device which pulls the film into position to photograph or project each frame; fingers move into the perforations to pull the film down and position it.

close-up: a scene in which the subject fills the frame; used to show detailed information.

console: the control panel for sound recording.

continuity: the arrangement of scenes to tell a logical story.

cookie: a flat sheet of metal cut into a pattern ;it is placed in front of a light to cast a shadow pattern on a flat wall.

core: a plastic hub on which motion picture film is temporarily wound.

cross-lighting: light coming from the sides of the set.

cut: an abrupt change from one scene to another by splicing one to the other; also the command to stop the action, camera, and sound recording.

cutter: another name for the film editor; he joins the scenes into the completed motion picture, adjusts scene lengths, matches action from scene to scene, and indicates the opticals to be used.

diffuser: a translucent screen to soften lighting.

director: the person who controls the action before the camera to interpret the wishes of the producer and writer.

dissolve: the change of scene wherein one scene gradually replaces the other.

documentary: an objective film intended to report a situation, giving background and causes, but usually not the solution.

dolly: a wheeled mount for the camera to enable it to be moved; also a scene photographed while the camera is being moved.

dubbing: adding a voice or other sound after a scene has been shot.

dupe negative: a negative made from a master positive print.

dynamic cutting: a method of editing in which scenes placed together create an impression not actually shown in the scenes.

edge numbers: a series of sequential numbers printed each foot on the negative stock; numbers are reproduced on the workprint to help in matching the negative to the workprint.

exciter lamp: a lamp which provides the light source for picking up the optical sound track in order to convert it to sound.

fade: a gradual disappearance of the scene (fade out) or gradual appearance (fade in).

fast motion: an effect of speeding up events by photographing at slower than screen speed.

film cement: a solution which is applied to the ends of film to join them together.

film gate: in a projector, a part which holds the frame of the film in proper registry for projection.

fine cut: the editing step which prepares the film in practically its completed form.

fishpole: a telescoping microphone boom.

flash-back: insertion of a scene that has taken place earlier than the previous action.

follow-focus: maintaining sharp focus on the main action as the distance from the camera to that action varies.

framing: adjusting the projector so that the picture is properly oriented vertically, with no frame lines showing.

gobo: an opaque piece of material used to shield the camera from unwanted direct light.

green print: a print just received from the processor; may stick in the projector unless lubricated or allowed to dry for a day or two.

head up (or heads out): the film wound on the reel with the beginning on the outside; ready to project.

inky-dink: a small incandescent spotlight.

jump cut: a cut where a discrepancy in the action is obvious; a short cut-away scene sometimes will cover.

lap dissolve: same as dissolve.

leader: blank film used to thread the film into a camera or projector.

light box: a sheet of opal glass set into the editing desk and illuminated from below; makes it easy to see what is on the film.

lip sync: the movement of a person's lips on the screen are matched to the sound of his voice.

long shot: a scene in which the camera is a considerable distance from the principal subject, showing it in relation to the surroundings; often used as an establishing shot.

magnetic head: a sound head for playing a magnetic sound track.

magnetic stripe: a strip of magnetic material placed along one edge of a film on which the sound track is recorded; may be erased and re-recorded

match-action: joining two scenes together so that the action is smooth and continuous from one to the other.

matte: a metal plate placed in front of the lens; a part is cut out to give the scene an outline of that shape, e.g. keyhole, binoculars, etc.

matte box: a large sunshade also used to hold mattes.

medium shot: a shot intermediate in distance between a long shot and a close-up; the distance at which the majority of filming takes place.

montage: the blending of a series of scenes to create meaning which is not contained in any scene by itself.

Moviola: a machine used in editing to run scenes forward and back; can run sound in sync with the film.

non-theatrical: film showings other than in theaters or other places where admission is charged.

opticals: effect created in the laboratory; fades, wipes, dissolves, etc.

pan: to swing the camera in a horizontal arc while filming.

photo-electric cell: a device which emits an electrical current when light falls upon it.

post-scoring: recording the sound after the photography has been done.

pre-scoring: recording the sound track first, then fitting the action to it.

process projection: a background is projected onto the rear of a translucent screen while the actors perform in front of it; looks as if the actors were actually at the locale where the background was shot.

producer: an independent motion picture company which has contracted to produce a film for a client; or, the executive on the client's staff responsible for the production.

production unit: the team which photographs and records the film.

props: anything on the set that is movable (except the actors).

raw stock: film that has not been exposed or developed.

recording, live: simultaneous recording and photographing.

release printing: completed copy of the film ready for projection or distribution.

re-recording: recording of one sound track from another; sometimes called dubbing; may combine sounds from several tracks onto one.

retake: shooting a scene again because the first time was not good enough.

reversal film: film which can be processed directly to a positive image.

rewinds: devices for the rapid winding of film from one reel to another.

rough cut: first edited version of a film with scenes in order but not adjusted for pacing or matching action; sometimes called the stringout.

safety base: film base which is nonflammable.

scene: one continuous bit of action photographed and/or recorded.

scoop: a light with a reflector but no lens, used to provide general illumination for the set.

screen: the reflecting surface onto which a motion picture is projected for viewing.

scrim: transparent material placed in front of a light source to soften the effect.

script: the blueprint for a motion picture; a parallel listing of the dialogue and action opposite the photographic instructions; may be general or detailed.

set: the place where the action of the film takes place; may be natural or artificial.

shot: a separate and continuous photographic record of an action or vista; practically synonymous with the scene.

silent speed: 16 frames per second.

single frame: exposing one frame at a time; used in animation or time-lapse photography.

single system sound recording: recording the sound and photographic material simultaneously on the same film.

slate: a small blackboard on which is written the identification of the scene, take, and whatever other information is desired; photographed on a few frames at the beginning of the take it identifies.

slow motion: photographing a scene at higher than normal camera speed so that when shown at normal speed the objects will appear to have slowed down.

sound effects: all intentional sound other than dialogue, narration, and music.

sound head: the portion of a recording device which records sound or which converts the recorded signal back to sound.

sound speed: 24 frames per second.

sound stage: an area equipped to photograph and record the sound for motion pictures.

sound track: the portion of the film where the sound is recorded.

special effects: a branch of motion picture photography which is concerned with the photographing of scenes that are difficult to stage or spectacular, such as earthquakes, fires, auto wrecks, etc.; often done in miniature.

spider: a junction box at the end of a cable with several outlet receptacles.

splice: a joint that unites two pieces of film end to end.

sponsored film: a film made by an organization for the purpose of public relations and usually distributed free or at a nominal cost.

sprockets: the teeth on the sprocket wheels which engage the sprocket holes in motion picture film to move the film through the machine.

stage: the area where photography takes place.

stock footage: footage of scenes which may be purchased for use in other films.

storyboard: a device to show the key scenes and ideas of a film so that those concerned with its development can get an over-all idea of the story.

strike: the set can be dismantled inasmuch as all the shooting on that particular set is completed.

swish pan: a rapid pan, blurring the background; used as a transition from one scene to another.

tail: the end of the film; tail up or tails out means that the end of the film is on the outside of the reel.

take: each time a scene is shot it is given a take number; take 1, take 2, etc.

thread: insert the film in a camera or projector so that it will be fed properly through the machine.

tilt: turning the camera vertically while filming.

time-lapse photography: a method of compressing time by photographing a single frame at regular intervals; projection at 24 frames per second speeds up the action.

transition: moving from one sequence to another; may be done by opticals, music, or dialogue.

treatment: a synopsis of the way that the subject matter of a film is to be handled.

trims: footage that was photographed but not used in the completed picture.

truck: movement of the entire camera to follow a person or to provide movement for a static shot.

turret: a mounting for several lenses so that the change from one to another can be made quickly.

TV framing: allowance for the fact that a TV set often does not cover the entire field of the broadcast; important details are kept near the center of the picture.

variable area sound track: recording of the sound track in such a way that the area through which the exciter lamp can send light to the photoelectric cell varies; this fluctuation of the light is converted to a fluctuating electrical current, built up by the amplifier, and sent to the speaker where it is changed to sound.

variable density sound track: light which strikes the photo electric cell is varied by the changing density; see variable area sound track above.

wild: shots made or sound recorded without use of a script. Also, photographing action when the camera and sound recorder are not synchronized.

wipe: an optical transition in which one shot seems to push the other off the screen.

workprint: original footage is never projected because of the danger of damage; a workprint is made from it and this is used in the cutting and editing; when the workprint is finished to everyone's satisfaction, the original footage is cut to match it.

wow: undesirable fluctuations in the sound reproduction.

zoom: the enlarging or contracting of the image on the screen caused by changing the focal length of the camera lens; gives an effect similar to dollying but is accomplished without moving the camera.

BIBLIOGRAPHY

Brodbeck, Emil E., *Handbook of Basic Motion Picture Techniques,* New York, McGraw-Hill Book Co., 1950

Brown, James W., Richard B. Lewis, and Fred F. Harcleroad, *AV Instructional Materials and Methods,* Second Edition, New York, McGraw-Hill Book Company, Inc., 1964, 592 pp.
        Chap. 8 Films
        Chap. 20 Photography
        Reference Section 1 Projection Equipment Principles,
            pp. 535-538
            Motion Picture Projectors, pp. 545-554

Brown, James W., and Richard B. Lewis (Ed), *AV Instructional Materials*

Manual, Second Edition, New York, McGraw-Hill Book Company, 1964, 188 pp.
>   Exercise Twenty-two Making Motion Pictures
>   Exercise Thirty-two Films
>   Exercise Forty-six Motion Picture Projectors
>   Exercise Forty-seven 8mm and 16mm Magnetic Projectors

Buchanan, Andrew, *Film Making from Script to Screen,* New York, Macmillan Co., 1951

Colburn, George W., Laboratory, *Colburn Comments on 8mm Magnetic Sound,* Chicago, George W. Colburn Laboratory.

Cross, A. J. Foy, and Irene F. Cypher, *Audio Visual Education,* New York, Thomas Y. Crowell Company, 1961, 415 pp.
>   Chap. 3 The Instructional Motion Picture

Dale, Edgar, *Audio-Visual Methods in Teaching,* Revised Edition, New York, The Dryden Press, 1954, 534 pp.
>   Chap. 15 Motion Pictures

De Kieffer, Robert, and Lee W. Cochran, *Manual of Audio-Visual Techniques,* Englewood Cliffs, New Jersey, Prentice-Hall, Inc., 1955, 220 pp.
>   Unit Three Projected Materials and Equipment
>   Motion Pictures and Motion Picture Projectors, pp. 123-139

Dugan, J. M., J. S. Jones, S. A. Hawk, and L. E. Walkup, *Guide to Audio-Visual Presentations,* New York, Wolf Business Publications, Inc., 1964, 149 pp.
>   Use of Projectors
>   Presentation of 16mm Moving Pictures

Eastman Kodak Company Publications
>   Industrial Motion Pictures, 76 pp, 50¢
>   Magnetic Sound Recording, 64 pp, 50¢
>   Kodak Movie Photoguide, 32 pp, $1.75
>   Storage and Preservation of Motion Picture Film, 80 pp, 50¢
>   Eastman Motion Picture Film for Professional Use, $1.25
>   Basic Titling and Animation
>   Planningboards (single copy free)

Eboch, Sidney C., *Operating Audio-Visual Equipment,* San Francisco, California, Howard Chandler, Publisher, 1960, 73 pp.
>   Chap. II Motion Picture Projection

Educators Guide to Free Films, Educators Progress Service, Randolph, Wisconsin, (Published yearly)

Fielding, Raymond, *The Techniques of Special Effects Cinematography,* New York, Hastings House, Publishers, 1965, 396 pp.

Finn, James D., *The Audio-Visual Equipment Manual,* New York, The Dryden Press, 1957, 361 pp.
>   Section 1—Projectors
>   16mm Sound Motion Picture Projectors, pp. 17-77
>   Sound Motion Picture Projectors (Magnetic) pp. 78-84
>   Good Projection Practice, pp. 189-220

Gordon, Jay E., *Motion Picture Production for Industry*, New York, Macmillan Co., 1961

Haas, Kenneth B., and Harry Q. Packer, *Preparation and Use of Audio-Visual Aids*, Englewood Cliffs, New Jersey, Prentice-Hall, Inc., 1955, 381 pp.
    Chap. 1 Motion Pictures

Kemp, Jerrold E., *Planning and Producing Audiovisual Materials*, San Francisco, California, Chandler Publishing Company, 1963, 169 pp.
    Part Three: Producing Your Audiovisual Materials
    5. Motion Pictures

Kinder, James S., *Audio-Visual Materials and Techniques*, 2nd Edition, New York American Book Company, 1959, 592 pp.
    Chap. 7 Motion Pictures: The Classroom Film
    Chap. 8 Motion Pictures: Appreciation
    Chap. 9 Motion Picture Equipment
    Appendix F Motion Picture Projector Check-out Form

Livingston, Don, *Film and the Director*, New York, Macmillan Co., 1958

Offenhauser, William H. Jr., *16mm Sound Motion Pictures: A Manual for the Professional and Amateur*, New York, Interscience Publishers, 1958

Sands, Lester B., *Audio-Visual Procedures in Teaching*, New York, The Ronald Press Company, 1956, 670 pp.
    Chap. 20 The Motion Picture
    Appendix F Motion Picture Projectors and Threading Diagrams

Spottiswoode, Raymond, *Film and Its Techniques*, Berkeley, California, University of California Press, 1953, 516 pp.

Strauss, L. Harry, and J. R. Kidd, *Look, Listen, and Learn*, New York Association Press, 1948, 235 pp.

Thomas, R. Murray, and Sherwin G. Swartout, *Integrated Teaching Materials*, New York, Longmans, Green and Company, Inc., 1960, 545 pp.
    Chap. 7 Motion Pictures
    Chap. 11 Creating Slide Series, Filmstrips, Motion Pictures

Wittich, Walter Arno, and Charles Francis Schuller, *Audio-Visual Materials: Their Nature and Use*, Third Edition, New York, Harper & Brothers, 1962, 500 pp.
    Chap. 13 The 16mm Sound Motion Picture Film

MOTION PICTURES

Film Editing: Interpretation and Values, American Cinema Editors, 6775 Hollywood Boulevard, Hollywood, California, 1958, 16mm sound, black-and-white, 25 min.

Sound Recording for Motion Pictures, Indiana University, Bloomington, Indiana

CHAPTER 11

SLIDES AND FILMSTRIPS

While motion pictures may be the "glamour" treatment for information that is to be transmitted by means of a projected image, other methods are often as good and sometimes even better than the use of movies. One such method is in the use of projected still pictures in the form of slides and filmstrips.

Slides are individual transparencies in color or in black and white which are mounted in some form that will hold them rigidly in position in a projector so that the image can be transmitted to a screen. The usual form for a slide is that of a photographic image, although handmade slides can also be utilized.

A filmstrip (also known as a stripfilm or slidefilm) consists of a number of individual transparencies printed on a strip of 35mm film. Once the film is started through the projector properly, no further attention is required except the flipping of a wheel which advances it from one frame to another.

A slide set or filmstrip may be self-explanatory, with title frames and captions on the individual pictures. A script which the leader or instructor reads aloud may accompany the pictures, or a disc or tape recording may provide the necessary information.

Advantages of Still Projection

Projection of still pictures has some advantages over all other types of communication when it is used to its best advantage. The advantages discussed here are primarily those over the motion picture. Some of them, however, apply to other media as well.

One of the chief strong points of the projected still picture is that it enables the group leader to pace the presentation of the material to fit the audience. The discussion of a series of pictures projected for a group of experts in a field would be quite different from that for novices. Since each individual picture can be held on the screen for whatever time is necessary and changed whenever the group is ready to go on, the use of this medium is very flexible. Compared to this, the motion picture goes along at the pace and timing that the producer feels is appropriate for some audience that he has in mind, and if this audience is different from the one actually present, the timing and pacing may be inappropriate.

Not only does the timing of the comments vary from one group to another, but more important, the actual content of the comments will be different. A group of executives viewing a series of pictures relating to the assembly of the company's product will be interested in vastly different aspects of the pictures than a group of new employees who are about to go to work on that assembly line. The person leading the presentation of the materials will be able to sense the reactions of his audience and modify the commentary to suit that particular group of people, deleting or augmenting the material as necessary.

If a person viewing a motion picture presentation has a question or a comment, he will have to wait until the film is finished before he has the opportunity to say anything. Otherwise he will interrupt the flow of the film as the projector is stopped and the room lights turned on while his point is discussed. If the question is asked while the projector continues to run, then the group is likely to miss out on the film's commentary during the time of the interruption. The only other alternative is to wait until the motion picture has been completely shown, and the viewer will probably have forgotten his question by this time. At best, it is out of context, and it might be necessary to rerun part of the film to reestablish in the minds of the viewers and the leader the situation which prompted the comment.

This problem of referral to an earlier part of the material that has been projected is much more easily accomplished when using still pictures than with a motion picture. True, if the scene of the motion picture has just been passed and the group wants to see it again, the projector can be put into reverse and backed to the beginning of the scene. However, if the scene has been passed several minutes earlier, then it will take that long to go back to it. If it is quite a long distance, it might be better to unthread the film and rewind it back to the spot desired. This, too, is time consuming and the position of the particular scene can only be estimated. When showing a filmstrip or set of slides, the presentation can be delayed while points are discussed. Even if it is a sound filmstrip, the record player or tape recorder can be turned off temporarily. Also, if a question comes up that requires referral to one of the early frames, it can be found quickly. A filmstrip can be backed rapidly by turning the film advance knob in the reverse direction. If slides are being used, the proper one can be picked out of the pile of projected ones. In either case, the disruption of the presentation is at a minimum.

Still picture projection combines readily with other media of communication. They can be combined very well with a recorded message, with either the recording or the pictures carrying the bulk of the communication—or this might vary even during a single presentation. A live speech presentation can be enhanced by the use of illustrative material in the form of a set of slides. While in this case the word may carry the bulk of the information, the slides are there to make otherwise abstract ideas more concrete, to help hold the interest of the audience, and to add punch to the material when it is needed. A set of slides or a filmstrip on a continuously repeating projector fits very well into an exhibit, particularly when the rear-projection technique is used. An example of combining the audio with the visual is in the desktop machine such as the DeKane Micromatic projector. The audio message is provided by a recording. The visual portion is projected onto a standard screen or onto a small screen scontained in the case. The filmstrip is changed automatically by a special subsonic tone on the recording which activates the changing mechanism. With only a source of power needed, the unit is ready to tell the sales or other story with no other equipment needed. This machine is pictured in Figure 63.

The operator of a 16mm motion picture projector should be a person who has had a considerable amount of training and experience, or else damage may result to the costly film or the machine, or the presentation will not be as smooth and effective as it should be. A person can operate a slide or filmstrip projector with a minimum of training or experience, and the materials are not subject to costly damage if a malfunction should occur. By means of the remote control cord, the leader or instructor can change the frame from any place in the room.

Materials for projection are lighter and less bulky for the still projector than for the motion picture projector. Approximately 20 filmstrips in individual containers can be mailed for the same cost as one 20 minute 16mm film. Four filmstrips with a 10″ record for

FIG. 63. DuKane Micromatic Projector.

each filmstrip could be shipped for the same cost or stored in the same amount of space.

Equipment for the projection of still pictures is likewise less bulky and heavy to move around and to store. This means that the projectors can be made available anywhere within the organization more easily.

Production and distribution of still materials are much less expensive than of motion pictures. The camera needs to be only the still variety, which in a professional quality machine is much less expensive than a motion picture camera. Special items of equipment, like dollies, blimps, etc., are not required. Motion pictures must have bright, continuously-burning lights for the photography. This means that it is necessary to have a power supply that will support a load of many amperes of electricity. Such sources of power supply are sometimes rather difficult to secure in certain lighting situations. Still pictures may be exposed for a long period of time where the light is poor, or they may use portable, battery-powered flash units. Motion pictures lack this flexibility. Simultaneous recording of sound is not necessary for still pictures, thus recording equipment is not needed at the site of the photography. Film costs are much less for still pictures than for motion pictures. The same holds true for the costs of film processing and release prints.

Security of information can be maintained more easily when preparing materials for a still picture presentation because processing can be handled within the organization without a large investment in processing equipment.

Random access slide and filmstrip projectors make it possible for a person to have available for instant projection a large number of photographs, maps, blueprints, forms, graphs, or charts, correspondence, schematics, wiring diagrams, engineering drawings, parts catalogs, tables, or nomograms. This type of projection is suited to almost any field where high-speed call-up of information is desired.

Typical of this sort of equipment are the projector systems produced and marketed by the Mast Development Company. This organization makes a random access slide projector and a random access filmstrip projector.

The slide projector utilizes a Kodak Carousel projector, which has a circular slide tray holding 80 slides. The projector rests on a case which contains the selection mechanism. Attached to the projection unit by a control cable is the keyboard selection unit. Selection of a slide is accomplished by depressing two buttons, one of which determines units location and the other decades location. When a request is entered, the actuator button lights up, but the slide in position continues to be projected. When the actuator button is depressed, the light goes out, the screen is darkened while the

FIG. 64a. Kodak Carousel Slide Projector and Mast Development Company Selection Mechanism with Digital Servo Unit.

desired slide is positioned, then the new slide is projected. The mechanism takes the shortest route to position the new slide, taking from 1.5 seconds to 3.0 seconds to place the new slide on the screen. Photographs of this projector and its control unit appear in Figures 64a and 64b.

The random access filmstrip projector combines the advantages of the similar slide projector plus a capacity many times that of the 80-slide capacity of the magazine. The decimal digital servo can handle count cycles of 100, 1,000, 10,000 and higher with equal facility. The projector takes the shortest route to the desired frame if a closed-loop filmstrip is used, or it can be factory modified to handle an open-end filmstrip. The random access filmstrip projector is pictured in Figure 65.

FIG. 64b. Mast Random Access Slide Projector Control Unit Model 136.
(Courtesy of Mast Development Company)

Filmstrips vs. Slides. While filmstrips and slides project quite similarly on the screen, they are different in their physical construction. When deciding which of the two forms of still projection to use, it is necessary to consider the advantages of each and choose the one which appears to be the more satisfactory in the light of the various factors involved.

Advantages of the filmstrip. One advantage of the filmstrip is that it is less bulky than a corresponding number of 35mm slides. To illustrate this, Figure 65 is a photograph of a 50-frame filmstrip and the same number of slides. Slides stored in projection magazines would, of course, be more bulky.

This is a factor of cost when mailing materials and a factor of convenience and sometimes cost when storing them. The filmstrip

FIG. 65. Mast Random Access Projector (Filmstrip) Model 132.
(Courtesy of Mast Development Company)

FIG. 66. Comparison of the Bulk of a 50-frame Filmstrip with 50 Slides.

consists of one long strip of film in which the individual pictures are maintained in the same relationship to each other. This means that once the strip is placed properly into the projector, individual frames cannot get out of order, upside down, or lost. This can make for a smoother presentation because the instructor's mind can be on the material that he is trying to put across rather than making sure one-by-one that each slide goes into the machine properly. In situations where the frames must be changed quickly to attain the proper pacing, the filmstrip advance can be operated more rapidly than slides can be changed, even with an automatic slide projector. Magazines for the slides help to overcome some of the fumbling, but they have the disadvantage of having to be changed every 36 or 40 slides, while the filmstrip can be as long as is necessary to tell the story. The filmstrips are more widely used in educational, sales, and training situations because of the advantages that they have. This, in itself, is another reason to use them because the use of slides would be out of the ordinary and the projectionists might not be set up to handle them. Finally, filmstrips are less expensive than slides when the distribution is rather wide. The reproduction costs are less because it is faster and easier to leave the individual frames attached in a long strip than to cut them apart and mount each one.

Advantages of slides. Of course slides have certain advantages over filmstrips or they would not be used. In the first place, the standard area for a 35mm slide is twice that of the standard filmstrip frame. This means that for the same size image on the screen, the slide will be twice as bright as the filmstrip frame; or conversely, the projected slide can be twice as large as the filmstrip and still be just as bright. Quality of the image is a factor of the degree of enlargement. Here, too, the slide has an advantage over the filmstrip frame.

While the order of a filmstrip is fixed by the producer, slides can be arranged in any order which suits the person doing the presentation. They can be rearranged for presentation to different groups. Obsolete material can be deleted from the group of slides and new material added without disturbing the remaining material.

Visual materials intended for inclusion in a filmstrip must be oriented horizontally because the filmstrip format is horizontal. In order to obtain a vertical format part of the frame must be lost. Slides in the 35mm size can be set up either horizontally or vertically according to the demands of the material being pictured. This provides more freedom and flexibility in preparing the visuals.

Finally, for small numbers of release prints, slides are less expensive. Color transparencies can be used directly in the slide projector without further treatment. Duplicate slides may be obtained from photographic processors rather inexpensively in medium size lots. The filmstrip is not generally economically feasible for small quantities because of the expense of the color negative which is made from the individual slides before the production of the filmstrip.

It is possible to cut a filmstrip into individual frames and mount them as slides. From then on it would be handled and used as a set of slides, and material can be rearranged, deleted, or added to.

The use of magazines to hold the slides overcomes some of the drawbacks of their use. Once they are in the magazines there is no concern about the order in which they will appear or that they will somehow get in the projector upside down or backwards. There remains the problem of changing the magazines, although certain brands of magazines are made so that they can be hooked together to avoid a break in the showing. The smoothest way of accomplishing the changing of magazines is to have someone stationed at the projector to replace the old one as soon as it is finished.

Special Techniques for Filmstrips and Slides. A still picture presentation can be very effectively tied in with a recorded narration, Unlike a sound motion picture in which the audio and video signals remain in synchronization throughout the projection, some method must be used to advance the frame at the proper time in the narration. Three methods of accomplishing this are in general use. One method is to provide the projectionist with a printed copy of the narration. Frame changes are indicated on the script and the projectionist changes the frame manually at the indicated time. The disadvantage of this method is that the person operating the projector must give the script his undivided attention. If he should lose his place, the picture on the screen would not correspond to the narration being heard at the time. If the filmstrip has frame numbers printed in one corner, it can easily be gotten back to the proper synchronization.

A second method of indicating the time to change the picture is to have a musical sound to indicate the advance. This rather common solution to the problem has two obvious drawbacks. In the first place, the "ping" can be rather annoying to people watching the filmstrip. They may find themselves listening for the change signal rather than concentrating on the oral part of the message. The second objection is that if the audio and visual parts of the filmstrip once get separated it is difficult to get them back together.

The third method of advancing the film at the proper time is to have a note of a certain pitch occur in the sound track at the proper time. This note is below the ability of the human ear to hear, but the pickup of the projector is sensitive to it. When it occurs, the changing mechanism is activated and the projector moves the filmstrip to the next frame. This system does not intrude an audible note onto the sound track, and a change cue cannot be missed through inattention. The drawback, of course, is the fact that the projector must be constructed for this sort of operation, and this kind of projector is considerably more expensive than one without this feature. Also, the record must be one which contains the proper tone signals to operate the automatic changer. A machine of this sort was pictured in Figure 62.

Continuous Automatic Projector. As a part of an exhibit or a store display it is occasionally desirable to display a series of film-strip frames or slides repeatedly and without attention. Various models of slide projectors operate with different methods of storing and projecting slides up to a total of about 100 different ones. Some of these machines operate a sound track with automatic cueing of the slide changes. Some models are made to sit on a table and pro-ject either onto a standard screen or use rear-screen projection. Others have a cabinet that stands on the floor with the screen at eye level to catch the viewer's attention. Some cycle continuously while others shut off at the end of the presentation and turn on when someone presses a button, interrupts a light beam trained on a photo electric cell, or steps on a pressure mat.

Using Slides to Illustrate a Talk. Normally, we think of a set of slides or a filmstrip as carrying the bulk of the message that we wish to put across, with the verbal component more or less auxiliary— to fill in the gaps of visual coverage. It occasionally happens that one is called upon to deliver a talk before his business or professional group. In this case, the oral part will probably carry the message, but it can perhaps be made much more effective if certain points are illustrated with appropriate slides. There are several purposes in using slides of this nature:

1. To help emphasize a point by presenting it visually as well as verbally.
2. To show the physical appearance of an object otherwise described verbally.
3. To show detailed material that would be too difficult to under-stand without the visual presentation.

In order to give the slides as much impact as possible in sup-porting the verbal material, these suggestions should be kept in mind:

1. Do not include too much data on one slide. The material is much

more easily assimilated if presented in small bits. Information that would cause overcrowding is better carried over to another slide.

2. Use no more detail than is necessary to convey the point. As the audience is viewing the major points, the speaker can be "hanging the meat on the bones," or filling in the details of the subject.

3. Get rid of the slide when you have finished with it. A slide that is left on the screen after the material on it has been discussed detracts from the impact of the points talked about later. The audience wonders why the material was left on and whether you are coming back to it.

What should one do if he has only two or three slides that he would like to interject into the speech at widely separated points? The best method is to have someone to control the room lights and another to turn the projector off and on at the appropriate times. The signal to them should not be obvious to the rest of the group, so that slipping into and out of the slide projection can be as smooth and unobtrusive as possbile.

Preparation of Slide Sets and Filmstrips

Standard Sizes. Of the many sizes of cameras that have been developed over the years, only certain ones have become the standard sizes for projection. Thus a few sizes of projectors will handle most transparency sizes.

Slides. The standard sizes of slides are determined by the size of the mounts in which the slides are placed for projection, rather than that of the transparencies themselves.

2″ x 2″ slides are those mounted in cardboard, glass, or combination mounts that are two inches square. Three common sizes of transparencies are accommodated in this size of mount. The size that is seen most often is what is called the double frame size. This has an opening cut to fit a picture 24 x 36mm (about an inch by an inch and a half), which is the size of picture that is taken by most 35mm still cameras. It is called double frame because it is twice the size of a motion picture frame on standard 35mm film. Mounts are also made to hold an 18 x 24mm single frame size picture. There are some 35mm still cameras that take a single frame size picture, but a more common use of this size mount is to modify a single frame size filmstrip by making it into a set of slides. The third size in common use is that known as the super-slide. This size utilizes 127 film instead of 35mm and yields a transparency that is 31 x 31mm.

The next standard mount size is $2\frac{3}{4}''$ x $2\frac{3}{4}''$ for the $2\frac{1}{4}''$ x $2\frac{1}{4}''$ transparencies taken on 120 or 620 film by single-lens or twin-lens reflex cameras. Photographs taken by $2\frac{1}{4}''$ x $3\frac{1}{4}''$ camera can be masked down to the square format. The larger size transparencies can be adapted by cutting away the excess area.

The Polaroid Company makes a special size of transparency film which yields a transparency $2\frac{1}{8}''$ x $2\frac{1}{8}''$ in size. The transparency is placed in a special plastic frame which is so constructed that it cannot be put into the projector incorrectly. This film, like the other Polaroid products, is made to produce the transparency within a matter of minutes after the picture has been snapped.

The $3\frac{1}{4}''$ x $4''$ slide is sometimes referred to as the "magic lantern slide" because it was one of the earliest sizes of slide format and this was its early name. This size of slide can be masked down to suit the size of transparency that is to be projected. Naturally, however, it should be used with transparencies that fill all or nearly all of the available area. The large size of this slide makes it ideal to use in an auditorium or other large space where it is necessary to have a large, bright image on the screen. Another advantage of this size is that it is possible to utilize handmade materials. One drawback to the use of this type of slide is that since it is rectangular rather than square, it can be placed in the projector only one way—horizontally. Thus every transparency must be organized in the horizontal format if it is to utilize the full slide area. The Polaroid Company makes a transparency size and plastic mount for the transparency with an overall size of $3\frac{1}{4}''$ x $4''$.

Slides or transparencies are also made in larger sizes—$7''$ x $7''$, $8''$ x $8''$, or $10''$ x $10''$. These are intended for use on another type of machine—the overhead projector—which will be discussed in chapter twelve.

Filmstrips. Filmstrips are made with two sizes of pictures, single frame and double frame. As described above, the pictures are 18 x 24mm and 24 x 36mm respectively. The vast majority of filmstrips are made in the smaller single frame size, although a few are issued in the double frame form. Since the double frame filmstrip pictures are made in a horizontal format, as is the case with the single frame filmstrips, the film must be run through the projector horizontally instead of vertically. This means that the projector must be made with the film framing and advancing mechanism that can be rotated through 90° to accommodate this direction of travel. Most filmstrip projectors are capable of this, but there are some that are not. In a case of this sort, it might be necessary to cut the frames apart and mount them as slides for individual projection.

Steps in the Preparation of Slides. The preparation of slides for communication, whether they carry the bulk of the message or just point up the major points, is not a difficult operation. We shall consider each of the types of slides individually.

Color Photographic Slides. The most commonly used color film for the preparation of transparencies is the type known as color reversal film. This type of film (of which typical brand names are Kodachrome, Ektachrome, and Anscochrome) is processed in such a way that the colors and tonal values on the original film correspond to those of the scene photographed. The same piece of film that was exposed in the camera comes back ready to be projected. The 35mm film is generally cut into individual pictures and mounted in cardboard mounts for projection unless the processor is asked to dc otherwise. Larger film sizes are generally returned in individual acetate sleeves which protect the transparencies until they are mounted. Little or no adjustment of the color balance can be made by the processor, so it is imperative that the correct type of light be used or that it be filtered to bring it to the correct color temperature at the time exposure. Duplicates of the transparencies can be made by a processor to provide additional slides. Duplicates can also be made locally by the use of a machine such as the Heiland Repronar (see Fig. 67). This machine makes it possible to reduce double frame to single frame, enlarge single frame to double frame, modify the color balance, and increase or decrease the density, all while copying.

Color or black-and-white prints can be made from the transparencies if the need for them should arise.

The color negative materials (such as Kodacolor) involve an extra step, but the advantages may outweigh the extra trouble and cost. After the film is exposed in the camera it is developed to form a color negative. In the color negative, the colors as well as the lights and darks are reversed. This negative is used as any other negative would be to print a positive. The positive, either on paper for a color print or on another piece of film for a color transparency, has the characteristics of the original scene. Only one type of film is used since the color balance can be corrected at the time of printing. Black-and-white prints or transparencies can also be made from the color negative.

Black-and-white photographic slides. These slides can be photo-

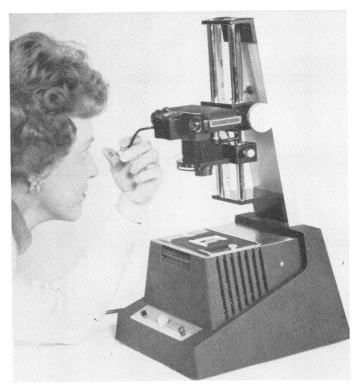

FIG. 67. Heiland Repronar Color Transparency Copying Unit.

graphed on ordinary black-and-white film and printed onto another piece of film, resulting in a positive transparency which is mounted in a slide binder and projected. Black-and-white reversal film is also available to make a positive image on the original film which was exposed in the camera. While this has the advantage of requiring only one piece of film, it also has a disadvantage of requiring an almost perfect exposure. Where the negative-positive process permits correction of overexposure or underexposure, the reversal film does not permit this. Also, additional copies are difficult to obtain.

When copying printed materials it is often desirable to use the negative as the slide. A slide that is predominately clear will cause a glare on the screen that makes the printed material hard to read. Use of the negative provides white letters against a black background and is much easier to read. When preparing slides from contrasty materials such as printed matter, one of the special high-contrast films (Kodalith, Reprolith, Ortho A) will give good crisp reproduction of the material.

Polaroid equipment, as mentioned earlier in the chapter, enables one to shoot and project a transparency in a matter or three minutes or so. After exposure in the Polaroid Land Camera, the transparency is allowed to develop in the camera just as an ordinary Polaroid print. After development, the transparency is placed in a solution to harden the emulsion to prevent it from being scratched easily. Upon removal from the solution (called Dippit), the transparency is placed in a snap-together plastic frame and is ready for projection.

Handmade slide can sometimes achieve results that photographic slides cannot, or at least can do it quickly and with less bother. Handmade slides can be prepared by drawing with pencil or ink on a $3\frac{1}{4}$ x 4 inch piece of etched glass or frosted acetate. Transparent colors—pencil, India inks, special transparent crayons, colored acetate with a pressure adhesive, or special slide inks can give the additional impact of color. Coating with a plastic spray makes the base material transparent and also protects the image from damage. Typewritten messages are prepared by typing on a piece of thin, transparent, colored plastic (preferably colored to prevent glare) that has been placed between two sheets of carbon paper with the carbon side inward. The carbon will come off on the plastic on the front and back and will be legible on the screen. Slides can also be made in silhouette form by cutting out a paper picture showing the outlines clearly or by using any flat, opaque object. The ease of preparation of these handmade slides makes their use practical in many communication situations.

The question of whether or not to mount slides in glass is one which is answered by the types of slides that one has and the conditions under which they are to be shown. Some years ago it was common practice to mount all slides that were used often. Otherwise, constant handling would result in fingerprints, scratches, and smudges that would reduce the quality of the projected image. Most projectors in current use are built so that they can hold slides in magazines. Figure 68 shows such a magazine with several slides in it. The slides are stored in the magazine and are removed from it and retured to it by the projector. Thus the magazine protects the slides from handling, dust, and the other normal hazards.

Glass mounts do, of course, protect the slide and prevent possible buckling in the heat of the projection lamp. Most modern projectors have efficient cooling systems that prevent the unmounted slide from

FIG. 68. Slide Magazine.

buckling, so this is not as much a problem as it once was. There are times when the extra expense of mounting the slides would be justified.

1. When the slide is an original and very valuable.
2. When the slides will be rearranged often, thus necessitating individual handling.
3. When the individual slide must remain on the screen for a long period of time.
4. Whenever the slide is larger than the 35mm double-frame size.

Steps in the Preparation of a Filmstrip. The first steps in photographing a filmstrip are the same as for a slide set. If the filmstrip is to be in color, a series of slides is prepared and edited so to contain the information desired, and to present information in the correct order of presentation. Titles are prepared and photographed so that they can be used separately or superimposed over appropriate frames. The slides, with the necessary directions, are sent to a color processor who specializes in the preparation of color filmstrips. The processor prepares a color negative (reducing the material to single frame size if this is to be a single frame filmstrip), masking and color balancing the individual frames so that they will fit well together. Cropping, insertion of frame numbers, and combining two or more photos in one frame can be accomplished at this time. When the negative is complete, the processor runs off several color positive answer prints, varying the density and color balance slightly so that the customer may pick out the print that suits his needs best. When the customer has selected the most suitable answer print, the processor runs off the number of release prints that have been ordered. The prints may be delivered all on one large reel or they may be separated into individual filmstrips and placed in cans. This latter operation adds to the cost of the filmstrip and can be done by the customer if he has the personnel.

Black-and-white filmstrips can be made by the company rather inexpensively. The number of copies that can be made without disrupting the operation of the photo section is somewhat limited, however. If a large number of duplicates is necessary, it would undoubtedly be better to have a processor produce the release prints.

After the negatives have been made, they are enlarged to the proportions of a standard 18 x 24 frame size Any touchup work, modifications, or titles can be placed on these prints. The next step is to rephotograph the print, reducing it to the single frame size. If a single-frame 35mm camera can be obtained, there is little problem. The material is simply photographed frame by frame to make the negative. If only a double frame camera is available, the prints are photographed two at a time with a black bar across the middle to divide the two pictures. Care should be taken so see that the negative is evenly exposed so that all of the frames of the filmstrip can be printed with the same exposure. Exposure of the print can be made frame by frame in a special contact printer or the entire strip can be exposed at once by using a contact frame the length of the filmstrip and with a pressure back to hold the negative and the film in good contact during the exposure.

It is possible to make either a color or a black-and-white filmstrip directly in the camera. This involves shooting each frame in the proper sequence, including superimposures and any other desired special effects. It is likely to involve a great deal of work and inconvience that will offset any saving that might accrue. It is most effective when a person desires just one color filmstrip.

Summary

Projection of still pictures is usually accomplished by the use of slides or filmstrips. Still pictures are sometimes preferred over motion pictures because they permit more flexibility in presentation and allow for adjustment to suit the individual audience. They permit variation of the speed of presentation and the content of the narration. Discussion by the group can be carried on while the picture is being projected. Reference back to earlier parts of the material can be easily accomplished by flipping back the filmstrip or by putting the correct slide in position. Materials and equipment are simpler, less costly, and more easily portable than those for motion pictures.

Filmstrips and slides each have certain advantages and disadvantages. The advantages are less pronounced because in slide magazines slides can be handled almost as easily as a filmstrip and a filmstrip can be cut into individual frames which are then mounted into slides.

These materials can be accompanied by a narration to be read aloud by the leader or a recorded narration with an audible or silent signal for changing the filmstrip frame.

Contents of a still picture projection unit will vary according to whether the visuals are intended to carry the bulk of the message or are merely to illustrate the information that is given orally.

A filmstrip normally originates as a set of slides. After editing, the slides are duplicated onto a single strip of 35mm film. A filmstrip can be prepared by photographing the material in order, directly in the camera, but this is often very inconvenient.

BIBLIOGRAPHY

American Standards Association, *American Standard Specification for Slidefilm Projection*, New York, American Standards Association, 1945

Brown, James W., and Richard B. Lewis (Ed), *AV Instructional Materials Manual*, Second Edition, New York, McGraw-Hill Book Company, 1964, 188 pp.
    Exercise Thirty-three Filmstrips
    Exercise Forty-three 3¼ by 4 Inch Slide Projectors
    Exercise Forty-four Filmstrips and 2 by 2 Inch Slide Projectors
    Exercise Fotry-eight Simple Equipment Maintenance.

Brown, James W., Richard B. Lewis, and Fred F. Harcleroad, *AV Instruction Materials and Methods*, Second Edition, New York, McGraw-Hill Book Company, 1964, 592 pp.
    Chap. 7 Filmstrips and Photographic Slides
    Reference Section
        2 by 2 Inch Slide Projectors, pp. 541-542
        Lantern-slide Projectors, pp. 543-544
        Filmstrip Projectors, pp. 544-545
        Projection-Equipment Principles, pp. 535-538

Kemp, Jerrold E., *Planning and Producing Audiovisual Materials*, San Francisco, California, Chandler Publishing Company, 1963, 169 pp.
    Part Three Producing Your Audiovisual Materials
        2. Slide Series
        3. Filmstrips

Dale, Edgar, *Audio-Visual Methods in Teaching*, Revised Edition, New York, The Dryden Press, 1954, 534 pp.
    Chap. 16 Still Pictures

De Kieffer, Robert, and Lee W. Cochran, *Manual of Audio-Visual Techniques,* Englewood Cliffs, New Jersey, Prentice-Hall, Inc., 1955, 220 pp.
 Unit Three Projected Materials and Equipment
  Slides and Slide Projectors, pp. 97-103
  Filmstrips and Filmstrip Projectors, pp. 104-110

Eastman Kodak Company Publications
 Adventures in Indoor Color Slides
 Adventures in Outdoor Color Slides
 Black and White Transparencies with Kodak Panatomic-X 35mm
  (Single copy free upon request)
 Simple Ways to Make Title Slides and Filmstrips
  (Single copy free upon request)
 Planningboards

Eboch, Sidney C., *Operating Audio-Visual Equipment,* San Francisco, California, Howard Chandler, Publisher, 1960, 73 pp.
 Chap. III Still Picture Projection

Educators Guide to Free Filmstrips, Educators Progress Service, Wandolph, Wisconsin (Published yearly)

Finn, James D., *The Audio-Visual Equipment Manual,* New York, The Dryden Press, 1957, 361 pp.
 Section 1 Projectors
  Filmstrip and 2″ x 2″ Slide Projectors, pp. 85-129
  Standard Slide Projectors, pp. 130-150
  Good Projection Practice, pp. 189-220

Haas, Kenneth B., and Harry Q. Packer, *Preparation and Use of Audio-Visual Aids,* Englewood Cliffs, New Jersey, Prentice-Hall, Inc., 1955, 381 pp.
 Chap. 2 Discussional Filmstrip and Sound Slidefilm
 Chap. 3 Teaching Slides

Holland, Ben F., Horace C. Hartsell, and Raymond L. Davidson, *Audio-Visual Materials and Devices,* Lubbock, Texas, Rodgers Litho, 1958, 157 pp.
 Chap. 5 Horizontal Slide Projection
 Chap. 7 Teaching with Filmstrips

Kinder, James S., *Audio-Visual Materials and Techniques,* 2nd Edition, New York, American Book Company, 1959, 592 pp.
 Chap. 5 Slides and Filmstrips

Lord, John, and Robert Larson, *Handbook for Production of Filmstrips and Records,* St. Charles, Illinois, Du Kane Corporation, 1962

Sands, Lester B., *Audio-Visual Procedures in Teaching,* New York, The Ronald Press Company, 1956, 670 pp.
 Chap. 17 The Filmstrip
 Chap. 18 The Two-Inch Slide
 Chap. 19 The Four-Inch Slide
 Chap. 21 Three-Dimensional Pictures

Wittich, Walter Arno, and Charles Francis Schuller, *Audio-Visual Materials:*

Their Nature and Use, Third Edition, New York, Harper & Brothers, 1962, 500 pp.

      Chap. 12 Still Projection

Woefel, Normal, *Amateur Filmstrip Production,* Columbus, Ohio, Ohio State University, 1958

MOTION PICTURES

Photographic Slides for Instruction, Bloomington, Indiana, Indiana University, 1956, Color, Sound, 10 minutes.

How to Make Handmade Lantern Slides, Bloomington, Indiana, Indiana University, 1947, color, sound, 14 minutes.

FILMSTRIPS

Handmade Lantern Slides, Columbus, Ohio, Teaching Aids Laboratory, Ohio State University

CHAPTER 12

OVERHEAD PROJECTION

What Is Overhead Projection?

Overhead projection is a method of providing a large, bright image which appears above and behind the speaker. Because of the focal length of the lens system and the brightness of the light source, a vivid image can be obtained at a short distance from the projector and in a fully lighted room.

In construction, the overhead projector differs from other projectors in that the path of the light through the machine is not straight, but passes through two right-angle turns. Two major types of overhead projectors have been developed. The first is typified by the Beseler Vu-Graph. The light source is a 750 or 1000-watt bulb located in the base of the projector at the opposite end from the operator. A fan system removes the heat generated by the light in such a way that it does not affect the transparency or the operator. Light from the bulb is reflected back toward the operator where it strikes a mirror set at a 45° angle. The mirror directs the light upward through the stage, where the transparency is located. The light is concentrated before it passes through the stage by a condensing lens. The transparency selectively transmits or absorbs the light coming to it. The light then passes upward to the projection lens which is mounted vertically on an arm extending above the machine. After the light passes through the projection lens it strikes a front surface mirror which sends the light to the screen. Only two adjustments are necessary besides the off-on switch. A knob adjusts the height of the head to focus the lens and a lever tips the top mirror to raise or lower the image on the screen.

The second type of projector is typified by certain models of the Thermo-Fax line. The light from the projection lamp is reflected upward by a concave mirror which also concentrates the light that is to pass through the transparency. The front-surface mirror, mounted on the vertical arm, reflects the light forward to the projection lens and from there to the screen. The image is raised or lowered on the screen by tipping the entire machine.

Figure 69 illustrates the two types of overhead projector.

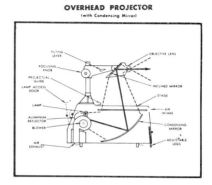

FIG. 69. Types of Overhead Projector. *(Courtesy of the Tecnifax Corporation)*

FIG. 70. Point Out Details with a Pencil.

The Advantages of Overhead Projection

One of the chief advantages of overhead projection is that it can be carried out in a bright, fully lighted room. Most types of projection require that the room be dark, or nearly so, for the projected image to be clearly seen. The overhead projector puts a large percentage of the available light onto the screen. In a semi-darkened room, the tendency is for the audience to relax a little too much and perhaps not give the material being presented as much attention as it should have. The normally lighted room encourages better attention.

In most types of projection, the leader must stand at the rear of the room if he is operating the projector as well as leading the discussion. This means that he is talking to the backs of the heads of his listeners, making it impossible for him to have eye contact or to watch facial expressions. If someone else operates the projector from the rear of the room, he will have to work out some system of signals to indicate when to change the visuals. This can be rather distracting to the audience. With an overhead projector, the speaker

FIG. 71. Writing on a Transparency with a Grease Pencil.

can stand at the front of the room where he can maintain eye contact with the audience and also operate the projector himself, keeping the projected image in synchronization with his remarks. He does not even have to turn away from the audience when pointing out details in the materials being shown. Using a pencil or other pointed object, the speaker merely points to the appropriate spot on the transparency (see Fig. 70). The shadow of his pointer appears on the screen to point to the particular detail on the projected image.

Only with the overhead projector does the speaker have access to the transparency while it is being shown. Thus he can manipulate the transparency in many ways during projection. He can use a grease pencil or china-marking pencil to write on the transparency, and then remove the marks easily by rubbing them with a soft cloth or a piece of facial tissue (see Fig. 71). For example, while the audience is looking at a transparency of the layout of a factory the path of the flow of materials through the plant can be drawn. This method of adding material while the group watches adds to the interest of the presentation and prevents the audience from getting

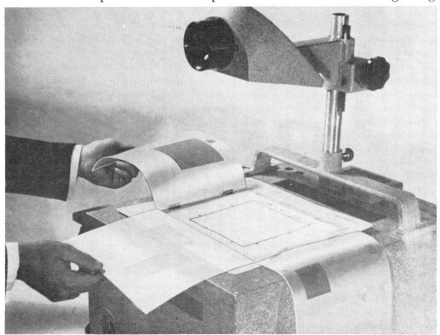

FIG. 72. Transparency with Overlays. *(Courtesy of the Tecnifax Corporation)*

ahead of you in your explanation. Any color of grease pencil will project as black, because this coloring material is opaque.

Overlays of additional sheets of acetate with additional information can be used. The basic information is put on the transparency sheet fixed to the cardboard mount. When it is time to add more details to the material, a second sheet of acetate is lowered into place. This sheet is hinged to the cardboard base with a strip of masking tape or with special hinges (see Fig. 72). As many acetate sheets as necessary can be hinged, provided that all of the layers can be kept in focus and the pile of acetate sheets does not cut down the light too much.

Material can be made to fade in or out very dramatically by placing the information on a piece of polarized acetate with another piece mounted over it so that the second piece can be revolved in place over the first (see Fig. 73). When the polarity of the two pieces are at 90° to each other no light can pass through. As one is rotated so that the polarity is parallel, the light can pass through onto the screen.

Since the stage is horizontal, specimens or small parts can be

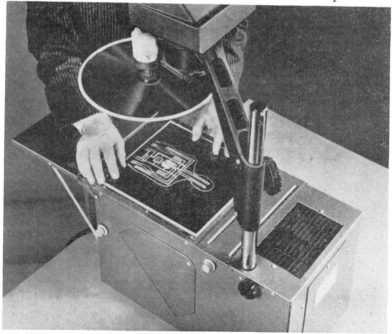

FIG. 73. Transparency with Polarized Film. *(Courtesy of Technical Animation, Inc.)*

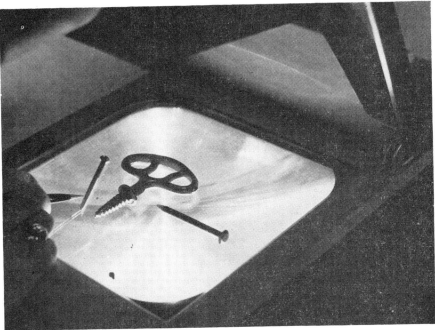

FIG. 74. Stage with Metal Parts.

placed on it and projected in silhouette onto the screen, as illustrated in Figure 74. Identification of parts and simple assembly can be demonstrated and differences between items can be pointed out.

Certain chemical reactions can be shown. For instance, Figure 75 shows how the reaction between a transparent liquid in a glass laboratory dish and an added chemical could be demonstrated. Any changes in the color or other state of the fluid can be shown to a large group.

Where size relationships are important, a transparent sheet containing grid lines may be placed under the materials. Regardless of the size to which the objects are projected, the grid lines will indicate the true size (see Fig. 76).

Working models showing mechanical actions can be made of heavy, flat plastic, as shown in Figure 77. The different parts can be made of colored plastic for easy identification.

Technamation is the name for a method of simulating action in an overhead transparency by the use of polarized light (see Fig. 78). A special plastic medium is placed over the top of the basic transparency. This medium, cut to fit the desired portion of the trans-

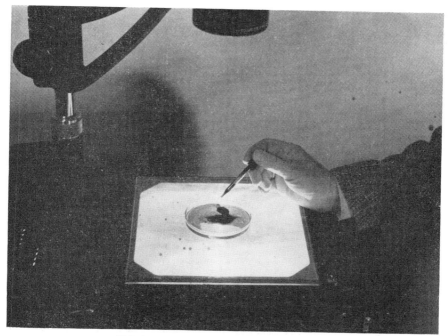

FIG. 75. Stage with Glass Laboratory Dish.

parency, is constructed so as to polarize the light differently in different parts of the transparency. Mounted just below the projection lens is a motorized disc of polarized plastic. The light passing through the polarizing plastic on the transparency and then through the turning polarizing disc causes a moving pattern of light in the appropriate part of the projected image. Available effects include linear motion in several different speeds, a turbulence effect for showing combustion or mixture, a blinking motion, gas action for simulating rising heat or jet propulsion, rotary motion for gears or wheels, and radiation motion from a central point outward. Speed of the motion can be regulated by adjusting the speed of the motor driving the revolving piece of polarized plastic at the projector lens and the direction of the action can be reversed by reversing the direction of the revolving disc.

Preparation of Overhead Transparencies

One of the advantages of the use of overhead projection materials is the fact that the transparencies are easily prepared without a great

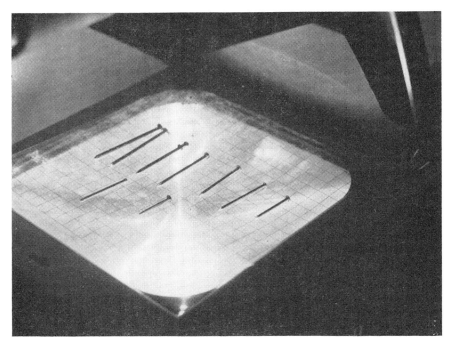

FIG. 76. Stage with Grid Lines and Opaque Objects.

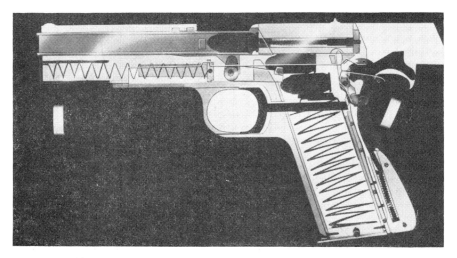

FIG. 77. Heavy Plastic Working Model of a .45 Caliber Automatic Pistol.
(Courtesy of the Charles Beseler Company)

FIG. 78. Technamation Kit.

deal of equipment or expense. While this is not intended to be a how-to-do-it type of discussion, the different techniques will be mentioned and described briefly. The bibliography at the end of this chapter contains a list of sources of information of a more detailed nature.

Hand Prepared Materials. The simplest techniques in the preparation of the overhead transparencies use handdrawn illustrative material. The basic method is to prepare the illustration in the proper size on a piece of paper, tape the acetate into place, and trace the material on the acetate.

Black India ink forms sharp, crisp outlines for drawing and lettering. Colored India inks will project in their true colors on the screen. These colored inks are satisfactory for lines or for small areas of color. They are not suitable for large colored areas because it is difficult to get the ink to dry smoothly. Since the acetate is non-porous, the ink is not absorbed by it as it is by paper. Instead, it must remain on the surface until it evaporates. Being still in liquid form, it tends to run down into puddles and dry in streaks.

Plastic inks which contain a solvent can be obtained. As they

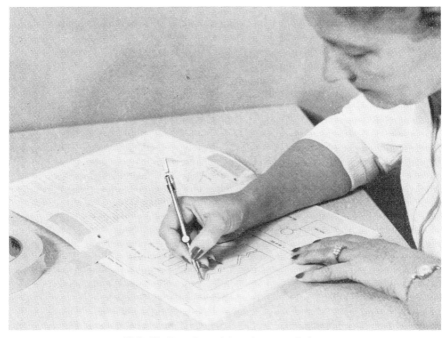

FIG. 79. Drawing with a Compass Point.

are applied to the acetate, the solvent dissolves part of the base
and the ink becomes an integral part of the base material. Transparencies subject to a good deal of handling and abrasion will last
longer if prepared with plastic inks rather than India inks.

Outlines that are more precise and clear-cut than those produced by India or plastic ink may be made by a scratching technique. An awl, large heavy needle, compass point, or any other heavy
tool with a fairly sharp point can be used for drawing by scratching the acetate deeply (see Fig. 79). The scratch is not very notice-
able when viewed directly, but shows up well upon projection.

Grease or china-marking pencil may be used to prepare temporary materials or to add information to a transparency while it
is being projected. After projection, the grease pencil material may
be wiped away, leaving the more permanent drawing for resue.

Smooth colored areas may be obtained on hand-made transparencies by use of sheets of colored transparent plastic that have
a pressure-sensitive adhesive on the back (see Fig. 80). The plastic
is cut roughly to shape, lifted off its backing, and placed in position

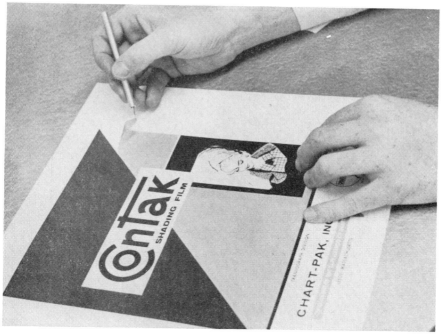

FIG. 80. Coloring an Area with Transparent Plastic. *(Courtesy of Chart-Pak, Inc.)*

on the transparency. After it is in position, the excess is cut away and the material is rubbed down into place. Increased rubbing will cause it to adhere more tightly and become more transparent.

Plastic sheets are also provided in various patterns of dots, lines, cross hatching, etc. These can be used to differentiate between parts of a drawing and can be used separately, in conjunction with each other, and with the colored plastic.

Another method of applying color smoothly is to use an airbrush (see Fig. 81). This method involves the use of compressed air to break the transparent liquid color into tiny droplets that are distributed evenly over the transparency. Areas that should not be colored are protected by paper covering the surface. The size of the area covered by the spray is determined by the adjustment of the airbrush and its distance from the surface.

Chapter 11 discussed the use of a thin sheet of plastic and two sheets of carbon paper to type slides for the $3\frac{1}{4}$ x 4 inch projector. The same method can be used for large transparencies for the overhead projector. The chief difficulty is the small size of the type in

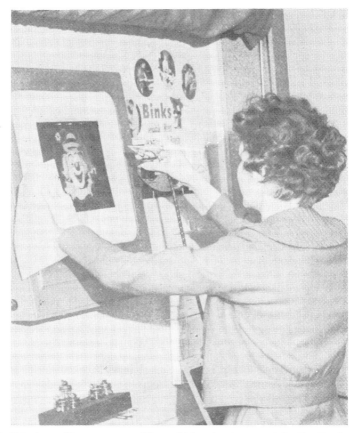

FIG. 81. Coloring a Transparency with an Airbrush. *(Courtesy of the Tecnifax Corporation)*

relation to the whole screen. This makes it rather difficult to read the typewritten material from the normal viewing distances, partly because the bright white area causes a glare. Use of a colored, rather than clear, sheet of plastic will help considerably. An even better solution is to use a special sheet of plastic which has an even coating of a material similar to the carbon on carbon paper. When this material is placed between two sheets of typing paper and typed on, the "carbon" comes off onto the paper and leaves a clear place on the plastic (see Fig. 82). When projected onto the screen, the typing appears as light against a black background. Although the letters are no larger than those obtained by typing on a piece of clear plastic, they are more legible.

FIG. 82. Preparing Carbon Film.

Another use for this carbon film material is to make drawings while projecting. This utilizes what is known as the "dot-dusting technique." A picture with rather simple outlines is chosen. With a sharp needle punch a series of holes along the lines of the picture. Place the picture on top of the carbon film—carbon side up—and pat a chalk eraser or other source of fine white dust over the picture. Where the holes have been punched, some dust will come through onto the carbon surface, giving an outline of the picture (see Fig. 83). Place the carbon film on the projector stage, turn on the light, and with a stylus or a hard pencil draw lines connecting the dots. As you do so, the line will appear to grow on the screen, giving quite an unusual effect.

A variation of the hand preparation of overhead materials is the use of a spirit duplicator for making the transparency. A sheet of frosted acetate can be run through the duplicator and will pick up the dye image that forms the spirit duplicator copy. After the spirit fluid has dried, the frosted surface can be sprayed with a clear plastic spray, which will make it transparent. This method of pre-

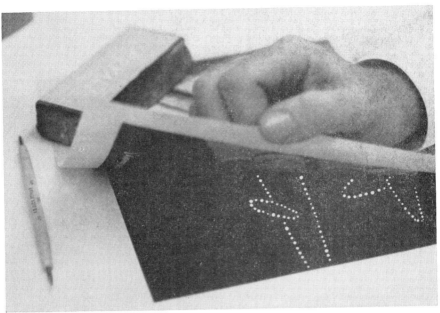

FIG. 83. Dot-dusted Carbon Film.

paring the transparency is particularly effective when you want to hand out a copy of the material that has been projected.

If many copies of a transparency are to be prepared, the silk screen method may be used. This method is pictured in Figure 84. A silk screen is prepared by stretching a piece of special silk cloth tightly over a frame. Attached to the silk is a stencil which covers the silk in areas where the printing medium should be held back and does not cover it in areas where the color should come through. The transparent ink is placed on top of the screen and the sheet of acetate is placed beneath it. The color is dragged across the silk with a squeegee. Where the stencil covers the silk it holds back the color and where there is no stencil the color passes through the silk and onto the acetate. Any number of colors may be applied in successive coatings and rather intricate designs may be developed. The preparation of a silk screen is an involved process, and is feasible only if a rather large number of copies is desired.

Photographic Materials. By means of the photographic process, materials can be quickly and accurately copied and reproduced for use on the overhead projector.

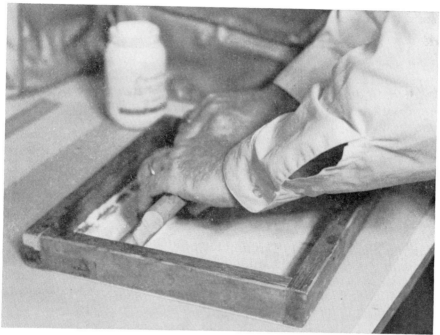

FIG. 84. Printing with a Silk Screen.

Color transparencies may be made by photographing the subject on large sheets of color reversal film. The material is ready to mount and project as soon as it is received from the processor. Or the material may be photographed on color negative film. Positive color prints returned by the processor can be examined to determine which ones are suitable for projection, and positive transparencies of the size desired can be made.

Black-and-white transparencies can be made very easily from black-and-white negatives by the in-plant photographic department. The process consists merely of enlarging onto a sheet of positive film from a negative. Black-and-white transparencies can be colored by using transparent oil colors. Natural coloring of a scene, however, is generally not too successful because any slight errors or imperfections in the coloring are magnified greatly on the screen, but general area colorings for identification purposes work quite well.

If printed or other written materials is to be reproduced for overhead projection, the high-contrast photographic method should be considered. It involves the use of a special high-contrast film, such as Eastman Kodalith, Ansco Reprolith, or Du Pont Ortho A. These films are designed to give solid blacks and clear whites, with no shades of gray between them. The images are very sharp and can be enlarged to many times their original size with little or no apparent loss in definition. After the negative is made, it can be printed to a positive or projected in its negative form. In general, printed materials are just as acceptable to the audience in their negative form and the projection of the white letters on the dark background is easier to read than the reverse because of the flare that is involved when the screen is predominantly white. Negative high-contract transparencies can be colored very easily by placing sheets of colored plastic over the proper areas or by coloring the clear lines with transparent photo colors.

Diazo Process. Many business organizations use diazo machines for the reproduction of business forms, blueprints, and other materials in their normal routines. These machines can be very easily used to prepare transparencies for use in the overhead projector. If such a machine is not already in operation, a substitute can be built at very little expense.

The diazo process uses one of the diazo salts and a coupler (the particular coupler depending upon the final color desired) mixed with a stabilizer and coated on a surface—in this case the surface of a piece of acetate. The diazo salt and coupler molecules will form a brilliant color dye when united. They are prevented from coupling by the stablizer, which is an acid. When ammonia vapor, which is alkaline, comes into contact with the emulsion, it neutralizes the acid stabilizer and the diazo salt and the coupler unite, forming the azo dye image. The diazo salt is subject to rapid deterioration by ultra-violet light prior to development. Where the material has been exposed to the ultra-violet light, it will remain clear upon development. Areas that have been protected from exposure will become colored when developed.

A diazo transparency is prepared from a master. This master must be transparent or translucent. Tracing paper makes an excellent master. Information can be typed or drawn on the tracing paper. Ink, pencil, and opaque materials of various sorts will block out the ultra-violet light while the rest of the paper allows it to pass through.

Exposure of the diazo foil is accomplished by putting the master, diazo foil, and backing sheet together under pressure in a frame that allows light to pass through the master to the foil. If a machine is not available in the organization, an exposure frame can be constructed from a picture frame that has a solid back and a device to apply sufficient pressure to keep the materials in contact (see Fig. 85). ultra-violet light source can be a mercury vapor lamp, an ultra-violet tube, a sun-lamp or the sun itself.

FIG. 85. Frame for Exposing Diazo Foil.

After exposure, the foil is exposed to ammonia vapor. A developing jar can be made from a wide-mouth one-gallon jar (see Fig. 86). A pad of blotting paper or paper towel will hold the ammonia and allow it to evaporate gradually. After the foil has been exposed, place it in the jar and replace the lid. The image can be seen developing as the ammonia vapor reacts with the stablizer and allows the dye to form.

Diazo transparent foil can be obtained in a wide variety of colors, plus black. Presentations may be designed to use overlays of various colors, with each color layer bringing out new information.

A moist process makes it possible to have more than one color on one foil. Exposure to ultra-violet light is the same as for the dry

FIG. 86. Ammonia Vapor Developing Jar.

materials. The coupler is applied after exposure. The color desired in the particular area of the transparency determines which coupler should be used. The coupler is applied with a brush or a piece of cotton. Avoid letting the couplers run together. If the transparency is to have different colors in close proximity or intersecting lines in different colors, it is best to use separate overlays for each color.

Reflex Processes. The reflex processes are particularly useful for making an overhead transparency from material on an opaque base, or where other material is printed on the back of the sheet to be reproduced. In neither case can the original be used as a master for the diazo process described above.

In the reflex process, the sensitive material is placed in contact with the material to be reproduced. Light is directed *through* the sensitive material from the back. A white original will reflect the light back to the sensitive material, and a black one will absorb the light. The reflex material can detect the difference between where the light is and is not reflected. Further processing brings out the image as either a positive or a negative image and on either a transparent, translucent, or opaque base, depending upon the variety of reflex material chosen. The transparent materials can be used on the projector and the translucent materials can be used as diazo masters.

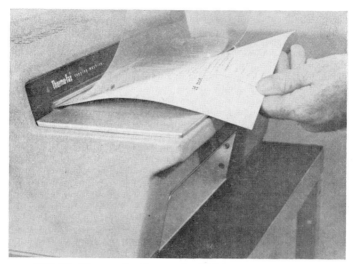

FIG. 87. Thermo-Fax Process for Making a Transparency.

Two brands of materials for the reflex process are the Thermo-Fax materials (see Fig. 87) which utilize heat generated by a special electric lamp to both expose and develop the image, and Autopositive paper and film which are exposed by the reflex method and then developed and fixed in photographic solutions.

A second Thermo-Fax system for producing transparencies is their Deluxe Transparency Maker which consists of two units as shown in Figure 87. The intermediate sheet (a thin piece of pink plastic) is placed in position over the material to be copied—even material in a book. A special translucent glass plate goes over the intermediate sheet to hold it in tight contact with the information to be reproduced. The unit at the left is then placed over the glass plate and a bright light inside is turned on for the time necessary to make the exposure. After exposure, the intermediate sheet is placed under a sheet of the projection transparency material and the two are put on the unit at the right. This is a heating unit that develops the transparency. The development process can be watched and stopped when the transparency reaches the proper density.

Technamation. To gain the advantages of simulated movement which Technamation materials can give, one starts with the basic transparency on high-contrast film or with a drawing on clear acetate. The Technamation material is applied to the base by means of the pressure adhesive on the back. The effect will be increased if the

FIG. 88. Thermo-Fax Deluxe Transparency Maker.

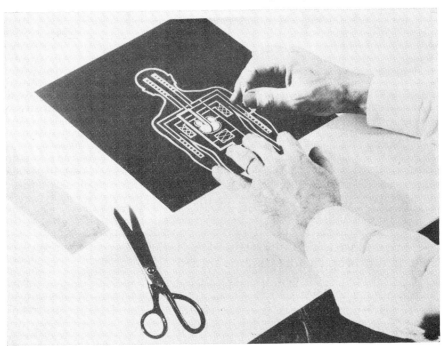

FIG. 89. Technamation. *(Courtesy of Technical Animation, Inc.)*

use of simulated motion is held to minimum consistent with accomplishing the communication purpose (see Fig. 89).

Mounting Overhead Transparencies. Mountings for transparencies must accomplish several purposes.

1. They must exclude extraneous light.
2. They must give rigidity.
3. They must protect the transparency.
4. They must provide for easy identification.
5. They must provide for the necessary manipulation of the material during projection.
6. They may provide space for notes or other information.
7. They must be convenient to use.

The basic mounts can be purchased from sources listed at the end of this chapter or they may be made from cardboard stock. One advantage of the locally prepared materials is that they can be made to fit the size and proportions of each individual transparency that you wish to use. The outside dimensions of the mount should be sufficient to cover the entire stage of the projector to block off any light that does not pass through the transparency. The outside dimensions should be standardized for efficient storage and easy retrieval from the file.

One excellent mount for a transparency is made from an ordinary manila file folder (see Fig. 90). An opening of the proper

FIG. 90. Manila Folder Transparency Mount,

size for the transparency is cut in the side having the file tab. The tab permits filing the material in a regular filing drawer, and easy location when needed. The front half of the folder helps to protect the transparency, its inner surface provides an area where notes or other data may be written, and when folded it provides a place where related information may be kept.

The transparency, or the basic transparency if there is more than one, should be mounted on the underside of the mount, using masking tape or staples on all four sides. This leaves more space for notes on the top and makes for a smoother surface. Overlays will be fastened by one edge to the mount, using masking tape or special hinges made for this purpose. If there is more than one overlay, the mounting will depend upon whether they will always be presented in the same order or if the routine will vary. If the order will always be the same and if the previous overlays are to be left in place as new ones are added, they should all be hinged on the same side. If the order will vary, or if only one overlay at a time is used, they should be hinged at the different sides up to a maximum, of

FIG. 91. Transparency Partially Covered with a Piece of Cardboard.

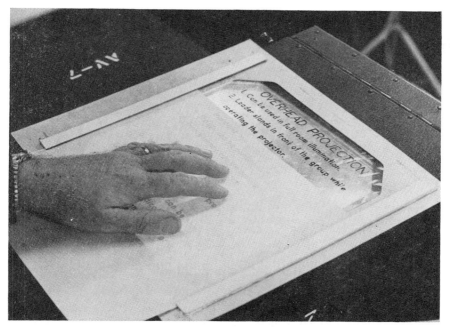

FIG. 92. Transparency with Cardboard in Grooves.

course, of four. If the combinations desired exceed four, the overlays can be separate from the basic transparency and made to fit against stops fastened to the mount. This provides for accuracy of placement of the overlays. Masking tape tabs fastened to the sides of the overlays will help to turn them over easily and without fumbling.

If the transparencies are used in the same order each time, it might be advantageous to mount them in a roll rather than in individual mounts. They can be fastened together side-by-side or end-to-end, depending upon the way that the roll mechanism operates on the particular projector. They should be fastened together with masking tape applied on both sides of where the edges meet.

Transparency sections may be cut out and placed on the background transparency and moved about on it as the need arises. If a transparent handle is left attached, the section can be moved about without showing the speaker's hand on the screen.

Projecting Overhead Transparencies

Revealing the Transparency One Part at a Time. Sometimes it

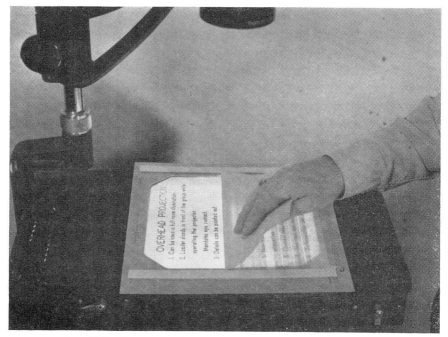

FIG. 93. Transparency with Hinged Cardboard Strips.

may not be desirable to use overlays, yet the presentation would be more effective if the audience could not see all of the material at the same time. In this case, the transparency may be partially covered until the psychological moment for disclosure (see Fig. 91).

The simplest method is to lay a piece of paper over the transparency before it is placed on the projector. As each point is discussed, the paper is slid down to disclose it.

A more permanent variation of this is to build up a groove on each side of the transparency which will hold a piece of heavy cardboard and let it slide up and down (see Fig. 92). A tab of masking tape will provide a handle for the slide and make it easier to move.

The material can also be uncovered by having a series of cardboard strips, each one as wide as the material that it is to cover, hinged together with masking tape and the whole assembly fastened to the mount at the bottom of the transparency. The pieces of cardboard are folded down to reveal the successive items of information (see Fig. 93).

Sometimes the material which is to be revealed does not appear in

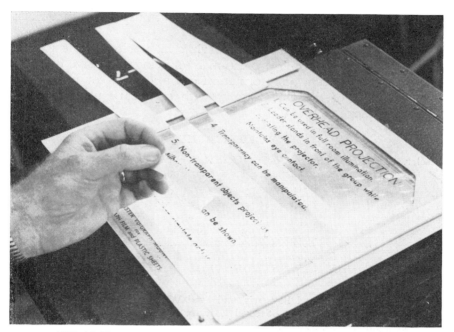

FIG. 94. Transparency with Cardboard Strips Hinged from the Side.

order on the transparency, but is scattered about on it. In this case, the information may be covered by pieces of cardboard individually hinged to the sides of the mount. The entire covering device may be of cardboard, or the part that covers the material may be cardboard and it may be fastened to a piece of acetate so that the rest of the transparency will show (see Fig. 94) .

Summary

Overhead projection is perhaps the most versatile of all of the projection devices. It enables a speaker to face his audience in a fully lighted room and at the same time control and manipulate his projected materials. Movement can be accomplished or simulated while the image is being projected. The speaker can add information as appropriate. Transparencies are inexpensive and easily prepared by hand, using India inks, plastic inks, grease pencils, scratching devices, a typewriter and carbon-coated plastic, and transparent colored plastic; photographic methods using colored or black-and-white photographs in either ordinary or high-contrast types; by the various diazo processes; reflex printing onto transparency materials; and by the Technamation process.

Mounting transparencies and overlays makes it possible to add to the information during projection by moving successive overlays into place. Revelation of information can also be accomplished by covering parts of the transparency with cardboard until you are ready to display it.

BIBLIOGRAPHY

Beseler, Charles, Company, *Vu-Graphics: A Manual on Vu-Graph Projection,* East Orange, New Jersey, Charles Beseler Company, 1952

Brown, James W., and Richard B. Lewis (Ed), *AV Instructional Materials Manual,* Second Edition, New York, McGraw-Hill Book Company, 1964, 188 pp.
    Exercise Fourteen Handmade Slides and Transparencies
    Exercise Fifteen Making Transparencies with Reproduction
        Equipment
    Exercise Forty-two Overhead Projection
    Exercise Forty-eight Simple Equipment Maintenance

Brown, James W., Richard B. Lewis, and Fred W. Harcleroad, *AV Instruction Materials and Methods,* Second Edition, New York, McGraw-Hill Book Company, 1964, 592 pp.
    Chap. 20 Using Still Pictures
    Reference Section
        Projection Equipment Principles, pp. 535-538
        Overhead Projector, pp. 540-541

Cross, A. J. Foy, and Irene F. Cypher, *Audio-Visual Education,* New York, Thomas Y. Crowell Company, 1961, 415 pp.
    Chap. 4 Projected Still Pictures

Dale, Edgar, *Audio-Visual Methods in Teaching,* Revised Edition, New York, The Dryden Press, 1954, 534 pp.
    Chap. 16 Still Pictures

De Kieffer, Robert, and Lee W. Cochran, *Manual of Audio-Visual Techniques,* Englewood Cliffs, New Jersey, Prentice-Hall, Inc., 1955, 220 pp.
    Unit Three Projected Materials and Equipment
    Overhead Projectors, pp. 111-116

Dugan, J. M., J. S. Jones, S. A. Hawk, and L. E. Walkup, *Guide to Audio-Visual Presentation,* New York, Wolf Business Publications, Inc., 1964, 149 pp.
    Preparation of Graphic Materials for Visual Presentation

Eboch, Sidney C., *Operating Audio-Visual Equipment,* San Francisco, California, Howard Chandler, Publisher, 1960, 73 pp.
    Chap. III Still Picture Projection, p. 42

Finn, James D., *The Audio-Visual Equipment Manual,* New York, The Dryden Press, 1957, 361 pp.

Section 1 Projectors
    Overhead Transparency Projectors, pp. 151-171
    Good Projection Practice, pp. 189-220

Haas, Kenneth B., and Harry Q. Packer, *Preparation and Use of Audio-Visual Aids,* Englewood Cliffs, New Jersey, Prentice-Hall, Inc., 1955, 381 pp.
    Chap. 4 Opaque and Overhead Projection

Holland, Ben F., Horace C. Hartsell, and Raymond L. Davidson, *Audio-Visual Materials and Devices,* Lubbock, Texas, Rodgers Litho, 1958, 157 pp.
    Chap. 6 Overhead Projection

Kemp, Jerrold E., *Planning and Producing Audiovisual Materials,* San Francisco, California, Chandler Publishing Company, 1963, 169 pp.
    Part Three Producing your Audiovisual Materials
        4. Transparencies for Overhead Projection

Kinder, James S., *Audio-Visual Materials and Techniques,* 2nd Edition, New York, American Book Company, 1959, 592 pp.
    Chap. 6 Opaque, Overhead, and Tachistoscopic Projection

Minor, Ed., *Simplified Techniques for Preparing Visual Instructional Materials,* New York, McGraw-Hill Book Company, 1962, 123 pp.
    Section 3 Visual Techniques
    Section 5 Photographic and Non-photographic Transparencies
        Diffusion-Transfer Transparencies, p. 86.
        Thermo-Fax Transparencies, p. 88
        Diazo Transparencies, p. 90
        Polaroid Transparencies, p. 92
        Large Transparencies—Making and Mounting, p. 100

Morlan, John E., *Preparation of Inexpensive Teaching Materials,* San Francisco, California, Chandler Publishing Company, 1963, 103 pp.
    Chap. I Materials for Projection
        Ammonia Process Transparencies, p. 2
        Heat Transfer Transparencies (Thermo-Fax), p. 11
        Carbon Negative Transparencies, p. 15

Tecnifax Corporation, *Diazochrome Projectuals for Visual Communication,* Holyoke, Massachusetts.

Tecnifax Corporation, *Visucom* (Free periodical)

MOTION PICTURES

Handmade Materials for Projection, Bloomington, Indiana, Indiana University Films. Color, sound, 16 minutes

CHAPTER 13

OPAQUE PROJECTION

What Is the Opaque Projector?

The opaque projector (Figs. 95, 96 and 97) is a device for projecting images of printed materials, books, specimens, small objects, mechanical parts, and other similar things onto a screen. Unlike other types of projectors such as motion picture, slide and filmstrip, and overhead projectors, does not require a transparency.

Applications of the Opaque Projector

The business applications of the opaque projector are chiefly internal. It can be used in training new employees in a number of different ways.

1. Training of employees can be expedited by showing them the proper ways of completing the forms that they will use in their work—sales slips, refund authorizations, work orders, time cards, materials requisitions, etc. The forms can be prepared in advance showing each step in the preparation of the material.
2. Photographs of accidents and unsafe practices can be shown to groups of new employees to make them safety conscious.
3. Actual small parts can be projected to illustrate to new employees the differences between acceptable and unacceptable products.
4. Material for instruction may be projected onto a chalkboard and additions written in chalk on the board. For example, a time card could be projected and filled in as an explanation of each part is made.
5. Organizational charts and similar materials may be projected and explained.

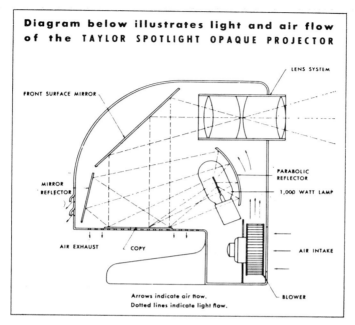

FIG. 95. The Opaque Projector. *(Courtesy of J. Y. Taylor Co.)*

Reporting to management may be improved through the use of the opaque projector to project such things as:

1. Financial statements and schedules.
2. Comparisons of the company's operations with its competitors and with its own previous records.
3. Photographs, documents, and other materials that should be shown to the management personnel as a group.

The opaque projector (Fig. 98) can be used in any situation where good light control is possible and where data is to be shown to a group of people simultaneously and at the least possible expense.

Advantages of the Opaque Projector

The main advantages of the opaque projector in its business applications are the inexpensiveness of the materials for projection, the availability of these materials, and the ease with which they may be used. It is not necessary to go through the costly and time-con-

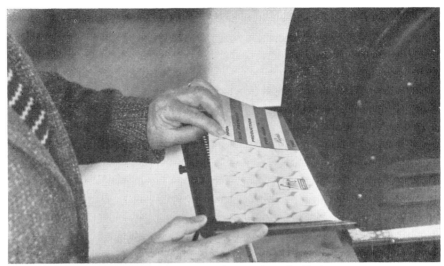

FIG. 96. Placing a Sheet of Paper into the Projector.

FIG. 97. Placing a Book into the Projector.

suming procedure of having to photograph or to duplicate by the diazo or reflex methods the materials to be projected. A report, a book, a document, or a small part can be placed on the projector stage and instantly a true, full-color image of the material is projected for all to see. There is sometimes an additional advantage to

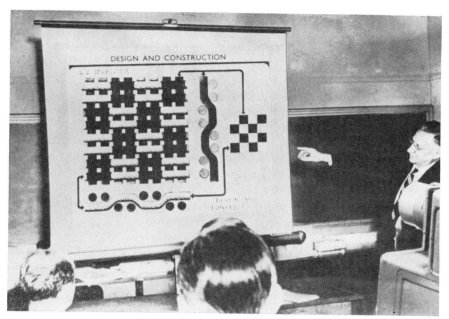

FIG. 98. Opaque Projector in Use.

be gained in interest when the acutal object or document can be seen rather than a mere photograph or reproduction of it.

A limited amount of manipulation of the materials can be accomplished while they are being projected. With stage in its lowest position there is room to put one's hands into the projection area. The length of time that one's hands can stay in the area is limited because the projection lamp generates a good deal of heat as well as light.

Disadvantages of the Opaque Projector

The chief disadvantage of the opaque projector is that it must be used in a room that is almost completely dark. This projector utilizes reflected light coming from the surface of the object while all of the others use transmitted light that passes through a transparency. Reflected light does not deliver as much illumination to the screen as does transmitted light, Therefore any ambient light degrades the image and makes it difficult to see. For this reason the opaque projector is not well suited to use in exhibits and other places where people are moving about during the projection. A room that is dark enough for efficient opaque projection is too dark to move about in safely.

Another disadvantage is the amount of heat that is generated by the projection lamp. Objects which are projected for a long period of time become quite hot to the touch and materials easily damaged by heat cannot be safely left under the light for long.

Preparation of Materials for the Opaque Projector

As mentioned above, materials from books, documents, and small objects can be projected just as they are without the necessity of making transparencies of them. Most materials can be handled more easily, though, if they are placed on a backing of some sort. Some of the reasons for mounting the materials are:

1. A stiff cardboard backing makes single sheets of paper easier to handle—both in the projector and elsewhere.
2. A uniform color around the picture or other material is less distracting than the design of the projector stage which otherwise is projected along with the material.
3. Numbers placed on the mountings where they will not be projected will help to keep them in order.
4. Materials which otherwise would get creased and dog-eared from handling will be protected by the mounts.
5. A series of materials can either be mounted on individual cardboard panels and hinged together with masking tape or mounted on a long roll of paper or cloth. The materials will move from one side of the machine to the other with very little disruption to the flow of the presentation.

The normal aperture of the stage is 10 x 10 inches. The mount for the material should be 10 inches high and a bit more than 10 inches, say 12 inches, wide so that it will protrude from the projector slightly on either side. This makes it easy to insert and remove individual items and to move them around to the best position inside the projector.

Materials that are to be used repeatedly should be fastened to their mounts with dry-mount tissue or some sort of cement so that they will project better. Materials that will be used only a very few times can be fastened on with paper clips, masking tape, or rubber bands. These methods enable one to remove the material after use.

Summary

Opaque projection is a method of presenting documents, printed materials, and small objects to a group of people with very little prior preparation. The actual objects rather than photographs of them can be used.

The chief disadvantages lie in the fact that almost complete darkening of the room is required and that materials projected for a long period of time become quite hot.

Mounting on cardboard backing preserves the material and makes it easier to handle during projection and in the files:

BIBLIOGRAPHY

Arthur, T. C., "Opaque Projector," *International Journal of Religious Education,* November, 1957, p. 19.

Blanc, Sam, "Preparing Opaque Projection Materials," *Teaching Tools,* Fall, 1956, pp. 172-178

Bowers, Kenneth L., *The Opaque Projector,* Austin, Texas, Visual Education Bureau, The University of Texas, 1960, 42 pp.

Brown, James W., and Richard B. Lewis (Ed), *AV Instructional Materials Manual,* Second Edition, New York, McGraw-Hill Book Company, 1964, 188 pp.
>>>>Exercise Forty-Five Opaque Projector
>>>>Exercise Forty-eight Simple Equipment Maintenance

Brown, James W., Richard B. Lewis, and Fred W. Harcleroad, *AV Instruction Materials and Methods,* Second Edition, New York, McGraw-Hill Book Company, 1964, 592 pp.
>>>>Chap. 20 Using Still Pictures
>>>>Reference Section
>>>>Opaque Projectors, pp. 538-539

Cross, A. J. Foy, and Irene F. Cypher, *Audio-Visual Instruction,* New York, Thomas Y. Crowell Company, 1961, 415 pp.
>>>>Chap. 4 Projected Still Pictures

Dale, Edgar, *Audio-Visual Methods in Teaching,* Revised Edition, New York, The Dryden Press, 1954, 534 pp.
>>>>Chap. 16 Still Pictures

De Kieffer, Robert, and Lee W. Cochran, *Manual of Audio-Visual Techniques,* Englewood Cliffs, New Jersey, Prentice-Hall, Inc., 1955, 220 pp.
>>>>Unit Three Projected Materials and Equipment
>>>>Opaque Projector, p. 117-121

Denno, Raymond, *Using the Opaque Projector,* Dallas, Texas, Squibb-Taylor, Inc., 1958

DuBois, Gladys, "Get Out the Opaque Projector," *Educational Screen,* March, 1956, p. 99.

Eboch, Sidney C., *Operating Audio-Visual Equipment,* San Francisco, California, Howard Chandler, Publisher, 1960, 73 pp.
>>>>Chap. III Still Picture Projection, p. 44

Finn, James D., *The Audio-Visual Equipment Manual,* New York, The Dryden Press, 1957, 361 pp.
>   Section 1 Projectors
>   Opaque Projectors, pp. 172-188
>   Good Projection Practice, pp. 189-220

Green, Ivan, *"Blow It Up with the Opaque Projector," Teaching Tools,* Winter, 1958, p. 22

Haas, Kenneth B., and Harry Q. Packer, *Preparation and Use of Audio-Visual Aids,* Englewood Cliffs, New Jersey, Prentice-Hall, Inc., 1955, 381 pp.
>   Chap. 4 Opaque and Overhead Projection

Holland, Ben F., Horace C. Hartsell, and Raymond L. Davidson, *Audio-Visual Materials and Devices,* Lubbock, Texas, Rodgers Litho, 1958, 157 pp.
>   Chap. 4 Opaque Projector

Kinder, James S., *Audio-Visual Materials and Techniques,* 2nd Edition, New York, American Book Company, 1959, 592 pp.
>   Chap. 6 Opaque, Overhead, and Tachistoscopic Projection

Lewis, C., "Results Are Giant-Size with the Opaque Projector," *Texas Outlook,* August, 1956, p. 12

Sands, Lester B., *Audio-Visual Procedures in Teaching,* New York, The Ronald Press Company, 1956, 670 pp.

Shaheen, T. S. "Board Uses Opaque Projector to Present School Budget," *Nation's Schools,* July, 1956, p. 76

Taylor, J. Y., *Opaque Projection,* Buffalo, New York, Scientific Instrument Division, American Optical Co., 1941

MOTION PICTURES

The Opaque Projector—Its Purpose and Use, Ames, Iowa, Iowa State University, 1952. Black-and-white, sound, 6 minutes

FILMSTRIP

The Opaque Projector, Columbus, Ohio, Teaching Aids Laboratory, Ohio State University

CHAPTER **14**

FLIPSHEETS

What Is a Flipsheet?

A flipsheet (or flipchart) is a device for displaying printed materials, graphs, charts, etc., to a group of people (see Fig. 99). It consists of a number of pages of material hinged or fastened together at the top so that as the speaker finishes with a page it can be flipped over the top and out of the way, revealing the following page. The information will be printed on sheets of tear-resistant paper or cloth and should be of a size appropriate to the distance at which it will be viewed. Blank sheets may be included where desired and information written in by the speaker. The flipsheet unit will be supported on an easel or stand which is placed on the floor or the table, depending upon the size of the material being displayed, or in a frame hung from wall brackets. A wall frame must have space behind the mounting to allow the paper to be slipped behind it.

Purpose of Flipsheets

The purpose of the flipsheet is to assist in the presentation of factual data to a group. The device is not intended to carry the bulk of the communication load, but to summarize the remarks of a speaker and add the impact of visual communication to that of the verbal. Some of the things it can accomplish are:

1. To show the title of the talk or presentation on the first panel.
2. To show key words, phrases, or slogans.
3. To show parts that go into a product.
4. To display charts of various kinds.
    Organization charts

FIG. 99. Flipsheet on an Easel. *(Courtesy of the Oravisual Company, Inc.)*

Flow of paperwork through the offices
Sources of raw materials
Areas where the company's product is sold

5. To present graphs showing the results of the company's operations.
   Bar graphs or line graphs showing sales, costs, etc., over a period
   of years, quarters, or months
   Pie graphs showing comparative sources of income, comparative expenses, etc.

6. To present intangible ideas in a tangible form.

7. To display drawings of various kinds.
   Cutaway drawings
   Enlargements of small areas
   Visualization of materials or actions that cannot be seen, such
   as the relation of the particles making up an atom or relation-
   ships of certain ideas to each other
   Successive steps in the performance of some mechanical action

8. To make comparisons by displaying contrasting materials side
   by side.

9. To organize the presentation in the minds of the viewers by the

FIG. 100. Using a Flipsheet. *(Courtesy of the Oravisual Company, Inc.)*

inclusion of transition devices, such as the headings of new sections of the talk.

10. To show reproductions of business forms which the viewers must learn to complete. The speaker may fill in the form with a grease pencil on the flipsheet or other medium that will show up from a distance as the viewers complete the copies of the form at their desk or table.

11. To keep the speaker from wandering far afield from the material that he should cover by serving as a reminder to him to get back to the subject under discussion.

12. To make it easy to refer back to a previous point by merely flipping the sheets back to the appropriate place.

13. To summarize the presentation by restating the major points.

Advantages in the Use of Flipsheets

Flipsheets have certain advantages that are not to be found in other forms of visual communication, even some of the more sophisticated types.

1. It does not require the area to be darkened.
2. It does not require electricity and so can be used wherever a group of people are assembled.
3. The speaker stands in front of the group while he manipulates the materials.
4. Materials can be completely prepared ahead of time, or information can be added in front of the group.
5. No elaborate equipment is required either in preparation or utilization of the device.
6. The speaker can easily prepare his own materials.
7. The presentation can be modified by skipping certain pages or by varying their order.
8. The visuals help to keep the speaker on the correct line of thought.
9. A review of the points covered can be accomplished by flipping through the sheets a second time.
10. Graphic materials may be reproduced by projecting them onto the paper and tracing over the image. (This is done during preparation, not in front of the audience, of course.)

Types of Materials Suitable for Flipsheet Presentation

Most types of information that can be reduced to visual terms are suitable for presentation on a flipsheet. Some special considerations are mentioned below.

1. Broad outlines and shapes carry best.
2. Detailed, involved ideas should be reduced to simple steps for the visual presentation.
3. Each detail should be large enough to be clearly seen by those at the maximum viewing distance.
4. Colored materials can emphasize certain points and show relationships that would not otherwise be noticed.
5. The visuals should not merely restate what the speaker says orally.
6. Wordage should be kept to a minimum consistent with the information that must be conveyed.
7. Printing should be of an easily readable style and large enough to be legible from anywhere in the intended audience area.
8. Drawings are generally better than photographs unless the photographs are prepared in such a way as to eliminate all extraneous detail.
9. If colors are used, the number of different colors should be kept to a minimum. Too many colors tend to confuse rather than to clarify.

10. No one sheet should be displayed for a long period of time. As soon as the information on the sheet has been absorbed, the next one should be uncovered.

11. Summary sheets may be included at several points during the explanation of an involved subject. These can serve also to stimulate questions from the group.

12. Handout materials should be held until after the presentation in order to assure the audience's attention on what the speaker is saying. People tend to read ahead of where the speaker is and not to give him their full attention.

Construction of the Flipsheet

The design of the stand for the flipsheet will depend upon two

FIG. 101. Light Stand Used as a Support for a Flipsheet.

factors. The first is whether the unit will stand on the floor or on a table or will hang from a wall. The second factor is whether the speaker will want to write on the flipsheet while it is being shown.

The stand must hold the material high enough so that all of the group can see the bottom of the page. This necessary height will vary according to the number in the group and the situation in which the material will be shown. The larger the crowd is, generally, the higher that the stand will have to be so that those in the back can see over the heads of those in front. However, if the stand is on a raised platform or if the floor slopes upward in the rear, the material will not have to be so high.

If it is not necessary to write on the flipsheet while it is being shown, an ordinary light stand of the sort used to hold studio lights makes a good support (Figs. 101 and 102). The stand is adjustable to about eight feet high and the top section is a steel rod approximately three-eighths of an inch in diameter. A hole this diameter bored in the center of the rear supporting board will hold the materials in place.

If the speaker wants to write on the flipsheet while it is being shown to a group, the support must be strong enough to withstand the pressure of the writing and must have a smooth, flat writing

FIG. 102. Light Stand Support from the Rear.

FIG. 103. Floor Easel for a Flipsheet. *(Courtesy of Advance Products Company)*

surface. An easel as illustrated in Figure 103 will provide the necessary support. The backing can be plywood, masonite, chipboard, or other fairly rigid, flat material. It can be made part of the easel or it can be fastened to the flipsheet pad and merely set into a grooved receptacle in the easel.

An easel for use on a table or desk will not need legs, of course, and can be smaller in size because the viewers will ordinarily be much closer than they will be when viewing material on a floor easel. This supporting device can be very simple, consisting merely of two pieces of rigid material hinged together at the top and connected with a chain or cord to prevent them from spreading too far. Even simpler, the piece at the rear needs only to be a piece of 1″ x 2″ lumber connected to the front piece with two lengths of chain or cord to keep it straight and preventing it from spreading too far (see Fig. 104).

FIG. 104. Table Easel for a Flipsheet. *(Courtesy of Chase Manhattan Bank)*

If a flipsheet is to be used in conjunction with projected visuals (perhaps to provide a summary of points covered) , it should be provided with a low-intensity light that is shielded from the eyes of the audience. The light should not be allowed to strike the screen, but should be directed onto the flipsheet only. A flipsheet with this sort of light is illustrated in Figure 105.

Flipsheet materials may be purchased to fit certain ready-made easels or they may be made to fit any size of backing desired. Pads of flipsheet paper may be purchased with mounting holes already punched. If a company intends to use this type of presentation, it

FIG. 105. Flipsheet with Low-intensity Light. *(Courtesy of the Advance Products Company)*

should standardize on all physical aspects of the flipsheets so that the materials prepared will fit any of the company's easels and backing boards.

The backing should have the same dimensions as one of the standard sizes in which sheets of paper come. This prevents the additional expense and bother of cutting larger sheets down to fit. Two or more holes should be drilled in the top edge of the backing. If pre-perforated pads of paper are to be used, the holes should correspond to those punched in the paper. If this type of paper is not used, the holes should be spaced evenly across the top of the backing, and the paper punched accordingly. A strip of ½″ x 1″ hardwood should be drilled to match the holes in the backing sheet. Bolts will be passed through the backing material from the rear, then through the pad of paper and the wooden strip and then fastened in front with wing nuts so that they can be assembled and disassembled quickly and easily (see Fig. 106).

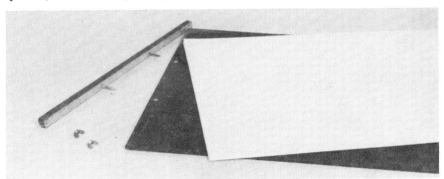

FIG. 106. Assembly of the Flipsheet.

Summary

The flipsheet is a device for displaying successive bits of information to a group. This method of communication is not generally intended to carry the entire burden of conveying the information, but to supplement the speaker's remarks. Many types of material can be shown on it but the most successful are those which do not contain too much detail. Materials and their support can be made easily by anyone. The great flexibility of this device makes it useful for communicating many types of information.

BIBLIOGRAPHY

Goetz, Rachel Marshall, *Visual Aids for The Public Service,* Chicago, Public Administration Service, 1954, 89 pp.
Chap. III Tips on Displays
Flip Charts, pp. 33-35

CHAPTER 15

AUDIO RECORDING

What Is Audio Recording?

Audio recording is the recording of sound material in order to preserve it for later recreation of that sound. Recorded sound may be used by itself to convey a message or it may be combined with visual material, such as motion pictures or a filmstrip, to provide an impact and degree of effectiveness that neither medium could attain by itself.

Types of Audio Recording

There are three types of audio recording that are in general use today—optical recording, disc recording, and magnetic recording. Each has its own advantages, disadvantages, and applications.

Optical recording is the most generally used method of providing sound for 35mm and 16mm motion pictures. The sound track is made so that a narrow beam of light shining through it activates a photo-electric cell. The sound track is constructed to allow a fluctuating amount of light to pass through. The fluctuations correspond to the vibrations of the original sound. The photo-electric cell changes the fluctuations of light into a varying electric current which is built up by the amplifier and sent ot the loudspeaker, where it is changed into air vibrations reproducing spoken words, music, or any other sounds.

Disc recording utilizes a spiral groove on a flat surface to provide the signal that is converted into sound. As a disc recording is made, a v-shaped stylus cuts a groove into the surface. Sound is fed into the system by a microphone that changes the sound into a fluctuating electric current. This current is amplified and fed to a mechanism that controls the operation of the stylus. An electro-magnet causes the stylus to vibrate in tempo with the sound vibrations. As the disc turns under the stylus, a wavy groove is carved into it. Upon playback, the needle following the groove is vibrated by the waves and this physical movement is transformed into a fluctuating electric current by the cartridge. This current is built up by the amplifier and sent to the loudspeaker where it is converted into sound. A mold can be made from the original recording (called the master recording) and copies can be made by casting the proper material in the mold. One important advantage of this form of recording is its universality. Record players can be found nearly everywhere and are quite inexpensive. Records are comparatively inexpensive to produce, distribute, and store. Disadvantages of this system are that the needle, preferably with a diamond or sapphire tip, is dragged through the groove, bouncing from side to side against the walls, so there is bound to be wearing of the track. Add to this the particles of sand and grit that can accummulate on a record and be ground in by the needle and one can see why disc recordings become worse with each playing.

Magnetic recording is based on the fact that certain types of materials will pick up a magnetic charge when they are pulled through a magnetic field. If this magnetic field is made to fluctuate as this material is being pulled through, some parts of the material will have a greater degree of magnetism than others. The amount of the magnetism varies according to the strength of the actuating magnet at the time that portion of the material was passing the poles of the magnet. In a magnetic recorder, the current from the microphone is amplified and fed into a electro-magnet which has poles very close together. The magnetic field varies according to the vibrations of the sound source and this fluctuating field is recorded on the magnetizable material which stores the signal in the form of tiny magnetic fields. When the material is again pulled past the magnetic poles (this time with no electrical current being fed into the magnet), the fluctuating magnetic field induces an electric current in the magnet which is amplified and sent to the loudspeaker where it is changed into sound.

Several variations of the magnetic material used to store the signal have been developed. The first was a fine steel wire that wound from one reel to another as it moved past the recording or playback head. Wire recording had several drawbacks and is seldom used today. Some of the disadvantages were: the volume fluctuated as the wire tended to twist as it wound from one reel to the other, the bare wires tended to pick up the magnetic charges from each other, splicing and editing were difficult, and if the wire should break during recording or playback, it tangled into a rat's nest. The wire was quite compact, however, and served the purpose for which it was first developed.

The successor to wire recording, and generally replacing it, is tape recording. In place of the steel wire as the device for storing the magnetic charge is a flat strip of plastic, usually an acetate or polyester base one-quarter of an inch wide and $1\frac{1}{2}$ mils (or less) thick, upon which a layer of finely ground ferric oxide has been coated. The magnetic field is retained in the ferric oxide coating. The tape overcame many of the shortcomings of the magnetic wire. The tape, being flat, does not tend to rotate, but keeps the same side always toward the magnet. There is no insulation for magnetism, but the separation of the thickness of the base between the layers of ferric oxide reduces the amount of magnetism that one layer can induce in another. Tapes can be spliced and edited very easily. Most tape recorders are made so that they record down only one side of the quarter-inch width of the tape. After the tape has been run through once, the reels can be turned around and the other half of the tape used. This makes it possible to double the amount of material that can be recorded on a length of tape. With tape it is also possible to record the signals from two microphones on the same length of the tape. When the tape is replayed, with each signal going through a separate amplifier to a different speaker, a stereophonic effect is obtained. A person sitting in front of and between the loudspeakers will receive a directional impression of the sound, making it seem much more realistic. When listening to an orchestral recording, for instance, one can almost determine where each of the instrumental sections was sitting when the recording was made.

Magnetic film is used when recording sound that is synchronized with a motion picture. The film is 16mm wide, is perforated with either single or double perforations, and is coated with ferric oxide rather than a photographic emulsion. The normal operating speed is the equivalent of 48 frames per second, just double that of the photographic film. The higher speed is used because it gives better quality on the original sound track and 48 frames per second was chosen because it makes footage computations easier to calculate.

A magnetic soundstrip is sometimes used on release prints of

16mm motion pictures, either alone or in conjunction with an optical soundtrack. The optical soundtrack cannot be changed once it has been put on the film, but the magnetic track can be re-recorded to suit the need. For instance, if a company has employees in several different countries and wants to communicate with them by motion pictures with optical soundtracks, there would have to be a different print for each language that was involved. With a magnetic soundstrip, one print can be used in many different language areas by recording the narration in the language spoken in the area to which it is going at the time. This method can also be used to record different narrations for a film to be used with various levels of employees.

All of the magnetic recording methods share two advantages in common. In the first place, materials can be recorded and re-recorded an infinite number of times without deterioration in the quality of the sound. The old magnetic patterns are erased each time that new material is recorded. The other advantage is that the recording can be played back an infinite number of times, again without deterioration in the quality of the reproduction.

The magnetic systems of recording are so much handier to use than other recording media that materials destined for release in other media are often recorded orginally in magnetic form. For instance, recording the orginal sound for a disc recording can be done more efficiently on tape than on the disc. If the recording is being done on the master disc and a mistake is made, say two-thirds of the way through, the whole disc must be discarded and the recording started again from the beginning. If the original is on tape, it is only necessary to go back a short distance and start again. The two portions can be spliced together, eliminating the error and saving a great deal of time for everyone concerned. Also, the recording can be played back immediately without endangering the master. Record companies almost universally use tape for the original recording of the sound and then dub from the tape onto the disc master recording.

Sound tracks for motion pictures were originally made on a length of special film that moved past a light gate for exposure of the optical sound track. The recorded material could not be played back for assessment of its quality until the film had been developed. This meant a delay of at least a day before the final decision could be made as to whether the sound as recorded was satisfactory or would have to be done again. By recording magnetically, immediate playback can be had, which makes it possible to re-record if necessary while conditions are still the same.

Uses of Audio Recording in Business Communication

Just as in the other communications media that have been discussed, the use of audio recordings in limited only by the imagination of the users. One example of the use of this method by the Pacific Telephone and Telegraph Company's accounting supervisors in training new personnel is given below.

1. We have used the tape recorder to help train interviewers. We prepare "typical" interviews of various sorts (employment, corrective action, get acquainted, etc.) and put them on tape as if actual.

   The training class is then exposed to the interview—line by line—with the recorder stopped after every line or so. Discussion is conducted on pros and cons of the interviewer's statements, questions, approach and then the group proceeds on to the next line or two.

2. We have used the recorder to try out talks to be given before groups so the speaker can hear in advance how he sounds. He can then edit, add, time, change, etc., his talk as is appropriate.

3. We are accumulating a tape library of talks made by prominent people. These are offered throughout our department as a lending library.[1]

This medium of communication is particularly useful as a training device where it is necessary to instruct employees in the proper ways of conducting themselves in their contacts with the public—customers, clients, prospects, debtors, etc.—and with people within the company—subordinates, co-workers, and superiors. It enables the employee to assess his own mistakes and discover just how he sounds to the other person. It also provides a record that can be played back as many times as necessary and one that is unchanging. Recordings made early in the training period can be saved until the end of the period to compare with those made at that time for the purpose of showing how much progress had been made.

Earlier in this chapter it was mentioned that an audio recording can increase the effectiveness of a sales or public relations presentation of a visual nature. The success of radio as an advertising medi-

---

1. Excerpt from a letter of March 28, 1961, from Mr. J. G. Luce, Public Information Supervisor, the Pacific Telephone and Telegraph Company.

um through the years bears testimony as to the ability of audio alone to carry a convincing message. Used appropriately, recordings can have the same sort of impact that radio has had. It is particularly useful in describing the characteristics of a product which cannot readily be seen in a casual examination.

In the field of employee relations, recordings may be used to maintain a closer feeling between the management of the company and the employees. For instance, the president of the company could not take the time to greet each new group of employees and welcome them to the company. He could, however, make a recording of a welcome speech and this recording could be played before the group at the end of their training period. This would be much more personal than a printed letter of welcome and less expensive than a motion picture of the same talk.

In reporting to management, an official of the company who is located at a long distance from the main office, in a foreign country for instance, and who could not personally travel to a directors' meeting, could submit the oral part of his report through a tape recording.

When reporting to stockholders' meetings, company officials could have their oral remarks recorded and sent to local group meetings of the company owners. This would usually entail recording the reports before the date of the meetings, since all meetings are usually held simultaneously.

Any time that a company official makes an address to employees, the public, management, stockholders, or governmental groups, it is a good idea to make a tape recording of the talk so that the material may be transcribed verbatim in the event a question arises as to what was actually said. It should be kept in mind that courts generally do not permit tape recordings to be submitted in evidence. These materials can be edited so deftly that words can be eliminated, added, or changed around so as to modify or completely change the meaning from what the speaker intended. A recording can, however, go a long way toward establishing what was or was not said during a speech.

Operation of the Tape Recorder

In the chapters on photography and motion pictures, it was assumed that the person responsible for the communication would not be doing the physical manipulation of the cameras, editing equipment, etc. In the case of sound recording, however, it must be assumed that the communicator will be responsible for the handling of his own recorder. For this reason, a discussion of the operation of the devices will be included in this chapter.

Because of the fact that the tape recorder is the most generally used device for sound recording, this type of machine will be the one discussed. There are many brands of machines on the market today and it would be impossible to illustrate the operation of each one. For this reason, one tape recorder, the Wollensak, has been chosen to demonstrate the controls. The actions which must be accomplished are the same on all machines, but the detail of how it is done varies from one machine to another. The operating manual accompanying each projector will explain the procedure for that particular machine. The manual should be read through carefully before attempting to operate the recorder.

Loading the Tape. The recorder has two spindles, one for the full reel (sometimes called the feed reel) and the other for the takeup reel. Generally the full reel goes on the left side of the machine and the takeup reel goes on the right. On some machines, however, this is reversed. The correct placement can be determined quickly by turning the machine on and pressing the play key (see below).

FIG. 107. Threading the Recorder.

The spindle for the takeup reel will commence revolving. The spindles have three projections, or keys, which engage slots in the reels and keep them from slipping. Make sure that the reel is the proper place on the spindle with the keys engaged in the slots.

If the full reel goes on the left spindle, it should be turned so that it revolves in a counter-clockwise direction as the tape is pulled from it. (See Fig. 107). The tape should be attached to the takeup reel by inserting the end into a slot in the reel and turning the reel about two turns in the same direction that the full reel turns. The tape is merely dropped into the threading slot and the threading operation is complete.

Controls. After plugging in the power cord, the next step is to turn the machine on. The off-on switch may be a separate switch or it may be combined with the tone or volume control. In the case of the recorder we are examining it is the tone control. (See Fig. 108). Pushing the top of the knurled wheel to the right turns the machine on. The recorder should be turned on for 30 seconds or so before actual recording or playback starts in order to give it time to warm up.

FIG. 108. The Off-on Switch.

The tone control (Fig. 109) regulates the relative intensities of the high and low (treble and bass) tones in music played back by the recorder. This control is generally not operative when the machine is recording. The bass setting gives deep, rich tones and also helps to minimize the noise and scratch present when a tape has been recorded from a worn phonograph record. The treble position gives greater clarity to speech and more brilliance to musical instruments. It also reduces turntable rumble, which is heard on some record players. An intermediate setting is a compromise between the two extremes and is generally more pleasing. The controls are continuously adjustable and the setting should be such as to give the best results in the particular room and for the conditions under which the tape is being played.

The volume control regulates the intensity of the magnetic field during recording and the volume of the sound when the recording is replayed. Volume is increased as the control is turned to the right to a higher number, as illustrated in Figure 110. The level setting for recording will vary according to the conditions under which the

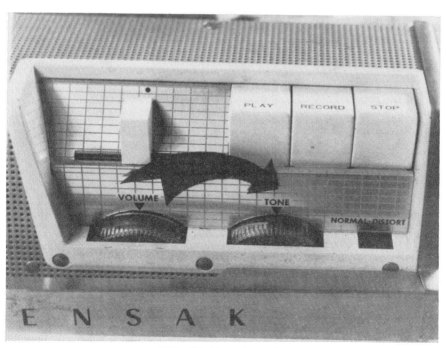

FIG. 109. Tone Control.

FIG. 110. Volume Control.

recording is being made, including the magnitude of the sound and its distance from the microphone.

The recorder will have an indicator to show the level of the signal that is being sent to the tape (Fig. 111). This indicator may take the form of a "magic eye," a green, fan-shaped light in a bulb. This fan widens as the volume increases. It may be a neon bulb that glows with an intensity proportional to the volume of the sound being recorded. The volume unit meter (often referred to as a VU meter) provides the most accurate indication with a needle that swings across a dial to indicate the volume. The purpose of all of these is the same—to insure that there will be sufficient signal to get a recording but not so much that it will cause distortion. Wollensak uses a split neon bulb. The volume control should be adjusted so that the "normal" half flashes when sound is being recorded, but that the "distorted" half does not flash, or does so only occasionally.

An index counter is provided so that it is easy to locate a certain section of the tape when it is played back. A dial, which records the number of turns that the feed reel makes, should be set

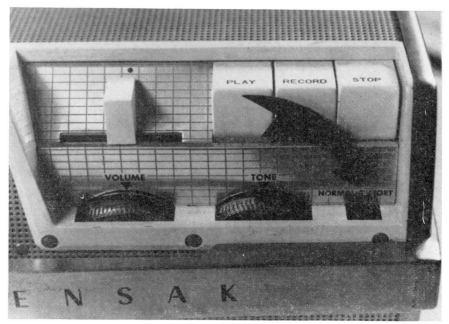

FIG. 111. Record Level Indicator.

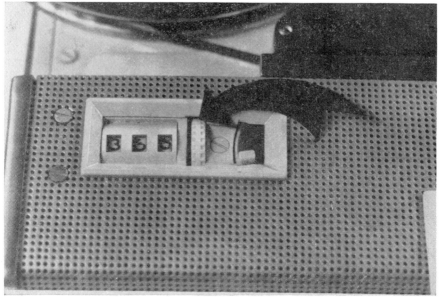

FIG. 112. Index Counter Adjustment.

to zero at the beginning of the tape. The reading at the beginning of each section of the recording can be jotted down on a place provided for it on the reel box. When it is decided to play a certain portion of the tape, it can be found quickly. This control is illustrated in Figure 112.

Before commencing recording, the desired tape speed must be set. Most recorders that are built for industrial use provide a choice of two speeds—7½ inches per second (ips) and 3¾ ips. The faster speed gives greater fidelity in recording and playback, while the slower speed results in greater tape economy, but at a loss in fidelity. The slower speed is adequate for speech but the faster one should be used when music is involved. On most recorders tape speed should not be changed while the tape is moving. This adjustment is shown in Figure 113.

The microphone plug should be inserted into the microphone jack to feed the signal from the microphone into the amplifier. In most tape recorders, a separate jack is provided for the microphone input and inputs from a radio or phonograph. The Wollensak machine provides for the differences in types of input by utilizing dif-

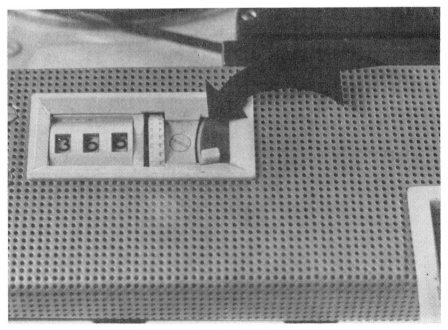

FIG. 113. Tape Speed Adjustment.

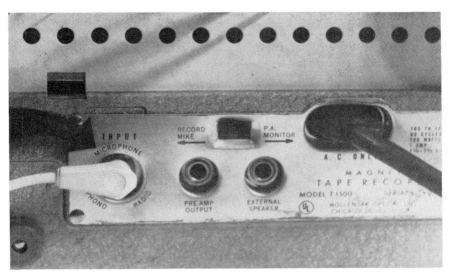

FIG. 114. Microphone Plug in Jack for Recording.

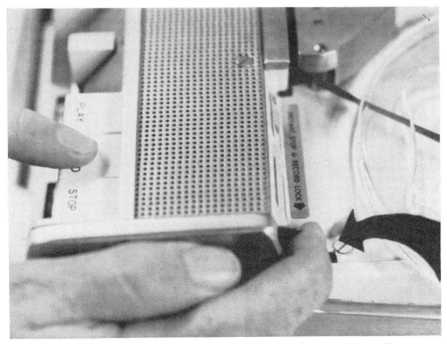

FIG. 115. Record Key and Lock Being Operated to Commence Recording.

ferent lengths of shaft on the plug. The microphone plug in position is illustrated in Figure 114.

The machine is set in operation to record sound by pressing the record key. However, to prevent inadvertent erasure of previously recorded material, a lock on the record key is provided. This lock must be released before the record key can be depressed. In the machine being illustrated, the lock lever is pulled toward the operator to release the record key so that it can be pressed, as in Figure 115. The record release lock also serves as an instant stop key for stopping the recorder briefly during recording or playback. To play previously recorded material, press the play key (Fig. 117).

To stop the machine during either recording or playback, press the stop key as in Figure 116. To resume recording, press the record key and release the record lock again.

A rapid advance and rewind control is provided for the purpose of moving the tape quickly forward or backward. The recorder may use two separate controls—one for advance and one for rewind—or as in the case of the Wollensak, a slide which is moved in the direction that the tape should travel (Fig. 118). On some recorders it is necessary to turn down the volume when moving the tape rapidly. Otherwise a high-pitched whine or garbled sound is heard.

FIG. 116. Stop Key.

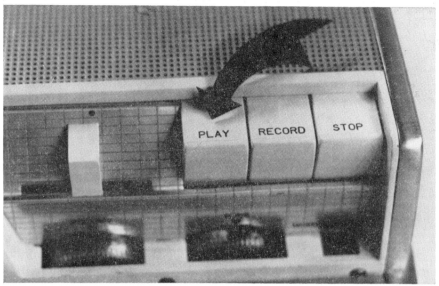

FIG. 117. Play Key.

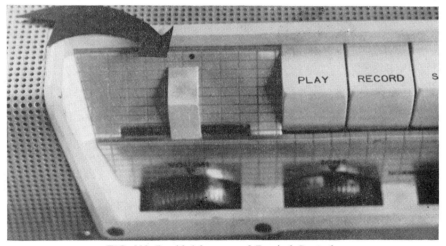

FIG. 118. Rapid Advance and Rewind Control.

The tape recorder may be made to play through external speakers by inserting the speaker plug into the output jack on the recorder. This disconnects the internal speaker system. (See Fig. 119). This makes it possible to make use of larger size and mounted speakers for better quality reproduction.

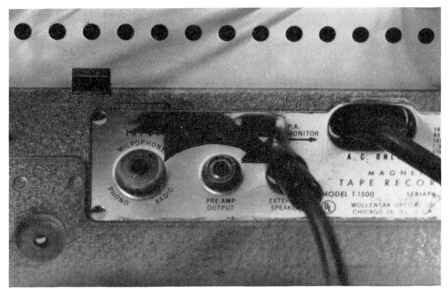

FIG. 119. Connecting an External Speaker.

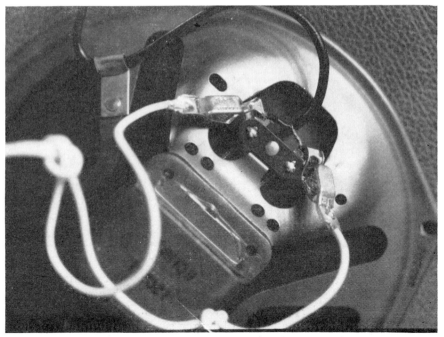

FIG. 120. Connecting to a Phonograph Output by Means of Alligator Clips.

Recording of material from the radio, television, or a phonograph record can be accomplished by connecting the output of one of the above with the proper imput of the tape recorder. If the source has an output jack, the plug connected with the tape recorder input can be inserted there. If there is no output jack, the cord to the recorder can be attached to the loudspeaker terminals of the radio, TV, or phonograph by use of alligator clips that enable a connection to be made, as illustrated in Figure 120. The clips are fastened to the terminals where the cords bringing the signal from the amplifier are connected to the loudspeaker. The loudspeaker will continue to put forth its sound and this can be used to monitor what goes onto the tape.

On some phonographs the plug from the speaker can be removed from the jack and the plug attached to the recorder inserted in its place. The signal is picked up and fed directly to the recorder, not passing through the phonograph loudspeaker at all. The recording, then, would be transferred in silence unless the speaker switch on the tape recorder is put on "P. A. Monitor", as in Figure 121. This enables one to listen to what is being recorded. The setting also makes it possible to plug a pair of earphones into the speaker output and monitor the recording of live sound without introducing the speaker sound into the room.

Splicing and Editing the Tape. One of the advantages of mag-

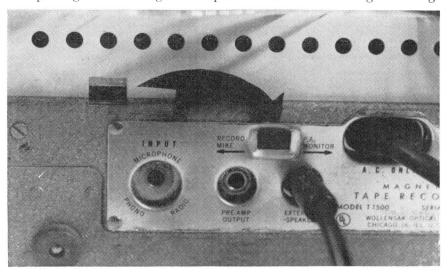

FIG. 121. Speaker Switch on P. A. Monitor.

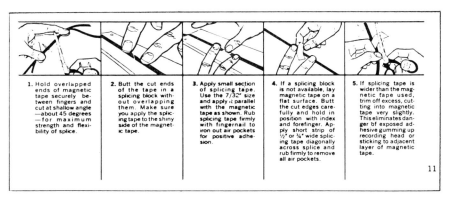

1. Hold overlapped ends of magnetic tape securely between fingers and cut at shallow angle —about 45 degrees —for maximum strength and flexibility of splice.	2. Butt the cut ends of the tape in a splicing block without overlapping them. Make sure you apply the splicing tape to the shiny side of the magnetic tape.	3. Apply small section of splicing tape. Use the 7/32" size and apply it parallel with the magnetic tape as shown. Rub splicing tape firmly with fingernail to iron out air pockets for positive adhesion.	4. If a splicing block is not available, lay magnetic tape on a flat surface. Butt the cut edges carefully and hold in position with index and forefinger. Apply short strip of ½" or ¾" wide splicing tape diagonally across splice and rub firmly to remove all air pockets.	5. If splicing tape is wider than the magnetic tape used, trim off excess, cutting into magnetic tape very slightly. This eliminates danger of exposed adhesive gumming up recording head or sticking to adjacent layer of magnetic tape.

11

FIG. 122. Hand Splicing a Magnetic Tape. *(Courtesy 3M Company)*

netic tape is the ease with which it can be spliced. This makes it possible to remove parts which are not desired and in some cases even improve on the original. For instance, if a talk was recorded in which the speaker had many hesitations and "uhs", they could be removed by cutting out the sections of the tape where they had occurred. Tape splicing can be done either by hand or with the use of a splicer. Steps in hand splicing are shown in Figure 122.

It is best to use regular splicing tape such as "Scotch" Brand No. 41 Splicing tape rather than ordinary pressure sensitive tape. The ordinary tape will ooze and cause sticky splices which pick up dirt and grit which wears down the recording heads and will also cause the layers of tape to stick to each other. A tape splicer will enable one to make better splices and to do it much more quickly than it can be done by hand. Such a splicer is illustrated in Figure 123.

If a tape has been recorded on both tracks, one track cannot be edited without losing part of the other track also. If it becomes necessary to edit material recorded in this manner, it will have to be re-recorded onto a single track before it is edited. Also, it is a good idea to dub the material onto another tape so as to have a spare in the event that an error is made in the editing.

Recording on the Tape Recorder. Effective recording requires that one have a knowledge of the equipment and techniques best suited to the particular job at hand.

One choice that must be made is the microphone to use. The microphone supplied with the tape recorders are generally of the crystal or ceramic type. These are inexpensive types of equipment,

FIG. 123. Tape Splicer.

fairly rugged, but not capable of the fidelity of recording that the more expensive microphones can produce. It is a truism that any sound system is only as good as its poorest component. In many cases the quality of a good recording system is held down to that of the microphone. In general, a recorder should be supplied with the best quality of microphone consistent with the quality of the rest of the equipment and the conditions under which it will have to operate. In addition to quality, microphones vary in their selectivity of sounds from different directions. The most common of the inexpensive microphones are uni-directional in their sensitivity. This means that they are sensitive to sounds coming from one direction only. A microphone of this type can usually be identified by the fact that when it is standing upright it has openings for the sound waves on one side only. The solid back effectively blocks out sounds coming from other directions. Such a microphone is useful when it is used by one person and there are competing noises that should be eliminated. Bi-directional, or two directional, microphones accept sounds from the two opposite sides but not from at right angles to these sides. This type can usually be identified by the fact that both sides of the instrument are perforated and are identical in appearance. This sort of microphone is good to record a conversation between two people, such as in an interview situation. The third type of microphone is the omni-directional, or all directional, type. It is characterized by a round top like a button or a sphere. It is excellent for recording meetings and other situations where the sound may come from any direction.

Most people new to recording make the mistake of putting the microphone too close to their mouths when speaking into it. This may damage the instrument and most certainly causes it to pick up the worst faults of a person's speech. A person should keep his mouth at least six inches from the microphone and should talk past it rather than directly into it. This will eliminate breathing sounds and other noises. If the microphone is not a hand-held one, the hands should be kept off because handling it will cause it to pick up more unwanted noises.

The person in charge of the recording should stand by the machine whenever anyone is speaking or otherwise recording on the machine, so that he can adjust the volume for the best recording level regardless of the changes in voice volumes or distances from the microphone encountered in different speakers.

When using a public address system, whether in connection with a recording or not, the microphone must be carefully placed with regard to the loudspeakers in order to avoid what is known as feedback. Feedback occurs when the microphone is in front of a loudspeaker. The sound coming from the loudspeaker is picked up by the microphone and sent through the amplifier to the loudspeaker again. This causes the sound to build up until it becomes a high-pitched, ear-splitting shriek. The best solution is usually to place the microphone so that it is not in line with or close to the loudspeaker.

Summary

Audio recording is an excellent way of conveying information to communicatees, whether they are employees, customers, management, or others. The impact of the spoken word is often greater than the same material presented in written form.

Three major forms of audio recording are in use today. They are optical recording, which is used mostly in providing the sound tracks for motion pictures; disc recording, which is the basis of phonograph records; and magnetic recording, which is used in tape recorders, some motion picture sound tracks, and is the original recording medium for the other systems.

Many different makes of tape recorders are on the market, each one differing from the others in the location and appearance of its controls, but all having the same functions to fulfill. The operation of the Wollensak recorder as a typical machine was described, as well as the methods of splicing magnetic tape and the techniques for using a microphone.

GLOSSARY OF TAPE RECORDING TERMS

Tape recording has given new meanings to many words in the English language. Numerous terms long used in the field of sound have become important to the tape recorder user. Here—in non technical language—is a glossary of some of the most common tape recording terms, prepared by the 3M Company.

"A" wind: (rhymes with kind) magnetic tape wound on the reel with the dull, oxide-coated side of the tape toward the inside. The wind most frequently used today. Recorder design determines whether "A" of "B" wind is required.

A. B. test: direct comparison of sound of two tape recorders made by simultaneously playing identical recorded selections on both machines and successively turning on the speaker of first one, then the other.

acetate base: the transparent plastic film which forms the tough backing for most of the audible range magnetic recording tape made. It is very popular because it meets all normal recording requirements and costs less per foot than polyester backing.

audible tones: sounds with wave frequencies which the average human can hear and which range from 30 to 15,000 cycles per second.

automatic shut-off: special switch incorporated in some tape recorders which automatically stops the machine when the tape runs out or breaks.

"B" wind: magnetic tape wound with the oxide out (see "A" wind).

bass reflex speaker enclosure: type of extension loudspeaker cabinet frequently available as an accessory item for tape recorders. Design employs a "port" or opening which greatly reinforces the bass, yet requires but a relatively small cabinet.

bias: a high frequency alternating current fed into the recording circuit to eliminate distortion.

binaural recorder: a tape recorder which employs two separate recording channels or systems, each with its own microphone, amplifier, recording and playback heads and earphones. Recordings using both systems are made simultaneously on a single magnetic tape on two parallel tracks, which, upon play-back, reproduce the original sound with depth and realism unequalled by any other recording method. Use of headphones for listening is necessary for true binaural effect.

bulk eraser: a 110 volt A. C. device used to erase an entire reel of magnetic tape at once without running it through a recorder. It uses a strong magnetic field which neutralizes the magnetic patterns on the tape.

capstan: the spindle or shaft—often the motor shaft itself—which rotates against the tape, pulling it along at a constant speed on recording and playback.

ceramic microphone: inexpensive piezoelectric type microphone supplied with many tape recorders which employs a ceramic element to generate voltages. Extremely rugged, it requires more gain than does a crystal microphone.

crossover network: filter circuits for a multiple loudspeaker system which separates highs and lows and feeds each to the particular speaker designed to handle them.

crystal microphone: inexpensive piezoelectric type microphone supplied with many tape recorders which employs a natural crystal—usually Rochelle salts—as its element. As the diaphragm moves, it causes the crystal to generate electrical voltages. Should be handled with care, however, and never exposed to heat. Provides best quality of all inexpensive microphones.

cycles per second: the unit for measuring the frequency, or "pitch," of any sound. Abbreviated cps.

decibel: abbreviated "db," it is a relative measure of sound intensity, or "volume." It expresses the ratio of one sound intensity to another. One db is the smallest change in sound that the human ear can detect.

distortion: any difference between the original sound and that reproduced by a recording machine. Distortion takes on many forms, and although it can never be completely eliminated, it can be reduced to a minimum in a good recording and reproducing system. Tape offers the maximum in distortion-free recording.

dual track recorder: usually a tape recorder with a recording head that covers half of the tape width, making it possible to record one track on the tape, then turn the reels over and record a second track in the opposite direction. Sometimes called a half-track recorder.

dupe: sometimes called a "dub" or "dubbing." A copy of a tape recording made by recording on one machine what another machine is playing. Tape recordings are easy to duplicate simply by re-recording and there is a minimum loss in quality from the original to the copy.

dynamic microphone: high quality electromagnetic type microphone which employs a moving coil in a magnetic field to produce varying voltages.

dynamic range: the ratio between the softest and loudest sounds a tape recorder or other device can reproduce without undesirable distortion. Usually measured in decibels (db's) .

editing: selecting certain sections of a tape recording, or of a number of different tape recordings, then splicing them together in the desired sequence. Magnetic tape is unsurpassed for editing purposes, since it can be easily cut and spliced.

electromagnetic type microphone: microphone using an electromagnet to produce varying voltages. Includes ribbon or "velocity" microphones, dynamic or "moving coil" type, and reluctance or "moving vane" type.

erasure: neutralizing the magnetic pattern on tape by placing it in a strong magnetic field, thereby removing the recorded sound from the tape. An "erase" head on a tape recorder does this automatically to any sound previously recorded on the tape just before the tape reaches the "record" head. A permanent magnet can also be used to erase magnetic tape, but with a resulting increase in background noise.

equalization: either boosting or decreasing the intensity of the low, middle, or high tones of a recording during recording or playback or both. This compensation serves to correct any deficiencies in the recording system and to increase the signal-to-noise ratio.

extra play: also called "long play" or "extended play." Refers to tape which gives more than standard playing time on a standard reel because it employs an especially thin backing.

fast forward control: provision on a tape recorder for running tape rapidly through the machine.

feed reel: reel on a tape recorder which supplies the magnetic tape.

feed through: transfer of signal from one track to another on a multi-track tape.

fidelity: a measure of the exactness with which any sound is duplicated or reproduced. Magnetic tape is generally regarded as the ultimate for high fidelity sound reproduction.

flat response: the ability of a sound system to reproduce all tones—low and high—in their proper proportion. A high fidelity sound system might be specified as having an essentially flat response, plus or minus one db, from 30 to 15,000 cycles per second.

flutter: very short rapid variations in tape speed causing similar variations in sound volume and pitch, not present in the original sound. A form of distortion.

foot switch: electrical or mechanical foot pedal device for stopping and starting a tape recorder without use of hands. Especially useful for dictating and transcribing.

four-track tape: also called quarter-track tape. It is tape which has four separate tracks which can be used individually for monaural or in pairs in each direction for stereo. When four-track tape is used for stereo, the first and third tracks play during the run in one direction, while the second and fourth tracks play during the run in the opposite direction.

frequency range: the range between the highest and lowest-pitched sounds which a tape recorder or other sound system can reproduce at a usable output, or volume, level.

gain: the ratio between the input level and output level of a piece of sound equipment. Gain is increased by means of an amplifier.

gap: the tiny distance between the poles of a recording head, measured in mils. The smaller the gap, the higher the frequency range of the recorder can be.

head: the ring-shaped electromagnet across which the tape is drawn, and which magnetizes the tape's iron oxide coating in a series of patterns. Most tape recorders employ a combination record-playback head and also an erase head. Some professional machines also employ a monitor head for listening to the recorded sound a split second after it has been put on tape.

head alignment: positioning of the record-playback head on a tape recorder so that its gap is exactly perpendicular to the path of travel of the tape. Head misalignment would cause loss of high frequencies upon playback. Special head alignment testing tapes are available.

head demagnetizer: device to eliminate any magnetism built up and retained in a recording head. Some tape recorders feature automatic head demagnetization.

impedance: a rating in ohms of the input and output of any electrical component, generally referred to either as "high" or "low" impedance. Importance is that, in connecting any two components, the output and input impedances must match. Most home tape recorders use a high impedance microphone and require a relatively short, shielded connecting cable. Low impedance microphones used on professional reecorders can use much longer cables with no loss in high frequencies.

index counter: an odometer type counter which makes it possible to note the location of any particular selection of a tape, thereby making it easier to find. Most late model tape recorders feature built-in index counters.

in line heads: arrangement of stereophonic heads on a tape recorder so that gaps are directly in line. One head is mounted directly above the other. Also called "stacked" heads.

input: the electrical voltage fed into an amplifier.

inverter: device to change one type of electrical current to another type. Frequently used to change 6 volt or 12 volt direct current to 100 volt alternating current for operation of a tape recorder in an automobile.

ips: abbreviation for tape speed in inches-per-second.

jack: receptacle for a plug connector leading to the input or output circuit of a tape recorder or other piece of equipment.

leader and timing tape: special tough non-magnetic tape which can be spliced to either end of a tape to prevent damage or breaking off of the magnetic tape ends and possible loss of part of the recorded material. White in color, it features a one-inch plaid marker every 7½ inches. Used as a timing tape, therefore, it can be spliced between musical selections on a tape providing a pause of a given number of seconds, depending on the tape speed.

level indicator: a device on the tape recorder to indicate the level at which the recording is being made, and which serves as a warning against underrecording or over-recording. It may be a neon bulb, a "magic eye," or a VU meter.

low print tape: special magnetic recording tape which reduces print-through (transfer of signal from one layer to another) which could result when tape is stored for long periods of time. These tapes are especially useful for "master recording" (making an original recording from which copies will be made) .

magnetic tape: a high quality plastic tape which has been precision-coated by the manufacturer with a layer of magnetizable iron oxide particles. The result is a recording media that is subject to virtually no wear, can be erased and reused, and offers the highest fidelity of reproduction possible today.

mailing box: special durable carton designed to fit standard magnetic tape boxes and provide protection through the mails.

mil: one thousandth of an inch. Tape thickness is usually measured in mils.

mixer: device by which signals from two or more sources can be fed simultaneously into a tape recorder at the proper level and balance.

monaural recorder: standard type tape recorder which uses a single-channel system consisting of one microphone, amplifier and recording head (as opposed to a binaural or stereophonic recorder) .

monitor head: additional playback head featured on some tape recorders making it possible to listen to the material off the tape while the recording is being made.

motor board: also called tape transport mechanism: The platform, or assembly, of a tape recorder on which the motor (or motors) , the reels, the heads, and the controls are mounted. It includes those parts of the recorder other than the amplifier, pre-amplifier, loudspeaker and case.

NARTB curve: standard playback equalization curve set by National Association of Radio and Television Broadcasters. (The name of this organization has since been changed to National Association of Broadcasters.)

output: an electrical voltage coming from an amplifier and normally fed into a loudspeaker.

oxide: microscopically small particles of ferric oxide dispersed in a liquid binder and coated on a tape backing. These oxides are magnetically "hard"—that is once magnetized, they remain magnetized permanently unless they are demagnetized by exposure to a strong magnetic field.

patch cord: sometimes called "attachment cord." A short cord, or cable, with a plug on either end (or with a pair of clips on one end) for conveniently connecting two pieces of sound equipment such as a phonograph and tape recorder, an amplifier and speaker, etc. Not used for 110 volt current.

playback head: magnetic head used to pick up signal off a tape. Often same head as used for recording, but with circuitry changed by means of a switch.

plug: circuit connector which is inserted in a jack.

PM speaker: loudspeaker using a permanent magnet in its voice coil.

polyester backing: plastic film backing for magnetic tape used for special purposes where strength and resistance to temperature and humidity change are important.

portable recorder: usually any tape recorder designed to be easily moved or carried about, but in most cases requiring an A. C. power supply. Some portable recorders, however, are self-powered and use batteries or a spring motor; hence are completely portable.

power amplifier: an amplifier designed to operate a loudspeaker.

power cord: cord for connecting the tape recorder to 110 volt A. C. current.

pre-amplifier: an amplifier that raises extremely weak signal levels such as those from a microphone, magnetic playback head or a phonograph pickup to a level usable by the power amplifier. Others—especially the tape recorders designed for use in high fidelity music systems—may feature a separate pre-amplifier. In such cases, the pre-amp includes an equalization circuit. In addition, the bias oscillator (necessary to record on tape) is often mounted in a unit with the pre-amp.

pre-recorded tape: a recording on tape for commercial distribution.

pressure pads: felt pads mounted on spring-brass arms which hold the magnetic tape in close contact with the heads on some machines.

pressure roller: also called "capstan idler" or "puck." A rubber-tired roller which holds the magnetic tape tight against the capstan by means of spring pressure to insure constant tape speed and prevent slippage.

print through: transfer of the magnetic field from layer to layer of tape on the reel.

quick-stop control: feature of some tape recorders making it possible to stop the movement of the tape temporarily without switching the machine off "play" or "record" position. Essential for a tape recorder used for dictation.

raw tape: a term sometimes used to describe tape that has not been recorded. Also called "virgin" or "blank" tape.

recording noise: noise induced by the amplifier and other components of the recorder. High quality magnetic tape itself is inherently noise free.

reluctance microphone: inexpensive electro-magnetic type microphone supplied with many tape recorders which is extremely rugged and durable but generally not as high quality as crystal or ceramic types. Employs a metal "wand" which moves in a magnetic field to produce varying voltages.

rewind control: button or lever for rapidly rewinding tape from the take-up reel to the feed reel.

self-powered recorder: tape recorder containing its own power supply, either a combination of wet and dry cells to power the unit, or dry cells in conjunction with a spring-driven motor.

signal-to-noise ratio: the ratio between the loudest, undistorted tune recorded and reproduced by a recorder and the noise induced by the recording system itself. Normally measured in decibels (db's).

single-track recorder: a tape recorder which records only one track on the tape. Usually a full-track recording head is used which covers the full-width of the ¼-inch tape although some machines use a narrower, half-track recording head which records a single track down the middle of the tape.

splicing block: metal or plastic device incorporating a groove in which ends of tape to be spliced are inserted. An additional diagonal groove provides a path for a razor blade to follow in cutting the tape. Makes splices very accurately using narrow-width $\frac{7}{32}''$ splicing tape.

splicing tape: a special, pressure-sensitive, non-magnetic tape used for splicing magnetic tape. Its "hard" adhesive will not ooze and consequently will not gum up the recording head, or cause adjacent layers of tape on the reel to stick together. *Cellophane tape should not be used for splicing.*

stacked heads: arrangement of recording heads used for stereophonic sound where the two heads are located directly in line, one above the other.

staggered heads: arrangement of recording heads used for stereophonic sound where the heads are located $1\frac{7}{32}''$ apart. Stereo tapes recorded using staggered heads cannot be played on recorders using stacked heads, or vice versa.

stereophonic sound: "dimensional" or "directional" sound reproduction achieved through use of two or more sound tracks, or channels, heard simultaneously through loudspeakers arranged in the same relative positions as were the microphones during the recording. In practice two channels are used, one on each track of a standard tape, with a recording head for each channel. Differs from binaural sound reproduction in microphone placement during recording and in using loudspeakers rather than headphones (required for binaural sound).

take-up reel: reel on the tape recorder which accumulates the tape as it is recorded or played.

tape cartridge: "magazine" or holder for a length of magnetic tape which can be slipped into a cartridge-type recorder and played without threading it.

tape deck: tape recorder designed for use in a high fidelity music system. Usually consists only of motorboard mechanism and does not include preamplifier, power amplifier, speaker or case.

tape guides: grooved pins of non-plastic material mounted at either side of the recording head assembly to position the magnetic tape on the head as it is being recorded or played.

tape loop: a length of magnetic tape with the ends joined together to form an endless loop. Used either on standard recorders, special "message repeater" type units, or in conjunction with a cartridge device, it makes it possible to play back a recorded message repetitively without rewinding the tape.

tape player: unit for playback only of pre-recorded tapes. Sometimes called a tape phonograph.

tape speed: speed at which tape moves past the recording head. Standard speeds for home use are $3\frac{3}{4}$ inches per second (abbreviated ips) and $7\frac{1}{2}$ ips. Faster speeds are 15 ips and 30 ips. Generally speaking, faster speed makes possible improved high frequency response, while slower speed means greater tape economy. If a tape is recorded at $3\frac{3}{4}$ ips, then played back at $7\frac{1}{2}$ ips, all sound will be raised one octave in pitch. Cutting the speed in half lowers a tone one octave.

tape splicer: device for splicing magnetic tape automatically or semi-automatically similar to a film splicer. Different models vary in operation, most using splicing tape, some employing heat.

tape threader: device on the hub of a reel for securing the end of the tape to the reel.

telephone pickup: type of induction coil device which slips over a telephone receiver, or upon which entire telephone may rest, used to pick up both voices during a telephone conversation for recording on tape.

tensilized polyester: polyester backing which has been pre-stretched for added strength and thinness.

threading slot: slot in recording head assembly cover-plate into which tape is slipped in threading up the reels for use of the recorder.

tone control: control knob on tape recorder amplifier used to vary bass and treble response to achieve most desirable balance of tone.

volume: an acoustical—rather than electrical—measurement, which refers to the pressure of the sound waves in terms of dynes per square centimeter. The louder the sound, the greater the pressure. Most technicians prefer to talk in terms of decibels.

VU meter: a "volume unit" meter which indicates the relative levels of the various sounds being recorded by measuring the electrical voltage.

wow: slow variations in tape speed causing similar variations in sound volume and pitch not present in the original sound. A form of distortion.

Extracted from *99 Tape Recording Terms,* issued by the 3M Company.

BIBLIOGRAPHY

Anderson, Ronald, "How Your Tape Recorder Works," *Magnetic Film and Tape Recording Magazine,* October, 1954

Begun, S. J., *Magnetic Recording,* New York, Rinehart Books, Technical Division, 1951

Bernard, Edward G., and Clifford Ettinger, *Using the Tape Recorder,* Brooklyn, New York, New York City Board of Education, 1953

Brown, James W., and Richard B. Lewis (Ed), *AV Instructional Materials Manual,* Second Edition, New York, McGraw-Hill Book Company, 1948, 188 pp.
        Exercise Thirty-One Recordings
        Exercise Thirty-Six Radio Programs
        Exercise Thirty-Eight Record Players
        Exercise Thirty-Nine Tape Recordings
        Exercise Forty-Nine Simple Equipment Maintenance

Brown, James W., Richard B. Lewis, and Fred W. Harcleroad, *AV Instruction Materials and Methods,* Second Edition, New York, McGraw-Hill Book Company, 1964, 592 pp.

Chap. 16 Recording
Reference Section
Record Players and Disk Recording, pp. 527-529
Tapes and Tape Recorders, pp. 529-535

Brush Development Company, *101 Uses: How to Get the Most Out of a Magnetic Tape Recorder*, Cleveland, Ohio, Brush Development Company.

De Kieffer, Robert, and Lee W. Cochran, *Manual of Audio-Visual Techniques*, Englewood Cliffs, New Jersey, Prentice-Hall, Inc., 1955, 220 pp.
Unit Four Audio Materials, Equipment, and Television
Principles of Sound, pp. 141-148
Recorders and Recording, pp. 149-161
Radio, pp. 163-171
Central Sound Systems, pp. 172-177

Dale, Edgar, *Audio-Visual Methods in Teaching*, Revised Edition, New York, The Dryden Press, 1954, 534 pp.
Chap. 17 Radio and Recordings

Eboch, Sidney C., *Operating Audio-Visual Equipment*, San Francisco, California, Howard Chandler, Publisher, 1960, 73 pp.
Chap. IV Sound Reproduction

Educators Guide to Free Tapes, Scripts, and Transcriptions, Educators Progress Service, Randolph, Wisconsin. (Published yearly)

Finn, James, D., *The Audio-Visual Equipment Manual*, New York, The Dryden Press, 1957, 361 pp.
Section 1 Record Players and Radio Receivers
General Theory of Recording and Sound, pp. 221-230
Transcription and Record Players, Simple PA Systems, pp. 231-258
Good Practice with Sound Equipment, pp. 269-274
Section 3 Tape Recorders
General Theory of Tape Recording, pp. 275-281
Tape Recorders, pp. 282-324
Tood Tape Recording Practice, pp. 324-328

Haas, Kenneth B., and Harry Q. Packer, *Preparation and Use of Audio-Visual Aids*, New York, Prentice-Hall, Inc., 1955, 381 pp.
Chap. 13 Radio, Recording, and Playback Equipment

Hodgson, Dick, and Jay H. Bullen, *How to Use a Tape Recorder*, New York, Hastings House Publishers, 1957

Holland, Ben F., Horace C. Hartsell, and Raymond L. Davidson, *Audio-Visual Materials and Devices*, Lubbock, Texas, Rodgers Litho, 1958, 157 pp.
Chap. 2 Disc Recordings and Record Players
Chap. 3 Tape Recorders

Kemp, Jerrold E., *Planning and Producing Audiovisual Materials*, San Francisco, California, Chandler Publishing Company, 1963, 169 pp.
Part Two Fundamental Skills
3. Recording Sound

Kinders, James S., *Audio-Visual Materials and Techniques,* 2nd Edition, New York, American Book Company, 1959, 592 pp.

    Chap. 10 Educational Recordings

Le Bel, C. J., *How to Make Good Tape Recordings,* New York, Audio Devices, Inc., 1956

Marshall, Robert, and Mary Marshall, *Your Tape Recorder,* New York, Greenberg, 1955

Mellenbach, Julia, *The Tape Recorder in the Classroom,* Austin, Texas, Visual Instruction Bureau, The University of Texas, 1959, 67 pp.

Morlan, John E., *Preparation of Inexpensive Teaching Materials,* San Francisco, California, Chandler Publishing Company, 1963, 103 pp.

    Chap. IX Tape Recording for Instruction

Nisbett, Alec., *The Technique of the Sound Studio,* New York, Hastings House, 1962

Sands, Lester B., *Audio-Visual Procedures in Teaching,* New York, The Ronald Press, 1956, 670 pp.

    Chap. 23 Disk Recordings
    Chap. 24 Magnetic Recordings

Stancil, William V., *Magnetic Heads and Magnetic Recording,* Hollywood, California, Stancil-Hoffman Corp., 1954

Tall, Joel, *Techniques of Magnetic Recording,* New York, the Macmillan Company, 1958

Thomas R. Murray, and Sherwin G. Swartout, *Integrated Teaching Materials,* New York, Longmans, Green and Company, Inc., 1960, 545 pp.

    Chap. 15 Recordings—Disc and Tape

3M Company, *The How to Do It Booklet of Tape Recording,* St. Paul 6, Minnesota, 3M Company, 20 pp. (Free)

Turnbull, Robert B., *Radio and Television Sound Effects,* New York, Rinehart & Co., 1951

Tydings, Kenneth S., *Tape Recorder Guide,* Long Beach, New York, Tydings Book Publishing, Cin., 1954

Wittich, Walter Arno, and Charles Francis Schuller, *Audio-Visual Materials: Their Nature and Use,* Third Edition, New York, Harper & Brothers Publishers, 1962, 500 pp.

    Chap. 10 Audio Learning
    Chap. 11 The Tape Recorder

MOTION PICTURE

Tape Recording for Instruction, Bloomington, Indiana, Indiana University Films. Color, sound

CHAPTER 16

EXHIBITS

The Exhibit as a Communication Device

Many companies have come to recognize the exhibit as a device for communicating effectively with large numbers of people in certain situations. The exhibit makes it possible to combine all or any combination of the previously discussed communications methods into an integrated presentation of a message which the organization wishes to convey.

Exhibit Locations

Exhibits are generally found in locations where there are many people who have time to spend examining the material and following explanations. Some of the situations where an exhibit would be successful are listed below.

1. Fairs and expositions. People attending a fair are generally in a mood that is conducive to good communication. They are there to enjoy themselves and to see what there is to see. They are not in a hurry to get to another place and will take whatever time is necessary to examine anything that interests them. An exhibit designed for display at a fair must be one that quickly arouses the interest of the viewer and causes him to stop for a closer look. Otherwise the person will walk on by and not give the exhibit the opportunity to communicate its message. The method and level of communication should be chosen so that it has appeal to both adults and children, and both men and women. If one or more of these groups is not considered, those who are not interested will try to hurry those who are trying to absorb the message. Thus they move on before they have thoroughly examined the exhibit.

2. Company premises. The company may set up a permanent exhibit of its operations in or adjacent to its reception area. A person who is waiting for some reason can spend the time in becoming acquainted with the scope and activities of the organization. Also, school groups and others taking a tour of the company can be taken through the exhibit as a preparation for or as a summary of the tour.

3. Schools. An exhibit for use in schools can be made to accomplish a certain educational end and the viewers will be fairly homogeneous in their age, background knowledge of the subject, and motivation for examination of the exhibit. Schools welcome exhibits that fulfill their educational needs and are not too blatantly commercial.

4. Railroad and other terminals. People waiting between trains, planes, and buses or who are awaiting the arrival of one, have time at their disposal and usually not a great deal of interest to occupy that time. These people will welcome diversion to occupy their time and make their waiting less tedious.

5. Museums. Specialized museums, such as the museums of science and industry that are found in several of the larger cities, often feature exhibits prepared by business or industrial organizations which illustrate the application of scientific or mechanical principles related to the museum's own exhibits. Other museums maintained by certain industries or business organizations feature materials prepared by individual companies.

6. Conventions. People attending conventions are an excellent audience for an exhibit. They are a select group, interested in a particular field, have leisure time (in fact, time is often scheduled between sessions for the purpose of permitting the delegates to visit the exhibits), and often are in a position to order the materials they see displayed.

Audio-Visual Media for Exhibits

The exhibit is versatile in that it can make use of virtually all of the audio-visual media, either singly or in combinations. The following is a list of just a few of the possible applications.

1. Specimens and samples
    The completed product
    The product in various stages of completion
    Raw materials that go into the product
    Byproducts
2. Models
    Sources of raw materials

Extracting raw materials
Transportation of raw materials
The manufacturing plant
Machines used in manufacturing
Steps in the manufacturing process
The completed product
The product in use
Products made using this product as raw material

3. Still pictures

Photographic representation of the items listed under specimens and samples and models. While not usually as good as the actual thing, a good photograph can tell a great deal about the subject —maybe even more than could be portrayed by the subject itself. The photographs can be mounted or projected by slide projectors, overhead projectors, or opaque projectors. Projected materials will often be shown on a rear-projection screen to save space in the exhibit and to permit a higher level of light in the vicinity of the screen. Taped narration synchronized to the visuals will enhance the quality of the communication.

4. Motion pictures

The values of still pictures listed above are also attained with motion pictures, with the added impact and communication value of movement. The stopping power of a motion picture is much greater than that of the same scene projected as a still. The values of both can be attained by having large prints of the most dramatic scenes on continuous display at the exhibit plus an operating motion picture projector to give its additional dimension to the message.

5. Audio recordings

In addition to their use in explaining visuals such as still and motion pictures, audio recordings can be used to attract attention to and explain other parts of the exhibit. A recording can carry a group of people logically through an exhibit, directing them from one part to another. If the recording can be synchronized with the lighting system so that as each portion of the exhibit is spotlighted, the description of that part is heard, the effect will be even more pronounced.

6. Television

Closed circuit television may be used to bring to the exhibits a timeliness that they would not otherwise have. This is particularly valuable in an exhibit set up in the plant itself, where the viewer can read about the various steps in the production of the goods and then immediately observe those steps being performed,

Construction of the Exhibit

There are certain characteristics which should be incorporated into its design and construction if it is to be as effective as possible, some of which are discussed below.

Portable. Practically all exhibits (with the exception of those on permanent display at museums or company plants) must be shipped at quite short intervals from one place of display to another. In order to avoid excessive labor and shipping costs, these things should be kept in mind when designing the exhibit.

1. The display should be as light in weight as possible consistent with the desired quality and appearance.
2. Sections should break down into panels of uniform size to be packed efficiently into boxes and crates.
3. Electrical fixtures, wiring, etc., should be packed into a separate box or partition of the crate.
4. Fragile materials—glass, etc.—should be packed into a box that can be marked for special handling.
5. Displays must be rugged in order to withstand the wear and tear of constant shipment, setting up, and tearing down.
6. If company employees do not accompany the exhibit and perform the setting up and tearing down, the procedure should be very simple and should be explained thoroughly so that one unfamiliar with the exhibit can handle it properly.
7. Parts should be packed so that they are readily available in the order in which they are needed for setting up the display.
8. As many parts as possible should be of standard commercial design so that they may be replaced by local purchase if they become lost or broken.
9. The shipping crates can be designed so that the interior side may be used as part of the display.

Compact, Yet Capable of Expansion. Exhibit booths found in different fairs and exposition halls across the country are not of uniform sizes or shapes. The exhibit must be compact enough to fit into the smallest that might be encountered and at the same time be expandable to fill the largest area that might be assigned. Some of the ways of adjusting the size of the display to fit the available room are these:

1. Have certain panels that can be added to or removed from the display without *seriously* affecting the continuity or appearance of the exhibit,

2. Provide background draperies and side rails with draperies that can be adjusted in height or width.
3. Have top panels that can be removed or placed elsewhere if the ceiling is too low for the normal setup.
4. Include free-standing sections of the display which can be moved about to make the most of whatever area is available.

Colorful. Colorful displays naturally attract the eye more quickly than those that are not colorful. Gaudy colors put there just for the sake of color, however, do not hold attention for long. The color scheme should be in keeping with that of the product, to harmonize with it and lend dignity to the exhibit. For instance, a display of a product that is used in space exploration might very well be designed predominantly in silver and blue, with small areas of warm colors to give emphasis and contrast.

Arresting Appearance. Just as proper use of color does, the use of a device that causes passersby to notice it can call the exhibit to the attention of everyone. Also, like color, the device must be in keeping with the display itself and must be followed up by some-

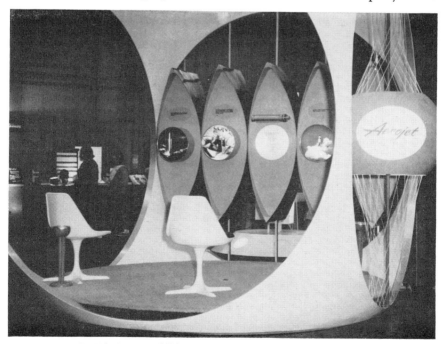

FIG. 124. Space Exhibit. *(Courtesy of Aerojet General Corporation)*

thing that can hold the attention that has been gained. An eye-catching display was recently observed which made use of a trick that is not new, but made an impression because of its size. A large model of a water faucet was suspended by wires about twelve feet from the floor. Gushing from it was a stream of water that fell into a barrel below. It was operated, of course, by an electric pump, concealed in the barrel, which pumped the water up through a clear plastic tube that was camouflaged by the water flowing down around the outside. The purpose of this device was to call attention to a display of home water softening equipment. If the booth had been demonstrating a product not connected with water or plumbing, this sort of device for attracting attention would not have been appropriate. Another display, illustrated in Figure 124, was built to explain certain concepts involved in the conquest of space. Design elements involving space material and equipment were appropriate to it.

Use of Motion. Like color and striking design, motion can call attention to an exhibit. Also, like them, the motion must be in keeping with the subject of the display. Random, meaningless motion that has no relation to the exhibit can attract only briefly. A common sight at fairs is a taffy-pulling machine which has a little figure of a man attached to a crank which makes it appear as if he is operating the machine. Placed eight feet or so above the floor so that everyone can see it, this little machine announces to all who see it that here is a place where taffy can be purchased. If the booth sold peanut brittle, chocolates, or any other kind of candy instead of taffy, the device would be inappropriate and misleading.

Use of Sound. Appropriate sounds from a tape recorder, record player, or the sound tack of a motion picture projector can attract people to an exhibit and arouse their interest in what is being displayed. The rest of the exhibit must be designed to hold that interest until the people have been given the message the exhibit is there to convey.

Forms of Construction. Depending upon the message that the exhibit is trying to put across, its elaborateness, and the size, shape, and location of the display area, an exhibit may take one of several forms. Some of them are described below.

1. The "walk-past" exhibit (Fig. 125). Viewers do not enter the exhibit but are held back by a rope or other barricade. This form of display is used when the effect desired is that of the over-all appearance rather than that gained by a close-up examination. The

FIG. 125. The "Walk-past" Exhibit.
(Courtesy of Thermador Division of Norris-Thermador Corporation)

FIG. 126. The "Walk-in" Exhibit. *(Courtesy of Sacramento Municipal Utility District)*

person can get an uncluttered view of the entire exhibit—something which he cannot get when a group of people are milling around in the display.

2. The "walk-in" exhibit (Fig. 126). This type of display is useful when there are detailed parts which must be examined closely or from different angles in order to be understood. Here the individual parts of the exhibit are as important as the general impression, and there is no special sequence in which the various components of the exhibit must be seen.

3. The "walk-through" exhibit (Fig. 127). It is very often desirable for a person viewing a display to see the various parts in a certain sequence. If a display shows such information as the steps in the manufacture of a product, it is important for the parts to be seen in the proper order. By directing people through the exhibit along a path outlined with markers or barriers of some sort, one can insure that they will view the parts in the proper order. This system also increases the number of people who can get a close-up view of the exhibit in a given period of time.

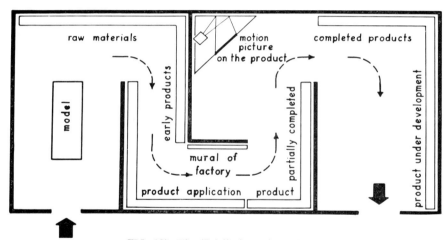

FIG. 127. The "Walk-through" Exhibit.

Summary

The exhibit is an excellent means of communicating with large numbers of people when they have the time and inclination to examine and absorb the material. Some of the places where exhibits can be shown successfully are fairs and exhibitions, company premises, schools, railroad and other terminals, museums, and at conventions. These are the places where people have the time and are in the mood to learn something.

Practically every medium of audio-visual communication can be utilized in the construction of the exhibit. Specimens and samples, models, still pictures, motion pictures, audio recordings, and television—all of these can contribute to the success of the exhibit.

The exhibit, in most cases, must be portable, collapsible, and rugged, to withstand constant setting up, tearing down, and transportation from one location to another. It should be adjustable in size to fit whatever size and shape area that is assigned to it.

Appropriate color and sound and an arresting appearance will help to attract the attention of passersby to the exhibit. After that, they will be held by the interest they have in the display—or lost through the lack of it.

Three major forms of construction are used in designing displays. They are the "walk-past" where the viewer does not enter the exhibit but views it from the outside, the "walk-in" where he can move from part to part in any order or succession that he wishes, and the "walk-through" where he is directed from one part to another in a predetermined order.

BIBLIOGRAPHY

Brown, James W., Richard B. Lewis, and Fred W. Harcleroad, *AV Instruction Materials and Methods,* Second Edition, New York, McGraw-Hill Book Company, 1964, 592 pp
  Chap 19 Real Things and Their Models
Cross, A. J. Foy, and Irene F. Cypher, *Audio-Visual Education,* New York, Thomas Y. Crowell Company, 1961, 415 pp.
  Chap. 7 Displays and Exhibits
Dale, Edgar, *Audio-Visual Methods in Teaching,* Revised Edition, New York, The Dryden Press, 1954, 534 pp.
  Chap. 13 Exhibits
De Kieffer, Robert, and Lee W. Cochran, *Manual of Audio-Visual Techniques,* Englewood Cliffs, New Jersey, Prentice-Hall, Inc., 1955, 220 pp.
  Unit Two Nonprojected Teaching Materials
  Exhibits and Museums, pp. 67-71
Gilbertson, H. W., *Educational Exhibits: How to Prepare and Use Them,* Washington, D.C., United States Government Printing Office, 1948
Kinder, James S., *Audio-Visual Materials and Techniques,* 2nd Edition, New York, American Book Company, 1959, 592 pp.
  Chap. 17 Three Dimensional Materials
Lockridge, J. Preston, and Gerda G. McMurray, *Educational Displays and Exhibits,* Austin, Texas, Visual Instruction Bureau, The University of Texas, 1960, 47 pp.
  Guidelines for Preparing Exhibits, pp. 8-10
  Exhibits, pp. 31-36
Sands, Lester B., *Audio-Visual Procedures in Teaching,* New York, The Ronald Press Company, 1956, 670 pp.
  Chap. 5 Using Real Things in Teaching

CHAPTER 17

TELEVISION

Communicating by Television

The widespread acceptance and popularity of television as a medium of entertainment has largely obscured its potential as a means of communication. Development of television as a device for the transmission of information of a business or industrial nature has yet to come into general use.

Television provides the only method of instantaneously sending both visual and audio information to another person at a distance from the event. Color television makes possible additional information about the object pictured.

Communication of Business and Industrial Information by Television

Television has been used in industrial applications which are not truly communication, at least in the sense in which it was defined in Chapter 1—that of conveying a message from one person to another. An example of this non-communication use of television is the case where a person can observe the different areas of a warehouse merely by looking at a bank of monitors connected to cameras trained on these areas. Another example is the observation of a manufacturing process from a distance to check on conditions such as the interior of a furnace or oven, where it would be too uncomfortable or dangerous for a person to make the observation directly. While these applications are unquestionably of value to the business concerned, we are not considering them as communication. They are more in the nature of extending one's senses.

Types of Dissemination of Telvision. There are three general methods of propagation of a television signal and transmitting it to the receiving set.

Regular broadcast television is the type used by commercial stations to send their programs to as many people as possible. The signal is sent out in all directions from the transmitter, which is located on the top of a mountain or a tall building in order to assist it in covering as large an area as possible. This form might be used by a company that wants to communicate with all of its employees when they are at their homes, scattered for many miles in all directions from the plant. Programs might be developed which would help to acquaint them with the company and its policies. Such telecasts might also be designed to develop good public relations with the people of the community and impress upon them the value of the company to the local area. Such a series of programs would not call for the establishment of a company-owned television station, but rather programming on the local commercial station. The program can be a sort of audio-visual house organ with film clips showing happenings and achievements of company personnel. They can also be an educational device by showing, for instance, the activities and operation of each of the company's departments or divisions. This would help each employee to understand how the work he does fits in with the entire operation of the company.

The second type of signal distribution is that known as microwave. Instead of being sent out in all directions, this signal is transmitted in very narrow beams to certain destinations. Receivers outside this narrow line cannot pick up the signal. This form of telecasting would probably be of most value when the organization has several plants or locations within a radius of thirty or forty miles. Communications can be sent from one to another of the selected locations without going to the general public.

The third type of dissemination is the closed circuit method. As the name implies, the signal is not sent out over the air, but is transmitted by means of cables. The closed circuit method is completely under the control of the company and there is no danger of the information being picked up by unauthorized persons. One advantage of this method is the fact that it does not come under the jurisdiction of the Federal Communications Commission and therefore does not require a license from that commission to operate as do the other two methods. This also means that it does not entail the preparation of many reports to the government which would otherwise be involved.

Types of Business Information Transmitted by Television. Some of the areas of usefulness for television in industry are listed below.

1. Indoctrination and training.

    Welcoming address from the company president.

    Demonstration of the operation of equipment. The TV camera can move in and give a better view of the operation than a person could get if he were actually there.

    Showing the operation of the assembly line and how other divisions of the company are geared to it.

    Showing the operations of the company where it would be too dangerous or too crowded to take the group of employees, or where the noise level would be so high that explanations and comments could not be heard.

2. Public relations and sales promotion.

    Groups visiting the plant for tours could be shown operations in places where they could not be taken because of the danger or discomfort.

    Prospective customers could be shown the high quality of materials and workmanship that go into the product.

3. Reporting to Management.

    Testing of new products can be observed by members of management from their offices or from their meeting room.

    Manufacturing activities can be observed as reports on them are made.

    Difficulties which arise or accidents which occur can be shown to management to get their decisions.

4. Reporting to stockholders.

    When the number of stockholders who wish to attend stockholders' meetings exceeds the capacity of the meeting room available, additional meeting rooms, even extending across the country, can be set up and the stockholders attending any of them can see and hear the business being transacted at the main meeting.

    Some companies whose stock is widely held buy time on commercial stations to convey messages to their owners, often as part of a regular advertising program.

Preparation for Television Communication

Preparation for the internal, closed circuit use of television involves two phases. First is the setting up of the connections and facilities for the origination, transmission, and receipt of the signal. Second is planning for what will be sent on it.

Facilities for Handling Televised Information. The amount and complexity of the facilities needed for the closed circuit television system will vary tremendously according to the variety of communication goals which the company wishes to accomplish with it. An organization contemplating setting up a system will confer with several companies supplying the components to determine which equipment is necessary for its intended operation. Some of the basic equipment is listed below.

1. Camera. Compact vidicon cameras are available for industrial use. They record images that are quite detailed and satisfactory for the purpose. Some of the variations in accessories and operation are these:

   Manual or remote controlled. (Remote controlled cameras have motorized mounts which can be adjusted in the horizontal and vertical planes.)

   Stationary or movable.

   Single or multiple lenses.

   Choice of lens focal lengths.

FIG. 128. Television Camera Used to Transmit Inventory Data.
(Courtesy of Cohu Electronics, Inc.)

Protection for the camera against heat, corrosive fumes or liquids, shock, hurtling objects, cold, sand blast, etc.

The type of camera needed to provide the quality demanded in the final image.

The type of mount—tripod, wall-hung, ceiling-hung.

2. Wiring. The coaxial cable for carrying the circuit must be laid out to provide connections for the cameras, the control facilities, and the receivers.

Conduit for this, as well as all other wiring, should be designed and built into the buildings at the time they are constructed. If closed circuit television is being added to an older building, the wiring can perhaps be added to existing ductwork and conduits.

Power requirements for all of the components must be provided for.

3. Control facilities. The requirements for types of control equipment needed vary from the very simple to the very complex. The degree of complexity will depend upon such things as:

The number of cameras in the circuit.

The amount of control necessary.

The number of receivers and the amount of selectivity desired by those receiving the signals.

The location of the control facilities will vary according to the type of control necessary. Locations might be at:

The camera, to compensate for varying conditions.

The receiver, for better control of the things the viewer wishes to see.

Elsewhere in the circuit, for choosing which camera's image to transmit, adjustment of the camera, etc.

4. Receivers. These will be located at the place where it is desired to view the image. The type and size of the receiver will depend on the number of people who are to view the picture and their distances from the receiver.

Utilizing the Television Facilities. Industrial television is not likely to require the extensive preparations, including the employment of the writers, producers, directors, etc., that are found in entertainment and educational television. The objectives of the use of this medium are quite clear-cut and the planning for its use will be equally direct. Cameras will be set up in the positions best suited to illustrate the action or situation and left in those positions until there is logical reason to move them.

As the different divisions of the company have need for the services of the television crew they will notify the person in charge,

FIG. 129. Viewing Industrial Closed Circuit Television. *(Courtesy of Cohu Electronics, Inc.)*

normally the audio-visual director or the engineer in charge of the television unit, and schedule the facilities for the day and time desired. A discussion with the person in charge of the TV crew concerning the purposes and intended outcome of the use of this communication medium will help in the planning of such things as:

1. Number of cameras necessary to cover the subject.
2. Types of lenses—telephoto, wide angle, etc.
3. Types of camera mounts—mobile, fixed, manually operated, remote controlled, etc.
4. Microphone placement for sound pickup.
5. Timing—overall time and timing of individual shots.
6. Cueing for synchronization of the visuals with the description and remarks of the leader of the group using the television.
7. Additional lighting beyond that normally found in the area.
8. Placement of cables, etc., so that they will not interfere with production.

Discussion with the audio-visual director will also help in the planning of the entire presentation, including all of the other communication media in addition to the television itself. Charts and graphs, still pictures, previously made motion pictures (which combined with the television might show a before and after situation), sound recording, etc., can combine to make the communication session very successful.

Summary

The industrial use of television can be of use in training new employees, in sales work, reporting to management, and reporting to stockholders. The most useful type of dissemination of the television signal in an industrial situation is by a closed circuit system. Under this system the signal does not go out over the air where unauthorized people might make use of it. Since it is not broadcast, no Federal Communication Commission license is needed to operate.

Facilities for televising material do not need to be elaborate, but there are minimum requirements one must have before he can operate. They include the cameras and mounts, wiring and cables, control facilities, and the receivers.

Scheduling television presentations should be done through the audio-visual director or the TV engineer. Either will confer with the other and plan, with the help of the person requesting the service, the arrangements for the television coverage and additional services to make the television more successful.

GLOSSARY

TERMINOLOGY–CLOSED CIRCUIT TELEVISION

From CLOSED CIRCUIT TELEVISION SYSTEM PLANNING GUIDE, published by the Philco Corporation, Government & Industrial Group.

ambient level: the overall lighting in a room; the general light level other than that focused on specific areas.

angle: or camera angle, is the point from which the camera views the action.

animation: a series of drawings or still photographs of models photographed on motion picture film in rapid sequence in order to simulate motion.

antenna: a mast-like device for transmitting radio frequency signals by television broadcasting stations; also, the device that picks up the television signal off-the-air for viewing on the television receiver.

aperture: the opening in a camera lens through which light passes; a means of regulating the amount of light picked up by the television camera.

aspect ratio: the relationship of width to height; the U.S. standard aspect ratio is 4:3; that is, the width of a television screen has four units to the depth's three.

audio: the sound portion of a television program; as opposed to the video or visual portion.

audio frequency signal: an electronic signal whose frequency lies within the limits of audibility; 20 to 20,000 cycles per second.

audio pair: a pair of wires connecting audio equipment such as microphones and speakers.

background: in video, that which is behind the people or action; in audio, the sound or music accompanying the action, but on a lower level of sound than voices or principal sounds.

beam: a directed radio signal such as a microwave beam directed in a straight line.

black: when the television picture is dissolved or faded from the television screen, the picture "goes to black".

bloom: the glare caused by too much light reflecting from an object into the camera.

booster: an amplifier which increases the television signal for distribution to distant points.

burn in: to cause the picture to remain in the television tube as an after-impression by overexposure of the camera on an object.

camera cable: the wire cable that carries the television picture from the camera to the control area.

camera monitor: a video monitor which is an integral part of the television camera or the camera's control unit.

coaxial cable: a wire cable having a center conductor within an outer shield; used to carry the signal from the camera to the control area, to the transmitter, to the receivers, and across country.

contrast: the light value between the lightest and darkest parts of the television picture.

depth of field: the limitations within which all action is in focus; measured from the nearest object to the camera to the farthest.

dissolve: the fading of the television picture, either to black or to another picture.

distribution amplifier: an amplifier connecting multiple television monitor circuits to a single source of television signal while retaining perfect electrical balance.

dolly: a mount enabling the camera to be moved to various areas in a studio or program originating room. Also to move the camera towards or away from the stage action.

fade: to lower the sound volume or dissolve a picture.

film clip: a motion picture film inserted into the television program.

filter: a glass disc fitted over the camera lens to produce a particular effect or to compensate for lighting conditions.

flood light: one that gives general illumination over the entire scene being televised.

foot candle: unit for measuring the intensity of light; one foot candle equals one lumen per square foot.

ghost: a shadow or additional image appearing in the picture; common to home television when the television signal is reflected from two points of the receiving antenna.

image: the picture on the television screen.

image orthicon: a camera pickup tube in which the granular elements of a photo-sensitive screen generate a current when activated by a light source and then internally amplified by electron mulipliers within the tube.

instructional television: the generally accepted term denoting the use of closed circuit television for formal classroom instruction on all educational levels.

kinescope recording: a motion picture of a telecast; recording equipment picks up the program as it is being performed; commonly referred to as a "Kine".

klieg light: a spotlight used to illuminate stage action.

light level: the ambient value of the overall lighting of a scene.

light meter: a device used in measuring the amount of light surrounding an object.

line: a single line across the inner surface of a television tube containing shadows and highlights; all standard television presentations have approximately 500 lines from top to bottom of the screen; standard home-type television sets have lines with horizontal detail referred to as a "325 line resolution". Special television monitors produce considerably greater horizontal detail.

line amplifier: boosts the strength of video signals for long distance transmission over coaxial cables.

live: a program telecast directly rather than one recorded on film and telecast later.

master monitor: a video monitor used in the originating area or studio, or a control room, enabling the previewing of pictures supplied by several different cameras.

monitor: a viewing screen on which the picture is seen; verb: to watch and appraise a television program.

pan: a horizontal movement of the television camera as it remains in focus.

pan and tilt head: a mounting device attached to a tripod enabling smooth horizontal and vertical movement of the television camera.

patch panel: an interconnecting device accepting incoming cables from various sources enabling the changing of circuits by patching-in short lengths of cable between connectors.

radio frequency signal: an electronic signal whose frequency lies above the limits of audibility; usually a carrier signal matching an established TV channel and modulated with picture or sound; commonly referred to as the RF signal.

remote: a television program originating from an area other than the studio or control area.

scanning: the function of the electron beam in sweeping across the surface of the television tube from left to right in forming the television picture.

signal: the sound or picture transmitted by radio waves.

sound: all parts of the telecast that can be heard; i.e., the audio portion.

spotlight: a light used to illuminate a specific part of the scene, such as the principal speaker or a specific object being discussed.

super-impose: the overlapping of two pictures by switching the scenes viewed by two cameras onto a single screen.

switch: to cut from the picture on one camera to that of another.

televise: the process of photographing with a television camera.

telecast: the broadcasting of a television picture.

tilt: the vertical movement of the television camera.

tripod: a camera support having three legs.

turret: a lens mount enabling rapid change of lenses; ordinarily has three or four lenses of different focal lengths.

video: that part of the television program which is seen as opposed to audio.

video frequency: an electronic signal which fluctuates according to the light and dark elements of a scene encountered by the scanning beam of the television pickup tube as it crosses and recrosses the sensitive surface of the tube.

vidicon: a camera pickup tube in which the outward flow of current is proportional to the amount of light falling upon the particular granular particle in a photo-sensitive screen upon which the scanning beam is focused.

zoom lens: a lens in which the relationship of elements can be altered to change magnification as well as focus, thus permitting smooth transition from close-ups to wide angle pictures without moving the camera.

Courtesy the Philco Corporation, Government & Industrial Group.

BIBLIOGRAPHY

Brown, James W., Richard B. Lewis, and Fred F. Harcleroad, *AV Instruction Materials and Methods,* New York, McGraw-Hill Book Company, Inc., 1964, 592 pp.
> Chap. 10 Television
> Reference Section 1 Television Receivers, p. 519

Brown, James W., and Richard B. Lewis (Ed), *AV Instructional Materials Manual,* Second Edition, New York, McGraw-Hill Book Company, Inc., 1964, 188 pp.
> Exercise Thirty-Seven Broadcast Television
> Exercise Forty-Nine Television Equipment

Cross, A. J. Foy, and Irene F. Cypher, *Audio-Visual Education,* New York, Thomas Y. Crowell Company, 1961, 415 pp.
> Chap. 2 Television

Dale, Edgar, *Audio-Visual Methods in Teaching,* Revised Edition, New York, The Dryden Press, 1954, 534 pp.
Chap. 14 Educational Television

De Kieffer, Robert, and Lee W. Cochran, *Manual of Audio-Visual Techniques,* Englewood Cliffs, New Jersey, Prentice-Hall, Inc., 1955, 220 pp.
Unit Four Audio Materials, Equipment and Television
Television, pp. 179-188

Dugan, J. M., J. S. Jones, S. A. Hawk, and L. E. Walkup, *Guide to Audio-Visual Presentations,* New York, Wolf Business Publications, Inc., 1964, 149 pp.
Television as a Method of Communication for Small Groups

Haas, Kenneth B., and Harry Q. Packer, *Preparation and Use of Audio-Visual Aids,* Englewood Cliffs, New Jersey, Prentice-Hall, Inc., 1955, 381 pp.
Chap. 14 Television

Kemp, Jerrold E., *Planning and Producing Audiovisual Materials,* San Francisco, California, Chandler Publishing Company, 1963, 169 pp.
Part Three Producing Your Audiovisual Materials
6. Television Materials

Kinder, James S., *Audio-Visual Materials and Techniques,* 2nd Edition, New York, American Book Company, 1959, 592 pp.
Chap. 12 Educational Television

Sands, Lester B., *Audio-Visual Procedures in Teaching,* New York, The Ronald Press, 1956, 670 pp.
Chap. 25 Radio and Television

Spear, John, *Creating Visuals for TV,* Washington, D.C., National Education Association, 1962

Thomas R. Murray, and Sherwin G. Swartout, *Integrated Teaching Materials,* New York, Longmans, Green and Company, Inc., 1960, 545 pp.
Chap. 16 Using Radio and Television Programs
Chap. 18 Creating Television Programs

Wittich, Walter Arno, and Charles Francis Schuller, *Audio-Visual Materials: Their Nature and Use,* Third Edition, New York, Harper & Brothers Publishers, 1962, 500 pp.
Chap. 14 Television in Education

CHAPTER 18

TEACHING MACHINES

What Are Teaching Machines?

The theory of learning which is today embodied in the teaching machine is not new, but actually one of the oldest techniques man has devised. It is based on the fact that a teaching device (including human instructors) should be ready to give the learner bits of information, test him to see when he has learned the information, and then go on to more advanced material using the previously learned material as a basis for what comes later. This was of the Socratic method by which the teacher, through carefully chosen questions, drew the information out of the learner. But it goes back even farther to when the father took his son out into the woods to teach him how to hunt wild animals. There was one teacher and one learner and the teacher provided information as fast as the learner could absorb it. If the boy made an incorrect response to the situation, the father corrected it on the spot. Today it is economically unfeasible to provide teachers on a one-to-one basis with the learners.

This situation is as true in industry as it is in the public schools and colleges. True, some instruction on-the-job is one-to-one for some of the time, but this would be too costly if long continued. The new employee must be trained and put into a productive position as soon as possible. Most training programs do not take into account the fact that some people can learn the necessary information more rapidly than others and they should not be held back with the slower learners.

If there could be an instructor who could work exclusively with one learner at a time, present the material to the learned in carefully planned small bits, check the performance of the learner at each step of the way, offer encouragement or correction at each step, repeat his instructions where necessary, and in all things retain infinite patience, then an approach could be made to the perfect learning situation. The teaching machine is the result of the attempts of educators and scientists to provide such a situation.

The teaching machine is designed to present the subject matter in a series of very small steps. After each bit is given to the student, he is asked to make a decision involving application of the material he has just received. The decision may be in the answering of a question or the working of a problem. At any rate, after the learner has made his response, the machine moves on. The machine's response to the learner's choice varies according to the type of machine, as we shall see below.

Two Theories in Teaching Machines. All teaching machines, regardless of their complexity, are of one of two types—linear and branching.

The linear type is the simpler. In this type of machine, the material advances from one frame (or question or problem) to the next when the learner has made the correct response. In this case, when the learner has read the instructions and has decided upon an answer, he presses one of several multiple-choice buttons. If he pushes the correct one, the material moves on to the next frame. If the response is incorrect, the machine does not move and the learner knows that he has made a mistake. The materials are generally arranged so that the learner seldom if ever makes an error. If he does make an error, he refigures the problem or reconsiders the question and selects another answer in accordance with his new line of reasoning. The machine may be constructed so as to record the number of incorrect answers that a learner makes. Also, it may record the cumulative number of errors that are made on each step of the program. Thus, if an inordinately large number of people miss certain questions, the organization of the material should be changed to improve those parts. This is not a testing situation, because correct answers are desired, not errors. A diagrammatic representation of the linear teaching machine program is shown in Figure 130.

FIG. 130. Diagram of a Linear Program.

The branching type of program is more sophisticated. When an error is made, it automatically takes the learner through a short review designed to clear up the specific difficulty which caused the student to make that particular error. After he has gone through the review, he is brought back to the original question and once more he makes his choice. Naturally, when the correct answer is made, the machine moves on to the next frame in the sequence. A diagram of the branching technique is in Figure 131. The learner answers frames 1 and 2 correctly. On frame 3, let us assume that the correct answer is A. Answer B would send the machine to frames a, b, c, and back again to frame 3. These three frames are designed to correct the misapprehension that led the learner to choose answer B. If C had been chosen in error, then corrective frames d, e, f, and g would be shown, then back to frame 3 to try again. This system modifies the presentation of the material to suit the needs and abilities of the learner. If the person makes the correct response each time, he can go straight through the material without using any of the remedial frames.

Programing. Programing is the preparation of the material presented by the teaching machine. One deterrent to a more rapid extension of machine teaching is the lack of good programs. It would appear that one could take a good textbook or set of lecture notes, break them up into small segments, and so construct a program. This, however, is not the case. In textbook learning and in the lecture method, the student is tested only infrequently and he has the opportunity to check with other authors or to ask questions of his instructor to clear up areas of confusion before he is asked to reveal his knowledge of the subject. In the teaching machine method, the material must be presented in such a way that gaps in the knowledge do not occur. For this reason, it is necessary to do a great deal of testing, experimentation, and revising before a program is ready for actual use in a teaching situation. One method of doing this is

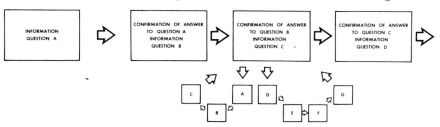

FIG. 131. Diagram of a Branching Program.

to work directly with a group of typical learners and present them with the material as you have it planned, with the learners making the choices and working the problems called for. If members of the group must ask questions or call for information that is not in the program, a note is made of the points at which the questions were asked. These indicate weak points in the program and must be corrected. This procedure must be repeated many times before the program is ready for use.

Advantages of Teaching Machines

The most obvious advantage of automated teaching for a business or industrial firm is the reduction in time that is necessary to prepare an employee for his job. If a particularly able person could in one week go through a course that would take three weeks under conventional methods, then he could start producing and returning the investment in his salary that much sooner. Another value is that the employee will avoid the frustration of sitting through the presentation of material at a much slower rate than he could absorb it. On the other hand, the employee who might have difficulty learning the information at the rate with which it would be presented to a class could learn it his own speed by the teaching machine method and perhaps turn out to be a valuable employee.

An additional advantage is that such a method would take less personnel to operate. Ordinarily the best producers are taken out of the production function to instruct new employees, in order to give them the best possible preparation for their jobs. Teaching machines could lessen disruption to normal operations.

Utilization of Teaching Machines

The following quotation, prepared by the Argyle Publishing Corportation (Lord Products Division) in cooperation with the American Institute of Executives, explains the philosophy behind their development of programing, and specifically their contract programing service.

Why Use Programed Instruction? More than $30 billion is spent every year by U. S. industry in training employees—about the same amount as is spent annually on the public schools. How can this cost be reduced? How can training be improved?

Programed instruction provides an answer to many of the problems that beset training directors. It can reduce substantially the time required to learn a subject, improve the final performance, insure a uniform quality of instruction to all trainees, conserve instructor time, decentralize training, and permit individuals to receive instruction without having to wait until the next training cycle begins.

Does PI sound like a panacea . . . a cure-all? It isn't. You cannot overcome the problem of poorly conceived training material simply by programing it. This is why an experienced programer will not be content simply to accept your existing training materials and convert them to frames (the basic units of PI) . Instead, the programer applies a "systems approach" to training. Here's how it works . . .

The Systems Approach In conventional training, the instructor starts with a predetermined set of facts and skills to be imparted through visual or auditory media, the assumption being that these materials will prepare trainees to do their jobs. However, it often happens in industry that job requirements change faster than the training for them. Thus, training materials become inadequate, or outdated, or not wholly relevant to the tasks for which they were originally intended.

This is why a programer does not start by translating your existing materials into programed instruction. Instead, he works with you in arriving at a statement of your training objectives . . . in very specific, observable, measurable terms. Then he prepares a "behavioral analysis" to determine how these objectives can best be met. In doing this, he'll simplify, combine, resequence, eliminate, and supplement your existing training material to arrive at a list of those facts, skills, and attitudes that are essential to the attainment of your training objectives. Then and only then will he write frames, try them out on a representative sample of learners, and revise them to produce the most effective training package possible.[1]

Areas Suitable for Use of Teaching Machines. As has been apparent throughout this chapter, the major contribution of the teaching machine in business is in the training of employees. The teaching of theory and the background of knowledge for the job are well suited to teaching machines. This can be done equally effectively for the new employee and for the one who is being prepared for a promotion or for a different job.

Organizations using programed instruction in training employees have, in general, certain things in common.

1. The positions for which the programed materials were prepared are those which require a knowledge of procedures, rates, etc., rather than physical skills as a base of performance.

---

1. Argyle Publishing Corporation (Lord Products Division) in cooperation with the American Institute of Executives, advertising brochure.

2. Employees vary considerably in their backgrounds of experience for the job.
3. Small numbers of employees beginning at one time, or wide geographical distribution of employees, makes it uneconomical to gather them together for formal classes.
4. On-the-job training would be too expensive because it would require a more experienced employee to supervise each action of the beginner. Errors which might otherwise slip through would be very costly.
5. After his training, decisions made by the new employee will be potentially costly to the company.

In addition to training their own employees, some companies make their course materials available to employees of their customers. For instance, one national van line allows customers' em-

FIG. 132. Videosonic Unit. *(Courtesy of Hughes Aircraft Company, Videosonic Systems Division)*

ployees to take the tariff course so that they can audit the charges correctly. This has reduced unnecessary correspondence and time spent in recomputing charges.

Many companies utilize printed programs in book form rather than those which require machine administration of the material, because of the smaller investment required. Also, the books may be used anywhere in the plant rather than just in a machines room. Another advantage is that the employee may take the book home and study it there if he wishes to complete the course of study as quickly as possible. If properly organized and presented, the program may be retained by the employee to serve as a reference in case that he needs clarification of certain material at a later date.

One may understand the theory of how a thing should operate or fit together and still not be able to make it work. Can teaching machines help in this kind of a problem? Can they show a person how to operate a complicated piece of electronic equipment or to run a piece of machinery? The answer is yes, there are devices designed to do exactly this.

One such device is the Videosonic System developed and manufactured by the Hughes Aircraft Company, Videosonic Systems Division. This device, which is pictured in Figure 132, is designed to sit directly in front of the individual worker at his work station.

The instruction provided by the machine consists of a series of color slides and magnetic tape narration. The slides are projected from the rear onto an 8″ x 5½″ translucent screen. The tape contains signals for the automatic changing of the slides in addition to the description of each step in the assembly or inspection of the product. The person starts the recording and slides as he commences the operation for which he is responsible. The narration tells him exactly what to do and the slide shows him what the assembly should look like at that time, pointing out the critical points. The tape can be stopped if the operator is not ready to go on to the next step when the tape has completed the normally allowed time. Programmed music plays during the interim periods between verbal instructions, to reduce worker fatigue and tension.

The Videosonic unit is located where the worker can see it most easily. In Figure 133, it is located just above the electronic assembly that is being made. The worker can look back and forth between the work and the unit by merely shifting her eyes. In this photograph the Videosonic unit appears just above the component being assembled.

FIG. 133. Videosonic Unit in Operation of an Electronic Component Assembly Line.
(Courtesy of Hughes Aircraft Company, Videosonic Systems Division)

The manufacturer claims these advantages for the use of the Videosonic System in a complex assembly operation:

Defects per hour—reduced by 40 to 55 percent
Productivity—improved by 30 to 50 percent
Learning cycle—reduced noticeably
Operator tension and fatigue—relieved

The inspection operation is improved in the following ways:

Inspection time is utilized more efficiently.
Inspection techniques and procedures are standardized.
Errors in judgment resulting in rejects are eliminated.
Paperwork is greatly reduced.

This machine, or variations of it, is also adaptable for use in sales activities and in employee recruitment by proper choice of slides and narration.

Programing for Industrial Teaching. As was mentioned earlier, any automated teaching device can be only as good as the program prepared for it. It was also mentioned that a good machine program takes a great deal of time and work to perfect. With the ordinary educational program, this cost can be amortized over a large number of students in many institutions. One developed by an industrial organization, on the other hand, would not, of course, be made available to competitors in the same line of business. Therefore, the cost of developing the program would have to be borne by the company. This cost might be more than the value of the program during the time that it would be in effect.

There are certain areas of knowledge which are of interest to all organizations, and in these areas programed materials can be purchased for use. The Argyle Publishing Corporation publishes standard programed books for general use. Those which are currently being distributed compose the Management Skills Series (see Fig. 134). Titles include:

No. 1 Improving Your Written Communication
No. 2 Understanding Public Relations
No. 3 Method Improvement & Work Control

FIG. 134. Programmed Book *Improving Your Written Communication.*
(Courtesy of Argyle Publishing Corporation, Lord Products Division)

No. 4 The Secretary: Jill-of-all-Trades
No. 5 Cutting Office Costs Through Work Simplification
No. 6 PERT for Management Planning & Control
No. 7 Application of Reliability Techniques

In order to provide a basis for accurate assessment of the value of these programs, a test kit is provided. This test kit includes:

The program desired
"Before" and "after" measurement tests
Complete instructions for administering a pilot training project
Statement of training objectives
Questionnaires to get employee reactions

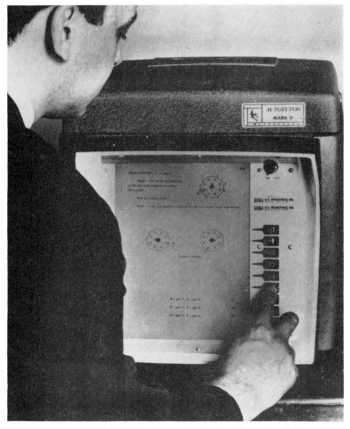

FIG. 135. Autotutor Mark II Manufactured by the Education Science Division, U. S. Industries, Inc. *(Courtesy of U. S. Industries, Inc.)*

Machine administration of the programed material is sometimes advantageous, particularly when more rigid control of the information being presented is desired. With this type of presentation, the learner does not have access to any part of the program except that bit of information that appears on the machine at any one time. He cannot look forward or back in the sequence of material, but must base his decisions upon what is before him. One such machine is the Autotutor Mark II (see Fig. 135). The information is projected from a 35mm filmstrip onto a rear projection screen contained in the unit. A number of buttons are provided for the learner to select what he considers the appropriate response to the question that is asked. A coding system on the edge of the filmstrip determines the machine's selection of the next material to be presented to the learner—whether it is the next step forward or remedial material given in the event of an incorrect answer.

Summary

The old ideal of a one-to-one ratio between teachers and students comes close to realization with the use of teaching machines (or to use the more inclusive term, programed learning) which permit the learner to proceed as rapidly as he is capable and gives him information, tests him, and gives remedial work when necessary. This makes it possible to place a new employee in a productive position just as quickly as he can learn the necessary information.

The program is the series of bits of information and questions which make up the presentation of the subject. There are two main kinds of programs—the linear and the branching. The linear program has one sequence of frames through which everyone goes. The branching program provides for variations in the sequence depending upon the errors the learner makes. As long as the correct answers to the questions continue to be given, the machine goes straight through the material. An error causes the machine to introduce appropriate remedial steps into the sequence. Construction of an adequate program requires much planning and testing before it is ready for use.

Industrial use of teaching machines will help to get the new employee on the production line just as quickly as he can learn the necessary material. There are companies which contract for the preparation of programs for individual companies and also have more general programs which could be used by almost any organization for the improvement of its operations. Certain types of machines are designed to be put in front of the employee as he works, providing a continuous reference and model for his work.

One deterrent to the use of these machines in any but the largest industrial organizations is the cost of developing the program in relation to the relatively small number of learners over which to amortize the cost. One solution is to utilize materials that have a wider base of use than just one company.

TEACHING MACHINE TERMS:
A GLOSSARY

Quoted from Desmond L. Cook, "Teaching Machine Terms: A Glossary," *Audiovisual Instruction,* April, 1961.

augmenting: one way in which guidance through a program is created is by augmenting, or introducing bits of information that will lead the student into a new concept.

auto-instructional methods: a comprehensive term suggested by Lumsdaine and Klaus to describe instruction characterized by the controlled presentation of material, the elicitation of appropriate response, guidance with respect to the subject matter, and control of the way in which learning proceeds.

automated instruction: instructional methods considered generally to comprehend any means, devices or material, whereby teacher or tutor functions (actual or desirable) are replaced, or provided, by a wholly or partially automated sequence of instructional segments that is prepared in advance and is capable of instructing effectively when presented without direct intervention or modification by a teacher. Also called "automatic teaching.

automatic teaching: see "automated instruction."

automatic tutoring: an individual instructorless method of teaching which is an automation of the classical process of individual learning.

choice: refers to the selection of an answer from several alternatives presented to the subject as opposed to having the subject construct or write out an answer.

construction: the process of requiring the subject to write out or prepare an answer as opposed to choosing one of several alternative answers.

confirming mechanism: a device or means by which the student has his response confirmed as being right or wrong. Correctness or error can be indicated through the presentation of visual or auditory signals, or, in the case of constructive answers, the presentation of the correct or model answers.

conversational chaining: a term introduced by Barlow to describe a program wherein the movement from item to item follows less the question-answer pairs in other programs and more the natural train of conversation so that the lesson becomes the main unit of concern for the student rather than the item.

cue, vanishing: a prompt presented originally, but gradually reduced or eliminated, thereby requiring the student to provide the response independently.

display mechanism: the mechanical means by which the programmed set of materials is presented visually or aurally to the subject.

error: an incorrect or non-appropriate answer to a specific item in the program.

error rate: refers to the number or percentage of a given group of subjects incorrectly responding to a specific item on the program. A high degree of error would probably indicate a need for revision in the program.

fading: the gradual withdrawal of stimulus support in presenting items.

feedback: communicating to the subject pursuing a sequence of programmed materials the information needed to modify responses so that failures or errors can be eliminated and correct responses maintained.

frame: a single item or statement is exposed at a time. The exposed material constitutes a single frame.

frame, forced: a stimulus frame presented to the student forcing him to respond correctly by the obvious nature of the answer.

frame, response: that part of a teaching machine or programmed textbook which permits the subject to record his response to the item presented by means of the stimulus frame. (See stimulus frame.)

frame, stimulus: that part of a mechanical teaching machine or programmed textbook containing the individual items, in the form of a question or statement, to which the student is to respond. Also refers to the mechanical part of the teaching machine which allows the examinee to see the item.

hints: devices used to direct the student's behavior in the desired direction. Used to increase the likelihood of a correct response.

item, augmenting: an item supplying new information but not requiring the student to make a relevant response.

item, delayed review: an item which allows for the distribution of practice. Differs from other items only in terms of presentation.

item, dovetailing: an item requiring the student to make separate responses to separate stimuli which otherwise may become confused.

item, fading: an item requiring the student to review what has been presented. In addition the item withdraws information successively. Similar to Skinner's "vanishing technique."

item, generalizing: an item presenting a verbal statement pointing to a common characteristic of several specific problems already presented to the subject.

item, interlocking: an item that requires a student to review the established skills while new information is being presented.

item, lead in: an item not requiring new information or rehearsal of old skills but functions to orient the subject to a problem and prepare him for new information.

item, restated review: an item, requiring a rehearsal of the skill where a problem is restated.

item, rote review: an item presenting a problem identical to one presented earlier.

item, specifying: an item which exemplifies a general rule or principle.

item, subject matter: an item classified with respect to its subject matter content.

item, tab: a specialized term referring to having the subject pull a tab to indicate his response rather than writing out an answer or selecting a choice.

leading: the student is first asked to talk about familiar things using his every-day vocabulary. He is then led to discuss relations among these. Technical terms are then slowly inserted.

learning machine: a term often applied to teaching machines. An inappropriate term for describing a mechanical teaching device since it implies that a machine learns.

matching: procedure used in some Skinner machines to inform student of correctness of his response. After writing his response, the student moves a lever which exposes the correct answer with which the student compares or "matches" his response.

operant behavior: behavior which operates or acts upon the environment. A fundamental concept in Skinnerian learning theory.

pace: the rate at which the subject is permitted to work through the pro-grammed material.

pacing, controlled rate: control of the subjects' rate of responding by features of the mechanical device utilized to present the program.

pacing, self: the rate at which the subject might complete the material at his own rate depending upon success on the previous steps.

panel: a short passage of prose material, graphs, and similar material which are presented or studied along with the discs in the Skinner device.

paper teaching machine: refers to the "scrambled" or "programmed" textbook type of self-instructional devices.

Porter device: a device similar to the Skinner disc machine, except instead of using round discs, a regular sheet of paper is inserted into the mechanism. The paper contains the programmed material and spaces for insertion of answers.

Pressey device: the earliest known device (1926) originally developed for use with multiple choice tests. Device could be set so that items missed could be skipped or repeated until success was established, a raw score obtained, and an item analysis or error count secured.

program: the subject matter that is to be learned by the student via the machine or other device.

programmed book: a special book in which the subject matter to be learned has been arranged into a series of sequential steps leading from familiar concepts to new materials. Differs from a "scrambled textbook" in that the content is arranged so that the student proceeds directly from one step to the next, or one succeeding page to the next, rather than skipping around. The student generally is asked to construct a response as opposed to choice.

programmed learning: a term sometimes used synonymously to refer to the broader concept of "auto-instructional methods."

programmer: generally, a curriculum specialist who subdivides the material to be learned into a series of sequential steps; usually moves the student from a familiar background into a complex and new set of concepts, principles, and understandings.

programming, intrinsic: a method of programming materials that directs the erring subject along certain corrective pathways before he is permitted to proceed to the next step in the program. Requires that each step contain multiple choice answers.

prompt: some type of verbal or symbolic cue which facilitates the desired response from the subject.

prompting: the method or sequence of providing verbal and symbolic cues to encourage responses. Can be visual, verbal, symbolic, or auditory.

reinforcement, immediate: the process of providing the subject with immediate feedback or information regarding the success or failure of his performance.

reinforcement mechanism: some type of reward for responding correctly to the items in the display. A motivational factor causing the individual to keep working at the set of materials. Sometimes considered as an integral part of the confirming mechanism.

reinforcer, immediate: a self-instructional aid which contains a built-in system of providing the student with immediate knowledge of the success or failure of his performance.

response device: a type of teaching aid which permits the student to practice certain types of responses. No stimulus is presented as part of this type of device.

response mechanism: a device which permits the student to record his response to the items presented in the display mechanism. Usually is either the selection of one or several choices of writing an answer to the item in the program.

response mode: the form of the response a student makes while working on a program.

scrambled book: a special book containing material to be learned in programmed sequential form, but in which the student is directed to different pages not necessarily in consecutive order. By means of alternate choice response at each step, branching to new or review material is made possible.

self-instructional device: a mechanical or paper device which presents a set of planned sequential materials to be learned and which the student can complete in the absence of a live instructor and at his own rate of speed.

shaping: the building of a behavior or set of behaviors through the differential reinforcement of progressively more adequate forms of behavior. (Skinner)

Skinner device: a mechanical device which presents a set of programmed materials. At each step the subject must construct an answer and evaluate its correctness with a model answer before proceeding further in the program. Generally considered the forerunner of later model "teaching machines."

Skinner disc: a round, flat record-like device which contains a set or series of program materials for the Skinner device. Contains the questions to be answered, spaces for recording student's answers, and the correct response, as well as for making a record of successful or unsuccessful performance.

step: the increment in subject matter level to be learned with each succeeding item or frame in the program.

step size: the amount of increase in subject matter difficulty with each step in the program. A large step size could result in relatively few frames while a low step would indicate a relatively large number of frames in the program.

stimulus device: a type of teaching aid which presents materials to the subject through one or several of the various senses. No active response is required on the part of the subject during the presentation of the materials.

stimulus-response device: a teaching aid which not only presents material to the subject through any or several of the various senses, but also requires a response to the stimulus presented in order to progress further in the program of instruction.

terminal behavior: the behavior a program is designed to produce.

track, multiple: a provision within the programmed material for allowing subjects to pursue alternative subdivisions of the program in terms of their successes or failures with earlier sections of the sequence.

track, single: a common set of programmed materials which all subjects work through, there being no alternative program such as in the multiple track situations.

vanishing: the basic problem here is to evoke a given bit of behavior, at least once, in the presence of an appropriate stimulus, so that it can be reinforced. One solution is to begin with stimuli which already control the behavior and to reduce them slowly as learning proceeds.

Desmond L. Cook, "Teaching Machine Terms: A Glossary," *Audiovisual Instruction,* April, 1961, pp. 152, 153.

BIBLIOGRAPHY

Brethower, Dale M., *Programed Instruction: A Manual of Programing Techniques,* Chicago, Educational Methods, 1963, 268 pp.

Brown, James W., Richard B. Lewis, and Fred F. Harcleroad, *AV Instructional Materials and Methods,* Second Edition, New York, McGraw-Hill Book Company, Inc., 1964, 592 pp.
    Chap. 11 Programmed Instruction

Brown, James W., and Richard B. Lewis (Ed), *AV Instructional Materials Manual,* Second Edition, New York, McGraw-Hill Book Company, Inc., 1964, 188 pp.
    Exercise Thirty-Four Programmed Materials

Coulson, John E. (Ed), *Programed Learning and Computer-Based Instruction,* New York, John Wiley & Sons, 1962, 306 pp.

Cram, David, *Explaining "Teaching Machines" and Programing,* San Francisco, Fearon Press, 1961, 86 pp.

Cross, A. J. Foy, and Irene F. Cypher, *Audio-Visual Education,* New York, Thomas Y. Crowell Company, 1961, 415 pp.
Chap. 13 Machines for Teaching and Learning

Deterline, William A., *An Introduction to Programed Instruction,* Englewood Cliffs, New Jersey, Prentice-Hall, Inc., 131 pp.

Dolmatch, T. B., E. Martin, and R. E. Finley (Ed), *Revolution in Training: Programed Instruction in Industry,* (American Management Report No. 72), New York, American Management Association, 1962, 160 pp.

Fine, Benjamin, *Teaching Machines,* New York, Sterling Publishing Co., Inc., 1962, 176 pp.

Finn, James D., and Donald G. Perrin, *Teaching Machines and Programed Learning, 1962: A Survey of the Industry,* (Office of Education Publication No. OE-34019), Washington, D.C., Government Printing Office, 1962, 85 pp.

Foltz, Charles I., *The World of Teaching Machines,* Washington, D.C., Teaching Research and Technology Division, Electronic Teaching Laboratories, 1961, 116 pp.

Fry, Edward B., *Teaching Machines and Programed Learning: An Introduction to Autoinstruction,* New York, McGraw-Hill Book Co., 1962, 244 pp.

Glaser, Robert, and M. Glanzer (Ed), *Training Research and Education,* Pittsburgh, Pa., University of Pittsburgh Press, 1962, 596 pp.

Green, Edward J., *The Learning Process and Programed Instruction,* New York, Holt, Rinehart and Winston, 1962, 233 pp.

Hughes, J. L., *Programed Instruction for Schools and Industry,* Chicago, Science Research Associates, 1962, 299 pp.

Hughes, J. L. (Ed), *Programed Learning: A Critical Evaluation,* Chicago, Educational Methods, 1964, 238 pp. (A report on programed instruction in industry)

Lumsdaine, A. A., and Robert Glaser (Ed), *Teaching Machines and Programed Learning: A Source Book,* Washington, D.C., National Education Association, Department of Audiovisual Instruction, 1960, 724 pp.

Margulies, Stuart, and Lewis D. Eigen (Ed), *Applied Programed Instruction,* New York, John Wiley & Sons, 1962, 387 pp.

Markle, Susan M., Lewis D. Eigen, and P. K. Komoski, *A Programed Primer on Programing,* New York, Center for Programed Instruction, 1961, Vol. I, 25 pp., Vol. II, 44 pp.

New Teaching Aids for the American Classroom, Washington, D. C., Office of Education, U. S. Department of Health, Education and Welfare, 1960, 173 pp.
A. A. Lumsdaine, "The Development of Teaching Machines and Programmed Self-Instruction," pp. 136-173

"Programed Instruction," *Audiovisual Instruction,* February, 1963

Schramm, Wilbur, *Programed Instruction: Today and Tomorrow,* New York, The Fund for the Advancement of Education, 1962, 74 pp.

"Self-Instruction," *Audiovisual Instruction,* April, 1961

Wiley, John, & Sons, *A Guide for Wiley Authors in the Preparation of Auto-Instructional Programs,* Second Edition, New York, John Wiley & Sons, 1963, 14 pp. (Single copy free)

Wittich, Walter Arno, and Charles Francis Schuller, *Audio-Visual Materials: Their Nature and Use,* Third Edition, New York, Harper & Brothers Publishers, 1962, 500 pp.
Chap. 16 Teaching Machine Programed Learning

MOTION PICTURES

Learning and Behavior (The Teaching Machine), New York, Carousel Films, sound, black-and-white, 26 minutes.

One Step at a Time, Pittsburgh, Pa., American Institute for Research, sound, color, 30 minutes.

Teaching Machines and Programed Learning, Washington, D.C., Norwood Films, sound, black-and-white, 29 minutes.

FILMSTRIP

An Example of a Teaching Machine Program, Pasadena, California, Basic Skill Films, color, 62 frames.

Teaching Machines, Pasadena, California, Basic Skill Films, color, 62 frames.

The Selection and Use of Programed Materials, Washington, D.C., National Education Association, sound (record), color, handbook, 63 frames.

CHAPTER **19**

FACILITIES FOR AUDIO-VISUAL UTILIZATION

Need for Proper Facilities

Efficient Utilization of Audio and Visual Devices. Chapter 1 discussed the need for the most efficient communication possible in the business and industrial world. The following chapters were concerned with the specific types of needs for this communication and with the tools which have been developed to assist in meeting these needs. Many of these tools are costly in time and money and can repay the investment in them only if they are permitted to do the best job of communicating of whch they are capable. This means that each person in the audience should be able to see and hear the material in order to have the opportunity to absorb all the information being presented to him. Anything that interferes with and makes this communication less effective decreases the return the company will get from the money it has invested in the preparation of the audio-visual materials.

In addition to the purely utilitarian advantage of more efficient communication afforded by properly constructed and equipped facilities for audio-visual presentation, there is another advantage to be gained by having a meeting place that makes possible the best quality of showmanship. This is the goodwill and respect of those with whom one is communicating. While this is admittedly a very small factor in the over-all reputation of a company, it is certainly a part of it. A smooth presentation of information about the company or its product may very well be the final thing that will clinch the sale or set up the final action—whatever that may be.

Location of the Room

The location of the room (or rooms) to be used for communications utilizing audio-visual devices will depend upon the major purpose of these communications. It should be convenient for groups who will use it.

A room to be used primarily in employee training should be the room in which the rest of the training activity takes place, or at least adjacent to it. The instructor should be able to go from other teaching methods directly into a motion picture, filmstrip, or whatever other teaching device will do the best job, without having to move the group from one part of the plant to another. An interruption of the flow of the routine makes it more difficult for the class to get all the information the material has to offer. The return to the regular classroom means that the instructor will have to get the students back into the proper frame of mind to proceed with the learning. The less interruption involved, the less will be the loss of time. The classroom or vestibule training shop should be equipped with as many of the facilities (listed later in this chapter) as are applicable to the situation.

A room used primarily for communication of a public relations nature should be a part of, or adjacent to, the reception area where people who are not employees of the organization gather. This will probably be where tours of the plant will start and finish, and where the first and last impressions of the company and its personnel will be formed. If the plant is operating under a security system that restricts the movement of non-employees to certain areas, the room should naturally be located so that it can be reached from the "public" access portions, so to avoid problems of escorting people back and forth. The reception area will also provide a convenient gathering place for the group before it moves to where the program is to be presented.

When salesman and company dealers are brought to the head office of the plant for an internal sales training program, their activities are usually under the control of the sales manager and the sales department. Efficient utilization of the audio-visual room will be enhanced in this instance if it is near the sales department, so that the group can move into it for filmed selling demonstrations and for information about new products being brought onto the market.

Groups of potential customers brought into the plant for external sales promotion can usually be handled most efficiently in an audio-visual presentation room located as the one described above for public relations. The same sorts of problems are involved and the solution is similar. The type of product that the company makes and the size of order that can be expected from individual customers will determine the feasibility of bringing them to the company premises for the sales presentation.

If the audio-visual facilities are primarily for reporting to management, they should, of course, be adjacent to the executive offices. The most logical place for this sort of activity is in the executive meeting room as described in Chapter 6.

Reporting to stockholders on the activities and condition of the company is a function that can justify the use of audio-visual methods, but in all but the most closely held corporations, the number of people who attend the meetings is so large that any meeting place on the company premises would not be large enough to hold them. It is generally necessary to rent some theater or auditorium, and even this may be insufficient to hold them all. The quarters obtained for such a meeting should have as many as possible of the features described below.

It is unlikely that a room with the equipment features necessary for the best utilization of audio and visual devices will be set aside for the exclusive use of any one of the activities described above. In practically every instance the room will have to shared by several or all of them. In this case, the location should be determined by the type of activity which will use it the greatest proportion of the time. Where the plant or office has already been built, the audio-visual room will have to be located wherever space can be found for it, but when new quarters are being designed, the location of the room can be determined on the basis of its planned utilization.

In addition to the utilization of the room, a factor in its location is its proximity to the preparation and storage areas for audio-visual materials and equipment. Actually, the major consideration should be the type of use the room will have, and the auxiliary rooms should be located where they can best serve the needs of those making use of the audio-visual room.

Suggested Facilities

Not all rooms set up for audio-visual presentations will have all of the features described below, but the features filling the needs of the organization should be included in the plans.

Efficient Light Control. The ideal location for audio-visual use from the standpoint of light control would be in a windowless room. There are several advantages to be gained from such a location.

1. It makes possible absolute light control, even to complete darkness.
2. Outside distractions—both visual and aural—are eliminated.
3. Better control over temperature and humidity is afforded.
4. An area not suitable for other activities can be put to good use.

If the room to be used for this purpose is not windowless, some method must be used to control the light coming through the windows for optimum utilization of various types of projection. Some of the light control methods in general use are the following.

1. Dark shades. Ordinary dark window shades reduce the light level in the room, but generally not enough to permit the best projected image, particularly when using an opaque projector. Too much light leaks in along the edges, especially if the window is open and a breeze is blowing.
2. Dark shades running in grooves. By adding grooves in which the shades will operate, the problem of light leaking in at the edges is eliminated. These present a problem, however, when outside ventilation is needed. An open window can allow the breeze to draw the curtain out of the grooves, letting light come into the room.
3. Floor-to-ceiling draperies running the length of the window side of the room. Opaque curtains running in a track in the ceiling provide a method of fairly satisfactory light control without blocking necessary ventilation. The draperies should be hung a foot from the outside wall and should end a foot to eighteen inches above the floor. Setting the track in from the wall will enable the drapery to clear the window sills and other obstructions that may be along the wall. The distance plus the space between the curtain and the floor make possible natural ventilation while the room is darkened for projection. Also, the small amount of light that enters the room makes it possible to move around in safety and to see enough to take notes during the projection.
4. Light-locking Venetian Blinds. These Venetian blinds have specially-constructed slats which are capable of better elimination of light than are the ordinary blinds. End grooves in which the slats fit prevent light from coming into the room around the ends of the blinds. Light is blocked out very effectively—but so is the air. If the room depends upon natural ventilation, it may be necessary to open the blind slightly. This allows some light to enter, but usually not enough to interfere seriously with the projected image.

Air Conditioning. Air conditioning, or at least forced circulation of the air, is a virtual necessity in a room designed for audio-visual presentations if the greatest possible value is to be received. A comfortable temperature is important in helping the members of the audience concentrate on the information being given to them. This is made more difficult by the fact that the projector lamps, which are 750 or 1000 watts, produce a great deal of heat which is blown out into the room by the fan. Equally important, though, is the provision of fresh, oxygen-laden air to help keep the people's minds alert. A room which depends upon air coming through the windows for its ventilation can become very hot and stuffy when those windows must be blocked in order to provide partial or complete darkness for viewing a projected image.

Electrical Outlets. A room in which various items of audio-visual equipment are to be used from time to time must have enough electrical outlets to take care of all of the different devices that might have to be used at any one time. Also, since the different items of equipment are used at various places in the room, the outlets should be located so that one will be handy from any place where a device might be used. Each outlet should be fused separately so that several projectors or recorders may be operated simultaneously.

Room lights should be operable from switches near the door and from the rear of the room. Multiple switches at each position make it possible to regulate the light level by turning on the desired banks of lights. More exact control can be provided by a rheostat switch which is continuously adjustable from full brightness to complete darkness. Thus, partial darkness can be maintained to permit notetaking or other activities and still have a bright image on the screen. A light switch at the rear of the room makes possible a smoother control of the process of moving into and out of the projected part of a program. When the room lights can be controlled from a position beside the projector, the procedures described in Chapter Ten for the process of starting and stopping a film can be accomplished easily.

Output and Input Connections for Electronic and Other Devices. Wires running across the floor from a projector to its speaker, from record players or tape recorders to external speakers, and from between types of equipment are unsightly, unprofessional looking, and likely to cause injury if people trip over them in the dark. In cases where equipment is set up on a temporary basis, the presence of wires on the floor cannot be avoided. In this sort of situation, the best solutions must be found, such as running the cords along the floor next to the wall where they will not be a source of danger. A room specially constructed for communication should be so planned as to make the use of audio-visual devices as efficient, safe, and professional as possible.

Multiple loudspeakers should be flush-mounted in the ceiling, to provide a low-level, non-directional sound reproduction for motion pictures and sound reproduction systems. At a minimum, jacks should be available at the front and rear of the room for connecting the sources of the sound signals (motion picture projector, tape recorder, etc.) to the speaker system.

Input jacks for microphone connections to the tape recorder and the public address system should also be available at least in the front and rear of the room.

Outlets for closed circuit and broadcast television should be at the front of the room, as well as connections for AM and FM radio.

An intercom or telephone (preferably the latter) should be available in the room so that calls to other parts of the company may be made when necessary, in order to save time or to insure the least possible interruption to the presentation in the event of equipment failure or the need for additional materials.

Projection Screen. A room that is used mainly for the purposes that we have considered for this one should have a permanently-installed projection screen. It can be mounted on either the wall or the ceiling and should be electrically operated. Switches controlling the lowering and raising of the screen should be located at both the front and rear of the room for the convenience of the person operating it and in the interests of a smooth showing. Portable screens on tripods are satisfactory where they are used only temporarily, but a permanently-mounted screen makes a much better impression on the viewer.

Several types of surfaces are available for the projection screen. Some of the surfaces and their characteristics are as follows.

1. Matte. This surface is a low-gloss white plastic which reflects the light from the projector over a fairly wide area. Dirt and smudges can be easily cleaned with a damp cloth. The majority of screens in use in schools and business organizations have this type of surface. More detail can be seen in images projected onto a matte surface than on any other kind.

2. Glass beaded. This surface consists of a great number of tiny glass

beads imbedded in a white background material. The light striking each bead is internally reflected and sent back in the general direction of the projector. This type of surface gives the most brilliant reflected image of any—but only to a viewer almost directly in line with the projector. The brightness falls off rapidly as one moves away from the direct line. If the audience is located directly in front of the screen in a rather narrow seating arrangement, this type of surface can give an image that no other surface can match. It is for this reason that the beaded screen is so popular for home movies and slide shows. The group is usually small enough so that everyone can sit very close to the direct line of the screen.

The beaded screen gives the least amount of detail in the image of any screen surface.

3. Lenticular. This surface consists of many tiny concave-curved grooves running vertically in a silvery plastic. Some screens are also grooved horizontally. The light from the projector is broken up by these surfaces and reflected in a wide arc. It is particularly useful when the screen must be placed on one of the long sides of a room. Sufficient light is reflected to the far sides so that the image is still bright when a person is sitting so far to the side that the material being projected appears distorted.

The screen generally should be placed against one of the short walls of the room, thus permitting a larger proportion of the audience to sit within the best viewing area. This best seating ranges in distance from two to six times the width of the projected image. The elimination of a center aisle makes it possible to put more people in the preferred seating area.

The bottom image of the projected image should be just a little higher than the tops of the heads of the audience.

The optical axis of the projector should be at right angles to the surface of the screen (vertically as well as horizontally) in order to avoid distortion of the image. Also, if the projection is made at an angle, it will be impossible to have all parts of the image in focus simultaneously.

The recommended seating areas for each of the major types of screen surface are shown in Figure 136.

Separate Projection Room. Where the room and facilities can be made available, a separate room for the projection of motion pictures and still pictures into the communications room has several advantages.

1. The distraction caused by the operator setting up and adjusting the projector is eliminated.

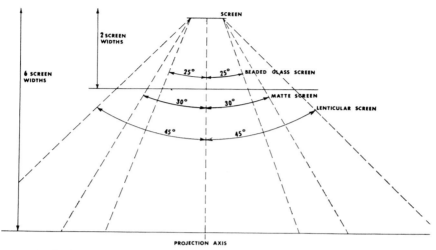

FIG. 136. Preferred Seating Arrangements with Glass-beaded, Matte, and
Lenticular Projection Screen Surfaces.

2. The running noise of the projector does not interfere with the sound track.

3. The operator does not have to move back and forth through the audience.

4. The projector is not physically in the way, making it difficult to move around and blocking the view of the people sitting at the rear of the room.

5. When more than one film is to be shown (or a long film on several reels) the distraction of rethreading the machine is eliminated.

6. Information discussed before, during, or after the showing may not be intended for general distribution throughout the company. If the operator is in the room, he may hear more than is intended for him to know.

The port through which the picture is projected should be covered with plate glass to keep out the projector sounds.

Comfortable Seating. The chairs in the communications room should be comfortable—but not *too* comfortable. They should be such that a group can meet for several hours without discomfort, but they should not be so relaxing that the people tend to go to sleep. Chairs with arms afford greater comfort than those without, but they require more room per seat. Some sort of padding will permit a person to sit and concentrate for a longer time. Remember, "The mind can absorb no more than the seat can endure."

Tables. Easily portable tables with collapsible legs should be provided for the room, to be used when the meeting is of a conference nature or when it is expected that the people in the group will be wanting to take notes or consult other documents, etc. Many meetings will not be of this sort, however, and therefore the tables should be easily movable so that they may be taken out when they are not needed. Storage space should be close by, or even opening off the room so that tables may be moved in and out quickly as the need arises.

The tables should be rather short, say six feet in length, so that many different arrangements can be made to increase the flexibility of use of the room.

Acoustic Treatment of Walls and Ceiling. Just as light control is necessary for projected pictures, acoustical control is essential for maximum understanding of material communicated by oral means. The chief cause of difficulty in understanding oral communication is unwanted reverberations. Sounds tend to bounce off hard, smooth surfaces and between parallel walls. Some methods used to reduce these reverberations, or echoes, are listed below.

1. Apply acoustical tile on the walls and ceilings.
2. Carpet the floor.
3. Hang draperies on the walls and at the windows.
4. Construct the walls so that they are not precisely parallel. This causes the echo to disappear quickly rather than bouncing back and forth.

The room must not be made too "dead" by absorbing too much of the sound. Some vibration must be permitted for better understanding and more pleasurable listening.

When planning the amount of sound deadening material to be used in a room, it must be remembered that human bodies absorb a good deal of sound themselves. Thus, a room that is crowded will sound deader than the same room when it is unoccupied. Some sound studios adjust for this by having wall panels that have a hard finish on one side and a sound-absorbing material on the other. The size of the crowd in the studio determines the proportion of the panels that will be in each position.

Lectern. The lectern provided to hold notes, etc., for a speaker may be free-standing or it may rest on a table. The former is generally the better type for a communications room because it makes the placement of the stand independent of the tables.

The lectern should have a place for the speaker's notes, plus shelves below for other materials. A shaded reading light should be attached to the side away from the speaker so that his material may be lighted regardless of the level of illumination of the rest of the room. A microphone can be installed on the lectern if the room is a large one, or if it is desired to record the speech on a tape recorder.

In addition to the usual features listed above, it is possible to make the lectern the control center for the operation of much of the audio-visual equipment in the room. A panel of controls on the right side of this piece of equipment can contain the switches, dials and regulators to operate such things as:

1. Control of the light level.
2. Raising and lowering the projection screen.
3. Starting and stopping the projectors.
4. Operation of a tape recorder.
5. Control of loudspeaker volume.

Movement of the lectern will be limited by the length of the control cable with which it is linked to the power supply and to the pieces of equipment which are to be controlled. Enough length should be allowed so that the lectern can be placed anywhere across the front of the room.

The arrangement just described permits control over the various components that make up a presentation, and permit the extra bit of showmanship that can result when all of the factors are under the complete control of one person.

Summary

Best utilization of the tools of communication requires a place where it is possible for these tools to do what they were produced to do. Proper facilities will also help to gain and to hold the attention of those people with whom it is desired to communicate. The room should be located where it is handy for the people who will be using it most. Facilities should be provided which will assist in the communication process, making it as efficient and effective as possible.

BIBLIOGRAPHY

Brown, James W., Richard B. Lewis, and Fred F. Harcleroad, *AV Instruction Materials and Methods,* New York, McGraw-Hill Book Company, Inc., 1964, 592 pp.
    Chap. 21 Improving the Room Environment

Brown, James W., and Richard B. Lewis (Ed), *AV Instructional Materials Manual,* Second Edition, New York, McGraw-Hill Book Company, 1964, 188 pp.
    Exercise Forty-One Projection Principles

Cross, A. J. Foy, and Irene F. Cypher, *Audio-Visual Education,* New York, Thomas Y. Crowell Company, 1961, 415 pp.
    Chap. 15 Planning and Equipping Instructional Areas

Dale, Edgar, *Audio-Visual Methods in Teaching,* Revised Edition, New York, The Dryden Press, 1954, 534 pp.
    Chap. 30 Administering an Audio-Visual Program

Department of Audiovisual Instruction, *Planning Schools for Use of Audio-Visual Materials,* Washington, D.C., Department of Audiovisual Instruction, National Education Association, 1952, 40 pp.

Dugan, J. M., J. S. Jones, S. A. Hawk, and L. E. Walkup, *Guide to Audio-Visual Presentations,* New York, Wolf Business Publications, Inc., 1964, 149 pp.
    Physical Arrangements of the Projection Room

Eastman Kodak Company, *Foundations for Effective Audio-Visual Projection,* Pamphlet S-3, Rochester 4, New York, Eastman Kodak Company. (Single copy free)

Holland, Ben F., Horace C. Hartsell, and Raymond L. Davidson, *Audio-Visual Materials and Devices,* Lubbock, Texas, Rodgers Litho, 1958, 157 pp.
    Chap. 13 Equipping and Furnishing Rooms

Kinder, James S., *Audio-Visual Materials and Techniques,* 2nd Edition, New York, American Book Company, 1959, 592 pp.
    Chap. 13 Room Facilities

Sands, Lester B., *Audio-Visual Procedures in Teaching,* New York, The Ronald Press, 1956, 670 pp.
    Chap. 26 Screens and Other Accessories
    Chap. 27 The Complete Classroom

Strauss, L. Harry, and J. R. Kidd, *Look, Listen, and Learn,* New York, Association Press, 1948, 235 pp.
    Chap. IV Principles of Utilization

INDEX

A

Advance Products Co., 241, 243
Advertising, 4
Advertising and Sales Promotion (Formerly *Advertising Requirements*), 149, 150-153, 170-171, 172
Aerojet General Corporation, 279
Aetna Life affiliated Companies, 42
Allis-Chalmers, 64, 70, 97
Aluminum Company of America, 42
American Telephone & Telegraph Company, 58
Annual reports, 92-103
Argyle Publishing Corporation, Lord Products Division, 298-299
Audience, choosing, 43
Audio, 8, 26, 37, 60-61, 92, 245-274
  disc (mechanical) recording, 245-246
  magnetic recording, 246-249
  optical recording, 245
  recording techniques, 262-264
  tape recorder operation, 250-261
  tape recording terms, glossary, 265-272
  tape splicing and editing, 261-262
  types of audio recording, 245-249
  uses of, 249-250
Audio-visual materials, 3
Audio-visual methods, reasons for use, 103
Audio-visual presentation,
  methods, 105-107
  reporting to management, 75
  preparation, 112
  tools of, 6
Audiovisual Instruction, 306-310

B

Borden Company, 38, 39, 81, 101
Beseler, Charles, Company, 208
Birth of a Giant, 41
Borden Reporter, 38, 39
Borden's Quarterly Report, 101
Brochures, 4, 14, 15, 16, 17, 20, 37, 45, 55-56, 66-69
Bulletin boards, 37, 62
Business communications, 3

C

Canadian Government, 41
Care and Handling of Buyers, 53
Case of the Chain Reaction, The, 31
Case of the Silent Yell, The, 31
Case of the Tuned-Out Mind, The, 31
Case of the Wrong Wave Length, The, 31
Caterpillar Tractor Company, 55, 56
Chart-Pak, Inc., 211
Charts and graphs, 77-80
Chase Manhattan Bank, 242
Cohu Electronics, Inc., 287, 289
Combination approach, 82
Communication Casebook, The, 31
Communication, 6
  barriers to, 109
  channels of, 6
  nature of, 1, 2
  what is it?, 107-109, 110-111
Company Manners, 41
Connecticut General Life Insurance Company, 13
Cook, Desmond L., 306-310
Crisis in Lindenville, 41

D

Demonstration, 18
Diazo process, 216-218
Dot-dusting technique, 213-214
Douglas Aircraft Company, 41, 48, 86-87
Douglas corporate chart room, 87
DuKane Micromatic Projector, 184
Du Pont de Nemours, E. I., and Company, 13, 78-80
Du Pont Story, The, 13
Dun & Bradstreet, Inc., 21, 22, 23, 24, 25

E

Eastman Kodak Co., 116, 157-159, 166
Education, 3
Employee advancement (upgrading), 22, 26

56846